THE
Sunday Dinner
COOKBOOK

Over 250 Modern Classics
to Share with Family and Friends

The
Sunday Dinner
Cookbook

Over 250 Modern Classics
to Share with Family and Friends

CIDER MILL PRESS

BOOK
PUBLISHERS
KENNEBUNKPORT, MAINE

The Sunday Dinner Cookbook

13-Digit ISBN: 978-1604337525
10-Digit ISBN: 1604337524

This book may be ordered by mail from the publisher.
Please include $5.99 for postage and handling.
Please support your local bookseller first!

Books published by Cider Mill Press Book Publishers are available at special discounts for bulk purchases in the United States by corporations, institutions, and other organizations.
For more information, please contact the publisher.

Cider Mill Press Book Publishers
"Where good books are ready for press"
PO Box 454
12 Spring Street
Kennebunkport, Maine 04046
Visit us on the Web! www.cidermillpress.com

Cover and interior design by Cindy Butler
Special thanks to Jaime Christopher, Annalisa Sheldahl, Abigail Spooner, Catherine Breer, and Marit Snowball for their design assistance.

Typography: Archer, Hoefler, Garden Grown, Minion Pro
Napkin folding illustrations pages 30-31 by Sherry Berger
All other images are used under official license from Shutterstock.com

Printed in China
2 3 4 5 6 7 8 9 0

Dedicated to the family cooks and chefs, who are keeping the tradition of sunday dinners alive.

Our hats are off to you!

Winter

Menus 1-11

Spring

Menus 12-25

Summer

Menus 26-37

Fall

Menus 38-52

Over the river, and

Now Grandmother's cap I spy! Hurrah for the fun!

No other poem in American literature quite captures the essence of Sunday dinner: the gathering, the family...and the food! It's as American as roast turkey and apple pie.

As long there have been families, there have been family dinners. Whether Sunday dinner is at the grandparents' house or if the tradition has passed along to another member of the family, it's a time to come together, to slow down a bit, to give thanks, and to celebrate both the major holidays and the everyday milestones from birthdays and anniversaries to graduations and promotions.

The Sunday Dinner Cookbook has 52 weeks of menus and recipes, plus special holiday menus, to help with your own celebrations and seasonal gatherings, from cold winter nights to the dog days of summer.

Many of the recipes will be familiar favorites, using traditional ingredients that have become synonymous with home-style American cooking. Likewise,

through the wood—

Is the pudding done? Hurrah for the pumpkin pie!

some of the recipes may not seem uniquely "American" at all, though they're staples in kitchens across the country—from the Italian households of Chicago to the Greek homes of Detroit, from the Mexican communities of Los Angeles to Chinatown in San Francisco, from the Jewish families of Brooklyn to the Boston Irish. The truth is that, going all the way to the colonial years, cooking in America has been as diverse as the country itself, as deeply rooted as our unique history, and as captivating as our many cultures. The stock pots in our kitchens reflect the "melting pot" of our country, and our daily meals range from the traditional to the exotic, with influences from every corner of the globe.

The menus have one thing in common: These are hearty, homemade family meals fit for "Sunday dinner"—whatever day of the week you can get the family together. Some of the recipes are new twists on old favorites. Others been prepared for generations, passed down with love from grandmothers to grandchildren, and now passed along to you.

Kitchen Essentials

A cook could go crazy in a kitchen supply store. This checklist of kitchen essentials is by no means exhaustive, but a kitchen provisioned with these items should have no problem preparing any of the recipes included here.

Cookware
Cast-iron skillet
Dutch oven
Large nonstick frying pan
Set of stainless steel saucepans:
Small 2-3 quart with lid
Large 4 quart with lid
10- to 14-inch sauté pan with lid
Steamer basket

Bakeware
9- to 10-inch round cake pan
Cheesecake pan
Cooling racks
5x9-inch loaf pan
Muffin tin
9- to 10-inch pie plate
9x13-inch rectangular baking pan
8- to 9-inch square baking pan
Sheet pans

Cutting
Bread knife
Chef's knife
Garlic press
Paring knife
Pizza cutter
Serrated carving knife
Vegetable peeler
Mandoline
Box grater
Microplane grater
Large wooden cutting board
Small plastic cutting board

Utensils
Can opener
Corkscrew
Ladle
Locking metal tongs
Melon baller
Oven mitts
Potato masher
Rolling pin
Rubber spatulas
Slotted spoon
Whisks
Wooden spoons

Measuring
Dry ingredient measuring cups
4-cup liquid measuring cup
Measuring spoons
Kitchen scale
Kitchen timer
Instant read thermometer
Oven thermometer

Bowls and Containers
Nest of mixing bowls
Large colander
Strainers

Small Kitchen Appliances
Blender
Food processor
Hand mixer
Standup mixer
Pressure cooker
Slow cooker
Salad spinner
Toaster
Waffle iron

How to Care for Your Kitchen Tools

We invest a great deal in our kitchens. Cookware, knives, and the like do not come cheaply, and to care for your kitchenware and keep these tools working well for an extended lifetime, it's best to clean and maintain your kitchen tools after every use.

Common sense is key when it comes to cleaning your kitchen tools. Be sure to follow the instructions of the manufacturer and, when in doubt, wash by hand. Most kitchen tools can be easily cleaned with just soap and water and dried with a clean cloth. When cleaning small appliances like a blender or food processor, take the pieces apart and clean them separately. Always ensure any electrical appliances, like slow cookers, are unplugged and have cooled.

Pots and Pans

When using a nonstick pan, avoid metal utensils that can damage the nonstick finish. Instead, use wood, plastic, or silicone utensils.

Once your pots and pans have cooled after use, be sure to clean them in a timely manner. Avoid leaving them soiled or soaking them overnight, which can damage the finish or cause rust. While many pots and pans claim to be dishwasher-safe, handwashing and drying will extend the life of your cookware.

For both stainless steel and nonstick pans, never use abrasive cleaners or a scouring pad, which will scratch surfaces and ruin nonstick coatings. Instead, use a nylon net pad or sponge. Copper bottom pots and pans should be cleaned with a copper cleaner after every use.

To avoid rusting or pitting, be sure your cookware is completely dry before storing, and avoid stacking your cookware.

Knives

First, make sure you use the right knife for the right job. Using a knife as intended will extend its life.

Knives perform at their best and last longer when sharpened. Before each use, hone your blade by using the steel found with your knife set, and have your knives sharpened by a professional once or twice a year. Local sharpeners can be found online or at many local farmer's markets, and the cost is inexpensive, particularly compared to the cost of a new, high-quality knife.

After you've used the knife, clean and dry it by hand. Never leave knives soaking, which can warp and wear the wooden handle. Likewise, never wash knives in the dishwasher where they can be damaged. Any rust can be removed with scouring powder and a gentle scrubbing.

Make sure knives are completely dry before storing, keeping them free from rust. Store your knives in a wooden knife block or sheathed in a drawer. Make sure your knife won't come in contact with anything that can damage the blade.

Wooden Items

Never soak wooden items like cutting boards or wooden spoons, nor wash them in a dishwasher, as this will heat, swell, and crack wood. Instead, wash and hand dry right away using mild dish detergent. Wood is prone to gathering bacteria, so wash immediately, and rub with a lemon first to help fight the spread of bacteria.

Wooden cutting boards and spoons need to be oiled to prevent from drying and cracking. Use a cloth to coat your wooden items with mineral oil or walnut oil, allowing the oil to soak in, and wiping away any excess oil after 30 minutes. Wooden items should be oiled every few months.

Plastic and Rubber Items

Most plastic and rubber plastic cutting boards, spatulas, and measuring cups are generally dishwasher-safe, but some cheaper plastic utensils may melt or crack with excessive heat. Be cautious when using plastic in the dishwasher; handwashing and drying your plastic and rubber items will ensure they last.

Coffeemakers

Coffeemakers can be cleaned using equal parts of white vinegar and water. Fill the coffeemaker with the mixture, and run halfway through a cycle. Turn the machine off and let sit for one hour. Then turn the machine on and complete the cycle. Next, rinse the filter chamber and the pot to eliminate the vinegar odor, and run a final cycle with only fresh water. Repeat as necessary.

Cast-Iron Cookware

Seasoning a New Skillet

When I went shopping for a new cast-iron skillet, I came upon Lodge pans—a company that has been making cast-iron skillets since the late 1800s. They brand themselves as "America's Original Cookware." Since nothing stands completely still, they have recently developed a method to season their cookware so that it will last as it always has but with minimal (consistent) care. That's a good thing! What they do is coat the pan with vegetable oil and bake it in at very high heat, which is just what you need to do to an unseasoned pan. With a new Lodge seasoned piece, you can be cooking from it almost immediately.

But let's start at the beginning, with an unseasoned skillet. Here's the procedure to bring it into use:

Wash with hot, soapy water.

Rinse and dry thoroughly.

If there's any rust on the pan, sand it lightly with fine-grained sandpaper. Apply Cola-Cola to the rust spots and leave on for 10 to 15 minutes. Wash again with soapy water, rinse, dry and put the skillet on a burner over low heat to dry any excess moisture.

If there's no rust, after drying the cookware all over, apply a light layer of cooking oil (vegetable oil, NOT olive oil, butter, or margarine!) all over the pan with a paper towel, rubbing even the handle. The pan should have a light sheen to it.

Place the skillet upside down on the middle rack of the oven and preheat the oven to 400 degrees F (with the pan inside). Put a piece of foil or a baking dish on the lower rack to catch any drips of oil. Let the pan cook in the oven for about 2 hours.

Turn the oven off and let the pan cool (upside down) in the oven.

Take it out, wipe it down with a clean paper towel, and it's good to go.

If your pan has taken on a slightly brown color, you can repeat the process, which will further season the pan and darken its color, improving its appearance. This will also happen over time.

Caring for Your Cast-Iron

Rule #1: Never wash your seasoned pan with soapy water!

Rule #2: Never put a cast-iron pan in the dishwasher!

Why? Soap breaks down the protective seasoning, and you have to re-season the pan all over again. Leaving any kind of water on the pan will lead to rusting, which will demand re-seasoning from the beginning. It seems counterintuitive, especially when you're used to thinking "it's not clean unless it's been washed in (really) hot, soapy water," but it's actually a great thing about cast-iron.

After you've cooked in your skillet, clean it with hot water (no soap) and a plastic, rough-surfaced scrub brush. Dry the cookware completely (all over) after washing. Put a teaspoon of vegetable oil in the pan and, with a paper towel, rub it in all over the pan until it has a nice sheen.

Rule #3: Never use steel wool!

Cast-iron is a softer material compared to steel. Any particularly abrasive sponge on your cast-iron has the potential to scratch the surface enamel or otherwise strip your pan's seasoning.

If there's a mess that water and sponge cannot handle, you can create a scrubbing paste by adding coarse kosher salt to your hot water before using your scrub brush or sponge to loosen the food off the pan. Stubborn residues may also be loosened from your cast-iron by soaking very briefly in water but do not leave your pan submerged in water. You can also simmer the mess over medium-low heat to aid in loosening up more extreme grime.

Never clean your pan by burning it in a fire! The rapid overheating of the metal can cause warps, cracks, red patchy scales, or brittleness that compromises the structure of your pan, and can sometimes make it no longer able to hold its protective seasoning.

Use it!

The thing I've learned about cast-iron skillets is that, once you start using them regularly, they truly become your go-to cooking instruments. They're so versatile and so easy to use. They conduct heat beautifully, and the fact that they can go from stovetop to oven is a real bonus. Here's why: Flavor. And, yes, the overall look of the meal served in the cast-iron. There's something very elemental about it.

Again, once scrubbed of leftovers, dry your cast-iron extremely well and rejuvenate the lovely sheen by rubbing in the vegetable oil, wiping excess off with a clean paper towel.

Rule #4: Store your cast-iron in a dry place!

Good air circulation and a moisture-free environment will ensure your pan stays rust-free and clean until the next time you wish to use it. If you need to stack it with other pans in your pantry or cupboard, put paper towels between the cookware to prevent scratches or other damage. Dutch ovens should be stored with their lids off, so that no moisture is trapped within.

Storing cast-iron within your oven is also a popular option, so that it is nearby and ready for use whenever you're cooking. Just be sure to remove any pans before preheating your oven (I couldn't tell you how many times I've discovered the pan I needed after the oven was warm)! Or you can leave it on your stovetop if you find you can't seem to cook a meal without it. An overhead rack is equally a good option, but if you have multiple cast-iron skillets, simply make sure that your cookware rack is well bolted to your ceiling and is prepared to handle the weight. Both of these options display your rustic, heirloom cookware proudly, and make a beautiful aesthetic statement for your kitchen.

Give It a Lot of Love

The best thing to do with your cast-iron skillet is USE IT! When you start using it for all the different things it can do (as evidenced by the diversity of recipes in this book), you'll probably find that the skillet lives on your stovetop, waiting for its next assignment. The more you use it, the better it gets. Nothing will stick to its surface. You can go from the frying pan to the fire, as it were, starting a dish on the stove and finishing it in the oven. You can cook your skillet to a very high heat (or put it in the campfire), and it'll cook up the food you put in it beautifully (so long as you keep an eye on it).

In short, with regular use, the cast-iron skillet truly is a pan that will just keep cooking and cooking, getting better and better with age and use. Just like you and me!

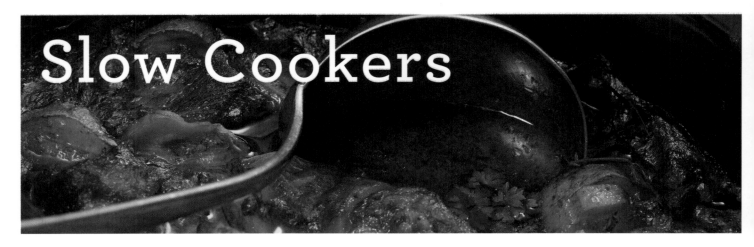

Slow Cookers

Slow cookers are inexpensive to operate; they use about as much electricity as a 60-watt bulb. They are also as easy to operate as flipping on a light switch. Slow cookers operate by cooking food using indirect heat at a low temperature for an extended period of time. Here's the difference: Direct heat is the power of a stove burner underneath a pot, while indirect heat is the overall heat that surrounds foods as they bake in the oven.

You can purchase a slow cooker for as little as $20 at a discount store, while the top-of-the-line ones sell for more than $200. They all function in the same simple way; what increases the cost is the "bells and whistles" factors. Slow cookers come in both round and oval shapes but they operate the same regardless of shape.

On the front of your slow cooker is the control knob. All slow cookers have Low and High settings, and most also have a Stay Warm position. Some new machines have a programmable option that enables you to start food on High and then the slow cooker automatically reduces the heat to Low after a programmed time.

Most of the recipes in this book were written for and tested in a 4- or 5-quart slow cooker. Either of those sizes makes enough for four to eight people, depending on the recipe. In a few cases, such as for lamb shanks that take up a lot of room as they cook, a large slow cooker is specified.

Slow Cooker Hints

Slow cookers can be perplexing if you're not accustomed to using one. Here are some general tips to help you master slow cooker conundrums:

- Remember that cooking times are wide approximations — within hours rather than minutes! That's because the age or power of a slow cooker as well as the temperature of ingredients must be taken into account. Check the food at the beginning of the stated cooking time, and then gauge if it needs more time, and about how much time. If carrots or cubes of potato are still rock-hard, for example, turn the heat to High if cooking on Low, and realize that you're looking at another hour or so.

- Foods cook faster on the bottom of a slow cooker than at the top because there are more heat coils and they are totally immersed in the simmering liquid.

- Appliance manufacturers say that slow cookers can be left on either High or Low unattended, but use your own judgment. If you're going to be out of the house all day, it's advisable to cook food on Low. If, on the other hand, you're going to be gone for just a few hours, the food will be safe on High.

- Use leaf versions of dried herbs such as thyme and rosemary rather than ground versions. Ground herbs tend to lose potency during many hours in the slow cooker.

- Don't add dairy products except at the end of the cooking time, as noted in the recipes. They can curdle if cooked for too long.

- Season the dishes with pepper or crushed red pepper flakes at the end of cooking time, because these ingredients can become harsh from too many hours in the pot.

- If you want a sauce to have a more intense flavor, you can reduce the liquid in two ways. If cooking on Low, raise the heat to High, and remove the lid for the last hour of cooking. This will achieve some evaporation of the liquid. Or, remove the liquid either with a bulb baster or strain the liquid from the solids, and reduce them in a saucepan on the stove.

While in many households slow cookers are banished to the basement when screens replace storm windows during the warmer months, in my kitchen at least one lives on the counter all summer. Running the slow cooker doesn't raise the kitchen temperature by even a degree, and you can be outside enjoying the warm weather while it's cooking away.

Slow Cooker Cautions

Slow cookers are benign, but they are electrical appliances with all the concomitant hazards of any machine plugged into a live wire. Be careful that the cord is not frayed in any way, and plug the slow cooker into an outlet that is not near the sink. Here are some tips on how to handle them:

- Never leave a slow cooker plugged in when not in use. It's all too easy to accidentally turn it on and not notice

until the crockery insert cracks from overheating with nothing in it.

- Conversely, do not preheat the empty insert while you're preparing the food because the insert could crack when you add the cold food.

- Never submerge the metal casing in water, or fill it with water. While the inside of the metal does occasionally get dirty, you can clean it quite well with an abrasive cleaner, and then wipe it with a damp cloth or paper towel. While it's not aesthetically pleasing to see dirty metal, do remember that food never touches it, so if there are a few drips here and there it's not really important.

- Always remember that the insert is fragile, so don't drop it. Also, don't put a hot insert on a cold counter; that could cause it to break, too. The reverse is also true. While you can use the insert as a casserole in a conventional oven (assuming the lid is glass and not plastic), it cannot be put into a preheated oven if chilled.

- Resist the temptation to look and stir. Every time you take the lid off the slow cooker you need to add 10 minutes of cooking time

if cooking on High and 20 minutes if cooking on Low to compensate. Certain recipes in this book, especially those for fish, instruct you to add ingredients during the cooking time. In those cases the heat loss from opening the pot has been factored in to the total cooking time.

- Don't add more liquid to a slow cooker recipe than that specified in the recipe. Even if the food is not submerged in liquid when you start, foods such as meats and vegetables give off liquid as they cook; in the slow cooker, that additional liquid does not evaporate.

Modern slow cookers heat slightly hotter than those made thirty years ago; the Low setting on a slow cooker is about 200°F while the High setting is close to 300°F. If you have a vintage appliance, it's a good idea to test it to make sure it still has the power to heat food sufficiently. Leave 2 quarts water at room temperature overnight, and then pour the water into the slow cooker in the morning. Heat it on Low for 8 hours. The temperature should be 185°F after 8 hours. Use an instant read thermometer to judge it. If it is lower, any food you cook in this cooker might not pass through the danger zone rapidly enough.

High-Altitude Adjustment

Rules for slow cooking, along with all other modes of cooking, change when the slow cooker is located more than 3,000 feet above sea level. At high altitudes the air is thinner so water boils at a lower temperature and comes to a boil more quickly. The rule is to always cook on High when above 3,000 feet; use the Low setting as a Keep Warm setting. Other compensations are to reduce the liquid in a recipe by a few tablespoons, and add about 5 to 10 percent more cooking time. The liquid may be bubbling, but it's not 212°F at first.

Pressure Cookers

Safety

If you own a pressure cooker, be sure to read these important safety precautions. This list is the part that you CANNOT skip.

- Read the manual. If you lost it, look up the manual for your model online. All pressure cookers are a little bit different, making it impossible for me to give 100% of my instructions to fit each and every pressure cooker. You need to know how big your cooker is, how long it takes to release pressure, and the minimum amount of liquid you need for the whole thing to work. Speaking of which...

- Never cook without liquid. It doesn't have to be plain old water. If you're cooking with broth or stock and the amount called for in the recipe meets or exceeds the minimum your pressure cooker needs to work, perfect. If the recipe calls for less liquid than necessary, you have to add water to it until it meets your pressure cooker's requirements. I can't stress this enough, NEVER cook in a sealed pressure cooker without having the minimum amount of liquid in there with everything else.

- Only seal the cooker when the recipe calls for it. A lot of recipes in here will have you browning meat or cooking onions before you actually use the pressure function of the cooker. DO NOT close the lid in these circumstances. There is no need to and it could actually damage your cooker.

- Know the max fill line. Different sized cookers obviously have different max fill lines, so it is important that you know where it is so that you can keep it in mind when preparing a recipe. Some of the smaller cookers may need to reduce the serving size in some of these recipes in order to fit everything in one go. Generally speaking, you should not fill most cookers more than ⅔ full with liquid because there needs to be room left for the steam to build. That said, you should have specific knowledge regarding how much liquid and food your pressure cooker can hold at any one given time.

- Most recipes in this book will include a sentence somewhere that reads "select the High Pressure function and let cook for X number of minutes." Keep in mind that the cooking time begins once whatever pressure was selected has been achieved. So, you're not cooking for 3 minutes after selecting High Pressure, you're cooking for 3 minutes once that High Pressure has been achieved. Every electronic pressure cooker that I've dealt with didn't actually start the timer until that was the case, though you should still check to make sure yours does the same!

- Know how to perform a quick and natural release and how to detect whether the pressure has been fully removed from your cooker. This is another area of differentiation between pressure cookers, making it extremely important that you know how to work your own.

- Check to make sure steam is removed before opening. Electrical pressure cookers handle this job on their own. However, you will have to check manually on the stovetop models. Depending on the model that you have, you're either going to jiggle the pressure regulator or the valve stem. No sound of escaping steam means that there is no more pressure in the cooker.

Grills

How to Care for Your Grill

The first order of business after heating up your grill to the optimal temperature is cleaning the grates for the upcoming meal. High heat gives great advantage here. Any lingering grime will smolder, and soot is a lot easier to scrape off a grate compared to a baked-on mess right after cooking. A sturdy grill brush will make this a breeze with a little bit of elbow grease—use brass wire brushes for stainless steel grates and stainless steel wire brushes for cast-iron.

Any large pieces of food that linger after cooking a meal may be scraped off with a quick run of the grill brush or a ball of heavy duty aluminum foil held between tongs. Grease or salt should be wiped up with a damp paper towel, because these accelerate corrosion. Leave the gradual buildup of blackened enamel on your grates. That encasing actually helps protect the metal from the elements and rust, and in the long run, the seasoning helps to hold and even out a specific temperature while grilling. If there is a burnt mess that absolutely refuses to move, a mixture of one part white vinegar and one part water sprayed over the area and left to stand for one hour will help make the mess easier to remove.

To prevent stuck-on messes, oil your grates every once in a while. This aids in ensuring that your grates can stay nonstick and easy to clean. To do this, simply dip a wadded paper towel in a little vegetable oil and wipe the oil over the metal evenly, making sure to get in between the crevices. Wipe off any excess oil.

A thorough cleaning of your grill, both inside and out, is recommended once or twice a year, ideally once in the spring and once in the fall. A mild soap and sponge should do the trick. In the event you find any spot of rust, use a fine steel-wool pad to gently rub away the build-up and spray the area with outdoor, water resistant paint (there are some options specifically made for grills). And of course, each grill is unique! Be sure to thoroughly read and follow your specific grill's maintenance guide to safely disconnect all pieces that require cleaning.

Your most important accessory is your grill cover! For a grill that stays outdoors, a cover helps protect it from the elements and exponentially extends your grill's life. Once your grill has cooled back to a safe, touchable temperature, always remember to re-cover it.

When winter comes, disconnect propane tanks and store in a dry place until spring. Moving your grill indoors to a garage or shed is ideal, but if this is not an option, make sure your cover is snug and, if possible, store it under a protected area such as an awning or porch.

The Toast Test

When firing up your grill for the first time, you want to do a couple dry runs without food to burn off any manufacturer's grease and practice how to hit the optimal temperature for cooking. Grills tend to have unique hot spots that cook food faster than other locations on its grates. You might want to do a Toast Test: A cheap sliced white bread loaf will do. After preheating the grill to a medium heat for fifteen minutes, lay out the sliced bread to cover your grill's grate (discarding the end slices, so their uneven width won't throw off the test). Allow the bread to toast for 1-3 minutes before moving the bread off to a large cutting board in the exact grid they were in on the grill. The more toasted pieces will clue you in to where the hottest spots of your grill are.

Charcoal vs. Gas Maintenance

For a charcoal grill, it is important to clean out the charcoal ash as soon as possible. Never allow moisture to accumulate in a grill full of ash. Wait for the coals to cool first before disposing of the ash. If you're in the middle of an outdoor party, it might be more convenient to have a bucket by the grill to quickly dump the remnants of your charcoal into. You can then store this bucket in a dry location until the ashes are completely cool and you're sure there aren't any coals left burning. You may then dispose of the remnants in the trash. Do not use this ash for your compost or garden!

For a gas grill, the upkeep is much simpler. You need only change or regularly clean the catch-pan and properly maintain your propane tank. When connecting your propane, only hand-tighten your grill's hose to the valve. Using any pliers can easily lead to over-tightening the threads together and damaging the connection. Always close the valve when you've finished grilling so no gas can escape. Be on the lookout for any leaks from your tank or hose. If you suspect a leak, brush some soapy water along the connections or hose to see if any gas bubbles and escapes. Immediately tighten the valve and connections if that is the case, and replace the fuel line if the hose has a hole. If tightening the valve does not stop the leak, move away from the grill and immediately call the fire department. Have your tank immediately serviced if you see any dents, damage, or rust.

Basic Safety

Accidents happen, but here are some basic steps to ensure that you and your family stay safe when grilling up a great meal!

- Propane tanks should be upright and stored away from direct heat in a shady location.

- Don't allow the propane to completely run out! You want to maintain some pressure within your tank at all times.

- Your grill should be at least ten feet away from your home, deck railing, and in an open area without any overhanging awning or tree branches.

- Keep decorations away from your grill, such as hanging baskets, outdoor furniture, pillows, and umbrellas.

- Make sure your grill is on even, stable ground.

- Never leave your grill unattended, and keep children and pets at a safe distance while the grill is on.

- Light your grill with the hood open. Fire needs oxygen to light, and you don't want to allow a buildup of gas or else you may get a fireball lit in your face.

- Never use additional lighter fluid or gasoline to start a fire in your grill. With charcoal, consider a chimney starter or newspaper to more easily light a flame. For a gas grill, turn the propane off and check the ignition system for a spark. Your ignition system's batteries may be dead if there is no spark, so a grill lighter may be used to light a flame.

- Check for gas leaks. Test the connections with soapy water as often as you change the propane tank, and regularly inspect the fuel line for cracks.

- Don't overload your grill with food, particularly fatty foods that will be producing a lot of grease and drips that catch fire.

- Always be prepared for a fire. You should have a fire extinguisher on hand when grilling, and never use water to put out a grease fire! This will cause the grease to splash, spreading the fire and potentially burning you. Baking soda is a solution to put out a small grease fire, but it probably won't be able to put out a large fire.

- But seriously, get a fire extinguisher, know how to use it, and know when to replace it.

Cooking

Many of our recipes say the grill is ready when it's about 450 degrees F, or when the coals lightly covered in ash. Another way to gauge that temperature is to hold your hand about 5 inches above the grates. If you can only hold it there for one to three seconds, the grill is at the medium-hot temperature we desire.

Only one fuel adds flavor: Wood. Sometimes we suggest you go for a smoky flavor by adding woodchips to your electric or gas grill. Wood chips burn quickly, making them great for smoking smaller pieces of meat, like chicken breasts, steak, or sausages. But if you want to smoke a large piece for a longer time, wood chunks—or even larger split logs— make more sense.

If you're the host, greet your guests with a smile and kind words. Answer questions politely and make your guests feel welcome. If you are a guest, greet the host in a friendly manner and compliment their efforts. As a guest, offer to help the host in any way. Always wash your hands before handling dinnerware, preparing food, or eating.

Take your seat at the table from the left side of your chair. Gentlemen will wait for ladies to be seated, and will offer to assist them. Once seated at the table, unfold your napkin and place it in your lap. Keep your elbows off the table and sit up straight, with your feet on the floor. When necessary, wipe your mouth with your napkin, not your hands or sleeve. Your napkin should remain in your lap when not being used, and if you need to excuse yourself from the table, place the napkin on your chair, not the table.

Pass food from left to right. Don't reach across the table; ask that someone pass the dish to you. Don't take more than you can eat, and make sure there are enough portions for everyone. Always say "please" and "thank you."

Be sure to wait until everyone is seated and served before you eat. Once you've picked up your flatware, it should never touch the table again. To avoid staining the tablecloth, flatware should be placed on the edge of your plate when not in use. When passing a plate for second helpings, flatware should be left on the plate. Don't eat with your hands.

When eating, bring your food to your mouth, not your mouth to your food. Take appropriate-sized bites, and chew with your mouth closed. When eating bread, break off a small piece and butter it using the butter knife. Likewise, it's not proper to cut all your meat before starting to

Grandma's Table Manners

Good table manners are vital to any meal, as they show courtesy to those with whom you dine. Practicing proper table manners creates a congenial atmosphere for everyone at the dinner party, and proper dining etiquette demonstrates one's modesty and social grace.

eat; instead cut only your next bite. When using a soup spoon, dip the spoon toward the back of the bowl. Don't slurp food or drinks. Should you have to burp or cough, cover your mouth and say "excuse me."

A lively conversation is the key to any dinner party. Conversations should include all guests, and topics of conversation should be in good taste and not insult any guest, and most importantly not your host. Flatware should be put down when one is gesturing while speaking. Do not monopolize the conversation, but rather wait for your turn to speak. Don't speak loudly or act rudely to other guests, and never speak with your mouth full.

Don't use a toothpick or blow your nose at the table, and don't do anything that would make your host or fellow guests feel uncomfortable, including the use of a cell phone. When food is served to you that you dislike, don't complain about the food, but rather eat what you can. Never point out another guest's ill manners. Be gracious, kind, and engaging, and compliment your host. Stay at the table until all have finished their meals.

When the meal is done, leave your plate in place, put your flatware on your plate, and place your napkin on the table to the left of your plate. Ask to be excused from the table, and always offer to clear your plate and flatware. Offer to help with any clean-up and care of the table and kitchen, but never overstay your welcome. Be sure to thank your host before leaving.

How To Set Your Table

A properly set table will add elegance to any meal and enhance the appearance of your table. Your dinner guests will appreciate the effort, as it makes the meal feel more exceptional. The following guide reflects a more formal meal, but it can abridged be for more casual dinners.

Place setting consists of three equal components: dinnerware, flatware, and glassware. Dinnerware includes plates, dishes, bread plates, and bowls. Flatware includes forks, knives, spoons, and serving utensils. Glassware includes water glasses, wine glasses, and dessert glassware. All of your dinnerware, flatware, and glassware should be freshly cleaned and sparkling, having been wiped of any spots. Please refer to the diagram below.

At each seat, a larger dinner plate, known as the charger, should be placed one inch from the edge of the table, and will act as the centerpiece around which the rest of the place setting will be laid out. A smaller salad plate will sit on the charger, and if serving soup, the soup bowl will sit atop the salad plate. A smaller bread plate will be placed on the upper left, above the forks. When the entrée is served, the charger will be removed and replaced with a clean dinner plate.

Flatware should be placed one inch above the table edge, with the handles lined evenly. No more than three of any utensil should be placed on the table. Additional utensils should be brought in with remaining courses.

Forks are placed to the left of the charger, arranged by order of use, with tines up. The larger of the forks, the dinner fork, is the main fork. If there is a fish course or salad, a small fork should be placed to the left of the dinner fork as it is the first fork used in the meal. If a salad course will follow the entrée, a small fork should be place to the right of the dinner fork. Forks should be used working in toward the charger. A dessert fork may be placed above the center of the charger.

A larger dinner knife should be placed to the right of the charger, with the blade facing the charger. A smaller fish or salad knife will be placed to the right of the dinner knife, to be used first, working in toward the charger. If soup or fruit is to be served as a first course, the spoon should be placed to the right of the knives, with the bowl up. A butter knife should be placed diagonally on the bread plate, with the handle on the right. A dessert spoon may be placed above the center of the charger.

Glassware is placed to the upper right of the charger, above the knives and spoons. A water goblet should be placed at the tip of the dinner knife. Next to the water goblet, on a slight diagonal, place a red wine glass, and finally, next to the red wine glass, place a white wine glass. If serving champagne during the appetizer, a champagne flute may be placed on the outside, next to the white wine glass. Cups and saucers should be brought to the table when tea or coffee is being served.

Freshly cleaned, pressed, and folded cloth napkins should be placed atop the salad plate, or to the left of the forks. When being removed, napkins should not disturb any of the flatware.

Napkin Folding

Napkin folding is a skill every dinner host should learn. A properly folded napkin will bring a touch of sophistication and flair to any dinner party, and it will impress your guests. A cleaned, starched, and pressed square cloth napkin should be used, although rectangular napkins may be substituted in a pinch. A few extra minutes spent folding your napkins will dress up your table at formal events and casual dinners alike. Below are easy instructions to help you master this art form.

Traditional Dinner Fold

You can't go wrong with this fold. Some even like to iron their linen napkins into this fold and store them that way so that when it is time to use them, they are ready to go and look great. This napkin can be placed to the left of the forks, underneath the dinner fork, or in the middle of the plate.

Instructions:

1. Using a square napkin, position it in front of you so that the flat sides face up and down.

2. Fold the top half down to form a rectangle.

3. Working from the left, fold the napkin in so that it forms a square.

4. Repeat this fold to create a rectangular fold.

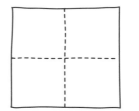

Traditional Luncheon Fold

Like its rectangular affiliate, the triangular fold makes an easy and elegant statement that, while slightly less formal, is always appropriate and always simple to accomplish. This napkin is best placed to the left of or underneath the dinner fork.

Instructions:

1. Using a square napkin, position it in front of you so that the flat sides face up and down.

2. Fold the top half down to form a rectangle.

3. Working from the left, fold the napkin in so that it forms a square.

4. Working from the bottom right corner, fold the napkin up to form a triangle with the corner facing left.

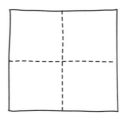

Classic Fan

This fold looks great placed either in the center of the plate or just above it. It is easy and fun to create, and it never fails to impress.

Instructions:

1. Start with the napkin in its open square configuration.

2. Fold it in half to form a rectangle.

3. Starting at one end, fold the edge over about an inch, pressing to create a firm crease.

4. Fold this over again so there is a double fold. This will create a solid base.

5. Next, create accordion pleats of the same size as your original fold.

6. Continue about halfway down the napkin. Firmly crease the pleats.

7. With the half of the napkin that remains, fold up from the bottom left, tucking the end into the pleats.

8. Stand the napkin up so that the pleats fall into place.

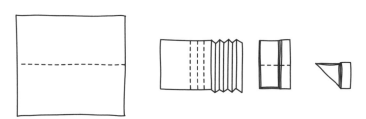

Server Serviette

The word for napkin in French is serviette. Here's a beautiful way to use a napkin to hold silverware rather than frame it.

Instructions:

1. Fold a large, square napkin in half horizontally to form a rectangle.

2. With the folded edge at the bottom, fold back the first layer so that it is folded in half toward the bottom edge.

3. Turn the napkin over, and fold the left edge over until it reaches the center.

4. Roll this part over two more times so that it forms a secure pocket.

5. Position the napkin with the loose fold in back, and fill with a fork, knife, and spoon.

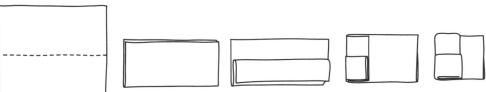

The Best Kitchen Secrets

While most of us like tinkering in the kitchen, not all of us have the skill-set of a professional chef. If you find yourself looking through these recipes and asking, "what does this mean?" here's a quick guide to some basic kitchen tips and techniques that will help you get these meals on the table with a minimum of difficulty.

Whisking: Used to combine ingredients, it's best to put your mixing bowl on an angle and utilize a side-to-side motion with your wrist, as opposed to stirring or beating (see beating below).

Folding: Combines ingredients without losing air in the mixture. Using a rubber spatula, add the lighter mixture (eggs, etc.) to the heavier mixture (e.g., chocolate) by running the spatula along the side of the bowl and "folding" the mixture on top of itself.

How to Separate an Egg: Yes, it seems basic, but some amateur chefs are uncertain how to get just egg white or just yolk. It's easy: Get a clean bowl, and crack an egg in half above the bowl. Separate the two halves of shell, and pass the yolk back and forth between the two halves, allowing the white of the egg to drip into the bowl below. Eventually all the white will be in the bowl, and the yolk will be in the shell.

Beating Eggs: Using a fork or whisk, first break the yolks, then combine the yolks and the white by mixing in a rapid circular manner.

Beating Egg Whites: Use fresh eggs at room temperature, and ensure your bowl is totally clean. When using a hand mixer, it's best to start on a slow setting and increase the speed, but do not overbeat, as overbeaten eggs will liquefy. When removing the beaters,

"soft peaks" will curl down, and "stiff peaks" will stand straight. Use beaten eggs right away.

Tempering Eggs: This is adding a hot mixture to eggs, or vice versa. While whisking, slowly pour the one mixture into the other, gradually bringing the eggs up to temperature without overcooking and creating scrambled eggs.

Creaming Butter and Sugar: Use butter that's been softened; butter that's too firm won't incorporate the sugar as well, and instead will be lumpy and create pockets of sugar. Mix butter and sugar together until the butter is fluffy with peaks.

Clarifying Butter: Butter is clarified by removing the water and milk proteins, leaving only the butterfat that stands up to high temperature. To make clarified butter, melt and then simmer unsalted butter in a saucepan. The milkfat will gather on top. Take the butter off heat, and skim off the milkfats. Then pour through a cheesecloth to remove any remaining or browned milkfats.

Whipping Cream: A fairly easy process; simply add the sugar and flavoring to heavy whipping cream, and whisk until there are stiff peaks. However, don't overbeat or you'll end up with something that tastes like butter.

Proofing Yeast: Proofing helps ensure you'll get the rise you want out of your baked goods. Proof your yeast by adding it to the water called for in the recipe, plus a pinch of sugar. Let stand for 10 minutes. The yeast will react with the sugar, and the resulting foam is "proof" the yeast is working.

Crimping a Pie Crust: Crimping creates a defined and decorative edge to you pie crust. Place one hand on the inside edge of your crust, and the other on the outside of your pie tin. Working your way around the pie tin, carefully press the edge of the dough together, creating a scalloped pattern, about an inch apart.

Melting Chocolate: The goal is to melt the chocolate without burning it. This is done by using indirect heat. Boil water in a saucepan and simmer. Place your pieces of chocolate in a metal mixing bowl, and place the mixing bowl in the simmering water (called a bain marie). Slowly stir the chocolate as it melts, heating evenly.

Zesting Citrus: Zest is finely grated citrus peel used to flavor. Using a microplane grater, gently grate the exterior peel of the fruit, but only as far as the pith (the bitter, yellow membrane between the peel and the pulp). Zest from end-to-end, and rotate as necessary.

Chopping an Onion: Here's a helpful hint to dice an onion easily. After removing the skin, cut your onion in half lengthwise (from "pole to pole"). Lay the onion on its side, and cut off the end where the stalk has grown, so the nub end still holds the onion layers together. Next, cut thin layers lengthwise with your knife parallel to the cutting board, stopping just before the nub. Finally, use your hand to hold the onion steady, and slice across the onion to dice.

Mincing Garlic: similar to dicing an onion (above), thinly cut a peeled garlic clove lengthwise. Then turn and cut thinly crosswise.

Grating Ginger: Ginger is easiest to work with when frozen, and it isn't necessary to peel. A microplane grater works well if you don't have a ginger grater.

Pitting an Avocado: Cut the avocado in half lengthwise, carefully rotating the blade around the large pit. Using your hands, slowly twist the two halves apart. Finally, using a chef's knife, carefully slap the blade into the avocado pit. Carefully twist the knife, pulling the pit out of the avocado.

Cutting a Mango: Mango is difficult to prepare because it has a long, thin seed in the middle that creates problems. Hold the mango and envision a centerline. Cut about a ¼ inch on either side of this centerline, avoiding the seed in the center.

Pumpkin Puree: While you can buy pumpkin puree at your grocery store, it's easy to make at home. Just cut a sugar pumpkin in half and clean out the seeds and pulp. Place face down on a baking sheet, and roast foil side up for an hour at 325 degrees F. Scoop the pumpkin meat from the shell and puree in a food processor.

Crushing Tomatoes by Hand: Just like it sounds, this is crushing tomatoes with your bare hands. Pull the tomatoes apart into small, coarse pieces, maybe an inch wide.

Sautéing: "Sautéing" means frying your ingredient with a small amount of butter or fat in a shallow pan over high heat. "Sauté" is French for "jump," and the trick is to keep the food moving so it doesn't stick to the pan and burn.

Basting: This is cooking a meat in its own juices, for flavor and moisture. Basting in these recipes refers to capturing the juices of your meat from the pan, and pouring it over the meat to keep it moist. This can be done with a baster, or by using a large spoon.

Flambéing a Steak: Be very cautious in flambéing, as it involves lighting flammable spirits. Use an ounce of brandy or cognac. Take the meat off the burner first for safety, then pour the alcohol over your steak, and return to heat. Wait until the alcohol has been heated, then carefully light using either a match or the open flame of your grill. The liquor should burn out on its own.

Deveining Shrimp: Once you've peeled your shrimp, it's best to devein them, which is removing the dark, unsightly digestive tract on the back of shrimp. Simply use a paring knife and make a shallow cut down the length of the shrimp. Then using the tip of your knife, or a lobster pick, scrape out the vein. With practice, the vein will come out as one continuous piece.

Cleaning and Filleting Fish: It's certainly easier to buy your fish cleaned and filleted, but it's not difficult to do at home. First remove the head just behind the gills, then cut off the tail at its most narrow part. Next make a horizontal cut along the body, running the blade along the ridge of the backbone, and separate the meat from the ribs. This may require a number of steady, small cuts. Once one side is done, repeat the process on the other side. Now remove the smaller pin bones with tweezers. Pin bones are smaller delicate bones, some just slightly thicker than a hair. If needed, turn the fillet over and remove the skin. This can be done with a knife, and sometimes simply by pulling the skin off carefully by hand.

How to Cook Eggs

Farm fresh eggs prepared properly will ensure your breakfast or egg recipe is a success. The instructions below are easy to follow, and remember that it's best to bring your eggs to room temperature before cooking, as this helps maintain even heating of the yolk. Be sure to wash your eggs before cooking, particularly if they've come fresh from the farm.

Scrambling Eggs

Scrambled eggs are a breakfast staple, and the lighter and fluffier the better. Feel free to add herbs in addition to salt and pepper. But don't overcook them or they'll get hard and rubbery.

1. Beat eggs with a splash of milk, and a dash of salt and pepper. The milk makes the eggs fluffier, but too much milk will make the eggs too watery.

2. Melt a teaspoon of butter in a nonstick pan over medium heat, and pour in the egg mixture.

3. As the eggs begin to set, use a spatula to pull the eggs away from the side of the pan, lifting and folding the eggs as they continue to thicken. Lower the heat as the eggs near completion, preventing any burning. Cook until fluffy, with no more liquid remaining.

Poaching Eggs

Poached eggs are the centerpiece of Eggs Benedict, and they're also the best part of a frisée salad with lardons. Fresher eggs will poach better. While poaching an egg seems difficult, it's really quite simple.

1. Bring a saucepan of water to a boil. Once the water is boiling, reduce to a simmer. Add a splash of vinegar to aid in thickening the whites.

2. Crack an egg in to a small bowl or measuring cup. This will help to gently place the egg in the simmering water.

3. Gently place the egg in the water and cook for about 4 minutes, or until the whites have solidified. One option is to use a spoon to slowly stir the water, creating a small whirlpool, which will contain the egg as it poaches.

4. Use a slotted spoon to remove the egg from the water, and dry quickly on a folded paper towel. Season and serve immediately.

Hard Boiling Eggs

Making hard boiled eggs is fairly easy, but an overcooked egg will have a tough, greenish yolk.

1. Place eggs in a saucepan, in one single layer. Cover with an inch of cold water. Heat the water on high heat until it begins to boil.

2. Take the saucepan off the heat, cover, and let sit for 12 minutes, slightly less for smaller eggs, and slightly more for extra large eggs, and longer at higher altitude.

3. Drain the saucepan and run cold water over the eggs, or submerge in ice water, to prevent the eggs from cooking further. Refrigerate any uneaten eggs.

Hard boiled eggs should be eaten within a week. It's easiest to peel eggs under running water.

Soft Boiling Eggs

While soft boiling eggs may be a bit trickier than hard boiling, it's not terribly difficult. The only difference is in the heating of the water and the timing.

1. Bring a saucepan of water to a boil, and then reduce to a simmer.

2. Add your eggs one at a time, carefully placing them in the saucepan. Cook no more than four eggs at once.

3. Boil for 5 minutes, slightly longer for a less runny yolk. But a runny yolk is the goal, is it not?

4. Use a slotted spoon to remove the egg, and run under cold water for 30 seconds. Serve immediately.

Serve soft-boiled eggs in an egg cup, using an egg cutter or a sharp knife to cut off the top of the egg. Dip toast points into the yolk, and use a small spoon to eat the remainder.

Essential Recipes

VEGETABLE STOCK

Makes 2 quarts   Active Time: 10 minutes   Start to Finish: 3 to 4 hours in a slow cooker on High

A lot of recipes can be made vegetarian-friendly (or even vegan-friendly) by simply using vegetable stock instead of chicken or beef stock. But even if you're just making a vegetable side dish, starting with stock creates a background for all the other flavors. Freeze some to have on hand next time you need it.

2 quarts boiling water

2 carrots, thinly sliced

2 celery ribs, sliced

2 leeks, white parts only, thinly sliced

1 small onion, thinly sliced

1 tablespoon black peppercorns

3 parsley sprigs, rinsed

3 thyme sprigs, rinsed, or 1 teaspoon dried

2 garlic cloves, peeled

1 bay leaf

1. Pour water into the slow cooker, and add carrots, celery, leeks, onion, peppercorns, parsley, thyme, garlic, and bay leaf. Cook on Low for 6 to 8 hours or on High for 3 to 4 hours, or until vegetables are soft.

2. Strain stock through a sieve into a mixing bowl. Press down on solids with the back of a spoon to extract as much liquid as possible. Discard solids.

3. Chill stock, and then ladle stock into containers.

Note: The stock can be refrigerated for up to 4 days or frozen for up to 6 months.

CHICKEN STOCK

Makes 2 quarts   Active Time: 10 minutes   Start to Finish: 4 to 5 hours in a slow cooker on High

This is a building block recipe that adds rich flavor to many other dishes that you won't get from water or even from store-bought stock (though, that will work in a pinch). Freeze whatever you don't use right away, and you can pull some out to defrost whenever you need it.

2 quarts boiling water

2 pounds chicken pieces (bones, skin, wing tips, etc.)

1 carrot, cut into ½-inch chunks

1 medium onion, sliced

1 celery rib, sliced

1 tablespoon black peppercorns

3 parsley sprigs, rinsed

3 thyme springs, rinsed, or 1 teaspoon dried

2 garlic cloves, peeled

1 bay leaf

1. Pour 2 quarts water in the slow cooker. Add chicken pieces, carrot, onion, celery, peppercorns, parsley, thyme, garlic, and bay leaf. Cook on Low for 8 to 10 hours or on High for 4 to 5 hours.

2. Strain stock through a sieve into a mixing bowl. Press down on solids with the back of a spoon to extract as much liquid as possible. Discard solids.

3. Chill stock. Remove and discard fat layer from top. Ladle stock into containers.

Note: *The stock can be refrigerated for up to 4 days or frozen for up to 6 months.*

Tip: *Starting the time in the slow cooker with the liquid already boiling saves hours of cooking time.*

Variations:

For Beef Stock, use 2 pounds beef shank or meaty beef bones instead of chicken parts. Preheat the oven broiler and line a broiler pan with heavy-duty aluminum foil. Broil beef for 3 minutes per side or until browned before adding to the slow cooker along with any juices that collected in the pan. The only other difference from the Chicken Stock recipe is the amount of cooking time: Cook on Low for 10 to 12 hours or on High for 5 to 6 hours, or until meat is very soft.

For Ham Stock, substitute ham bones for the chicken.

For Asian Chicken Stock, add 3 tablespoons sliced fresh ginger and 4 scallions (white parts and 4 inches of green tops).

For Hispanic Chicken Stock, use cilantro instead of parsley, and 1 serrano chile and 1 spring fresh oregano (or 1 teaspoon dried).

For browner stock, preheat the oven broiler, and line a broiler pan with heavy-duty aluminum foil. Broil chicken bones for 3 minutes per side or until browned, and use the browned bones for the stock.

Menus

Winter

The seasonal meals here are perfect for the winter: warm and filling, and sometimes spicy and adventurous. The change of weather brings with it a change in seasonal ingredients. Winter vegetables take center stage, while heartier stews and meaty entrees ward off the chill. There are also a number of special holiday menus for gathering the family together during these long winter months.

The start of the new year is also a cue to organize your kitchen pantry. Take all the cans and boxes off the shelves and check the expiration dates. Move commonly used items to the front of your pantry, and reorganize your shelves using a "first-in, first-out" system. And in the spirit of the season, anything that you may never use should go to your local food pantry.

New Year's Eve/Day

New Year's traditions extend beyond the singing of "Auld Lang Syne" to a customary New Year's meal. With progress and longevity in mind, the Chinese serve pork and fish, as they root and swim forward, portending progress. But don't serve chicken! Chickens scratch backwards, so let's not regress! Here we give two entrée options: Pork Chops with Cider and Apples or Simple Skillet Salmon. Lucky New Year's food includes peas, greens, and corn—"circular" foods that resemble coins or money, with a green and gold color palette indicating prosperity in the New Year. Again, we give some options, including Homestyle Baked Beans, Southern Stewed Collard Greens, and Spiced Corn. Chocolate Fondue is an elegant party treat. And Peanut Butter Blossoms start the year out with "kisses."

Shrimp Cocktail with Homemade
Cocktail Sauce

Pork Chops with Cider and Apples

Simple Skillet Salmon

Home-Style Baked Beans

Stewed Collard Greens

Spiced Corn

Chocolate Fondue

Peanut Butter Blossoms

SIMPLE SKILLET SALMON

Makes 4 to 6 Servings   Active Time: 20 Minutes   Start to Finish: 30 Minutes

3 to 4 pounds salmon filets

2 tablespoons unsalted butter, cut in pieces, softened

1 lemon

Salt and pepper

1 teaspoon herbes de Provence

1 tablespoon oil

1. Rinse the filets with cold water to ensure that any scales or bones are removed. Dry them in paper towels. Rub soft butter on both sides of the filets, squeeze lemon over them, and season with salt, pepper, and herbes de Provence.

2. Heat the skillet over medium-high heat and add the tablespoon of olive oil. Add the filets, flesh side down. Cook on one side for about 3 minutes, then flip them and cook only 2 minutes on the other side. Remove the pan from the heat and let the fish rest in it for a minute before serving. The skin should peel right off.

There are different cuts of salmon: steaks and filets. The steaks are cut from the meat around the backbone, and they contain that bone in the middle. Filets are cut from the flesh that extends from the head to the tail of the fish. For this recipe, use filets.

HOME-STYLE BAKED BEANS

Makes 6 to 8 servings   Active Time: 30 Minutes   Start to Finish: 1½ to 2 Hours

6 strips thick-cut bacon, divided in half

½ onion, diced

½ cup diced bell pepper (ribs and seeds removed)

1 teaspoon salt

2 (15.5-oz.) cans pinto beans, rinsed and drained

1 cup barbecue sauce (not too sweet!)

1 teaspoon Dijon mustard

2 tablespoons dark brown sugar

Baked beans are delicious and filling on their own, but they are the perfect accompaniment to grilled sausages, hot dogs, hamburgers, pork chops, or barbecued chicken. Their thickness is also complemented by coleslaw or a big green salad. Cornbread makes the meal.

1. Preheat the oven to 325 degrees F.

2. Heat the skillet over medium heat and cook half the bacon pieces. Cook until it's just soft, about 8 minutes. Transfer to a plate lined with paper towels to drain.

3. In the fat, add the remaining pieces of bacon, turn up the heat, and cook, flipping often, until pieces are browned. Reduce the heat to medium. Add the onion and pepper and cook, stirring occasionally, until the vegetables soften, another 8 minutes or so.

4. Add the salt, beans, barbecue sauce, mustard, and brown sugar. Stir, season with additional salt and a generous grind of fresh pepper, and leave on the stove until the liquid just starts to simmer.

5. Lay the partially cooked pieces of bacon on top and transfer the skillet to the oven.

6. Bake for 1 hour and take a look. The bacon should be crisp and browned, and the beans should be thick. This can go for another 15 to 30 minutes more if the consistency isn't right. Just be careful not to overcook them, in which case the beans will start to dry out. An hour and 15 to 20 minutes is about right.

7. Remove from the oven and allow to cool slightly before serving, preferably in bowls around a fire!

STEWED COLLARD GREENS

Makes 6 to 8 servings   Active Time: 15 minutes   Minimum cook time: 2 hours in a medium slow cooker

2½ pounds collard greens

1 cup Vegetable Stock (page 36) or purchased stock

2 garlic cloves, minced

¼ cup cider vinegar

¼ cup granulated sugar

½ teaspoon dried thyme

1 bay leaf

Salt and red pepper flakes to taste

1. Rinse collard greens well, rubbing leaves to remove all grit and sand. Discard stems and cut leaves crosswise into ½-inch strips.

2. Bring stock, garlic, vinegar, sugar, and thyme to a boil in a large saucepan. Add as many greens as will fit into the pan by pushing greens into boiling liquid. Add more greens as those in the pan wilt. When all greens are wilted, pour greens into the slow cooker, and add bay leaf.

3. Cook on Low for 4 to 6 hours or on High for 2 to 3 hours, or until greens are very tender. Remove and discard bay leaf, season to taste with salt and red pepper flakes, and serve hot.

Note: The dish can be prepared up to 2 days in advance and refrigerated, tightly covered. Reheat it, covered, over low heat until hot, stirring occasionally.

Variations:
Substitute kale or Swiss chard for the collard greens, and reduce the cooking time by 1 hour on Low or 30 minutes on High.

Greens were a mainstay of the poor Southern diet, and though the nutritional profile might not have been known at the time, it is certainly impressive. One serving of greens provides more than your daily requirement of vitamins C and A. Greens have a substantial amount of iron and calcium, fiber, and minerals. And they are one of the few good nondairy sources of calcium.

Spiced Corn
Makes 6 Servings   Active Time: 10 Minutes   Start to Finish: 20 Minutes

6 ears corn, husks removed and kernels separated

2 tablespoons unsalted butter

½ teaspoon cayenne pepper

¼ teaspoon ancho chile pepper

1 teaspoon coarsely ground black pepper

1 teaspoon fresh sea salt

1. Place a medium cast-iron skillet over medium-high heat.

2. Add the butter to the pan and when hot, add the corn, cayenne pepper, ancho chile pepper, coarsely ground black pepper, and fresh sea salt. Cook the corn for about 15 minutes, stirring frequently.

3. Remove the skillet from the heat and serve immediately.

Chocolate Fondue

Makes 4 servings
Active Time: 5 minutes
Start to Finish: 45-60 minutes

¾ pound good quality bittersweet chocolate, chopped

½ cup heavy whipping cream

3 tablespoons liqueur or rum extract

1. Combine chocolate, cream, and liqueur or extract in the slow cooker. Cook on Low for 45 to 60 min, or until chocolate melts. Stir gently toward the end of the cooking time.

2. Serve directly from the slow cooker, using large toothpicks or fondue forks to dip the selection of foods.

PEANUT BUTTER BLOSSOMS

Makes: 2 dozen   Active time: 20 minutes   Start to finish: 45 minutes

---

1¼ cups amaranth flour

¼ cup potato starch

½ teaspoon xanthan gum

½ teaspoon baking soda

Pinch of salt

¾ cup firmly packed light brown sugar

4 tablespoons (½ stick) unsalted butter, softened

½ cup smooth peanut butter

1 large egg

½ teaspoon pure vanilla extract

24 kiss-shaped chocolate candies, unwrapped

1. Preheat the oven to 350 degrees F. Line two baking sheets with parchment paper or silicon baking mats.

2. Combine amaranth flour, potato starch, xanthan gum, baking soda, and salt in a mixing bowl. Whisk well.

3. Combine butter and sugar in another mixing bowl and beat at low speed with an electric mixer to combine. Increase the speed to high, and beat for 3 to 4 minutes, or until light and fluffy. Add peanut butter, egg, and vanilla, and beat for 1 minute.

4. Slowly add dry ingredients to the butter mixture, and beat until stiff dough forms.

5. Roll dough into balls with your hands, and arrange them on the baking sheets. Chill dough if too soft to roll. Press an indentation in the center of each ball with your fingertip, and place one candy in the indentation.

6. Bake cookies for 12 to 14 minutes, or until firm to the touch. Cool cookies for 2 minutes on the baking sheets, and then transfer them with a spatula to cooling racks to cool completely.

Variations:

• Substitute sweetened almond butter for the peanut butter, substitute pure almond extract for the vanilla, and substitute ½ cup almond meal for ½ cup of the amaranth flour.

• Substitute ¾ teaspoon fruit jelly for the candy in the center of the cookies.

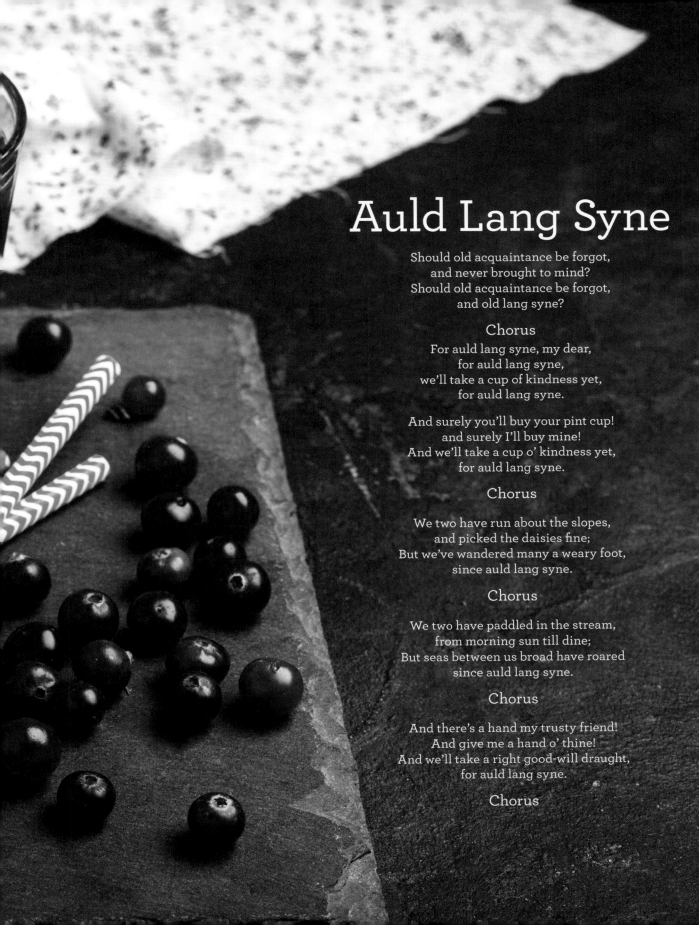

Auld Lang Syne

Should old acquaintance be forgot,
and never brought to mind?
Should old acquaintance be forgot,
and old lang syne?

Chorus

For auld lang syne, my dear,
for auld lang syne,
we'll take a cup of kindness yet,
for auld lang syne.

And surely you'll buy your pint cup!
and surely I'll buy mine!
And we'll take a cup o' kindness yet,
for auld lang syne.

Chorus

We two have run about the slopes,
and picked the daisies fine;
But we've wandered many a weary foot,
since auld lang syne.

Chorus

We two have paddled in the stream,
from morning sun till dine;
But seas between us broad have roared
since auld lang syne.

Chorus

And there's a hand my trusty friend!
And give me a hand o' thine!
And we'll take a right good-will draught,
for auld lang syne.

Chorus

Menu 1

Here, we start the new year with a sourdough starter you can use for making delicious sourdough bread all year round. Other than that bready goodness, we're starting the year off light and fresh. It's a time for new beginnings, and a time to work on those New Year's resolutions.
Let's get started!

Country Sourdough
& Sourdough
Starter

House Salad

Stuffed Bell Peppers

Baked Apples

SOURDOUGH STARTER

50/50 mixture all-purpose and whole-wheat flour

Water at room temperature

1. In a small glass, plastic, or stainless steel bowl, combine equal amounts of water and flour—I would say about 1 cup of each. Use a spoon and whisk it together thoroughly, scraping off the dough that lines the sides. Cover with a towel and place in a shady area at room temperature. Let rest for 2 to 3 days.

2. When you uncover the starter in the morning 2 to 3 days later, it may have risen slightly and bubbles will appear on the surface. If a dried layer of flour appears on the surface, peel it back and discard.

3. Discard about three-quarters of the starter and then replace it with equal amounts water and flour so that you recreate the original amount. Cover and return to a shady environment, and let rest overnight.

4. Repeat the process for about 1 to 2 weeks, until the starter has a bubbly surface and starts to smell slightly sour; when you obverse it over the course of a day, it should rise just after being fed, and then fall throughout the afternoon and night.

5. Your starter is now ready. For most of the recipes that follow, you will need only 1 cup of the starter. When you take the cup of starter from the original batch, be sure to feed the starter again to its normal amount. When it starts to get bubbly, transfer the starter to the refrigerator so the growing process is halted and you can return to it several days later, before planning to bake again.

COUNTRY SOURDOUGH

Makes 8 Servings   Active Time: 2 Hours   Start to Finish: 6 to 12 Hours

---

⅔   cup active starter

1   cup water, room temperature

2   tablespoons extra-virgin olive oil

2¼   cup 50/50 whole-wheat and all-purpose flour (see page 53)

2   teaspoons fresh sea salt

1.   In a large plastic, glass, or stainless steel bowl, combine the starter, water, extra-virgin olive oil, and flour using your hands. Make sure all the flour is incorporated into the dough, and then set aside and let rest for 30 minutes.

2.   Next, fold the salt thoroughly into the dough and continue to fold until the dough takes the shape of a ball. Cover the bowl with plastic wrap and place in an area that receives an average amount of sunlight. This is the bulk fermentation process and you should let the dough rest anywhere from 4 hours to overnight, until it has practically doubled in size. If you'd like to increase the volume (and essentially the density of the bread after it's baked), fold the bread over itself every 20 minutes for the first couple hours of the bulk fermentation. Simply lift one edge of the dough and fold it on top of the other.

3.   Dust a large carving board with a handful of flour and then transfer the dough from the bowl to the carving board. Using a bread spatula, fold all four edges of the dough to the center and then flip the entire loaf upside down, so that the seams of the folded dough press onto the carving board. Continue to do this until the dough begins to rise and take a round shape.

4.   Place the shaped dough inside a large bowl lined with a floured kitchen towel, seam side down. Let rest for 1 to 3 hours, until it rises significantly.

5.   Coat the inside of a medium Dutch oven with flour, and then preheat the oven to 400 degrees F.

6.   After the dough has risen, transfer the loaf from the bowl to the Dutch oven, and then cover and transfer to the oven. Bake for 20 minutes. Remove the lid and then bake for about 35 more minutes, until the loaf is golden brown and crisp.

7.   Remove the loaf from the Dutch oven immediately and let rest for about 15 minutes before slicing.

STUFFED BELL PEPPERS

Makes 2 servings   Active Time: 5 Minutes   Start to Finish: 17 Minutes

1 tablespoon olive oil

4 slices bacon, cut into ½-inch pieces

¼ pound ground beef

½ teaspoon salt

½ teaspoon pepper

2 tablespoons onion, chopped

⅛ teaspoon poultry seasoning

½ cup rice, cooked

2 green bell peppers, tops removed, cored and deseeded

1 egg, beaten

1 cup water

1. Add olive oil and bacon to the pressure cooker and cook over medium heat until crispy, about 5 minutes. Remove bacon and add the ground beef and onion, cooking until the beef is browned and the onion is softened and slightly golden brown.

2. Remove the beef and onions from the pressure cooker and place in a mixing bowl. Add the bacon pieces, salt, pepper, poultry seasoning, rice and egg to the bowl and mix well.

3. Fill each pepper with the meat mixture. Add the cup of water to the pressure cooker, along with the stuffed peppers on the rack. Seal the pressure cooker, select the High Pressure function, and let cook for 12 minutes.

4. Use the natural release method and slowly remove the lid once the valve has dropped.

Tip: Any color bell pepper works!

HOUSE SALAD

Makes 6 Servings   Active Time: 15 Minutes   Start to Finish: 30 Minutes

3 heads Romaine lettuce

1 small red onion, sliced into ¼-inch rings

10 Kalamata olives

10 green olives

4 plum tomatoes, stemmed and quartered

6 pepperoncini peppers

2 garlic cloves, minced

¼ cup red wine vinegar

¾ cup extra-virgin olive oil

Coarsely ground black pepper

Fresh sea salt

1. Rinse the heads of the lettuce and dry them thoroughly. In a medium bowl, combine the lettuce, red onion, Kalamata olives, green olives, tomatoes, and pepperoncini peppers and then set in the refrigerator.

2. In a small jar, whisk together the garlic, red wine vinegar, and extra-virgin olive oil, and then season with the coarsely ground black pepper and fresh sea salt. Chill in the refrigerator for 15 minutes.

3. Remove the salad and vinaigrette from the refrigerator and mix together immediately before serving.

Baked Apples

Makes 4 servings   Active Time: 30 Minutes
Start to Finish: 50 Minutes

4 firm apples

2 tablespoons butter

½ cup water

Maple syrup

1 teaspoon cinnamon and

½ teaspoon ground star anise

Vanilla ice cream or maple Greek yogurt

1. Preheat the oven to 350 degrees F.

2. Core the apples, getting as much out as possible without cutting the apple in half.

3. Heat the skillet over medium-high. Add the butter and let it melt. Place the apples bottom-down in the skillet. Add the water from the center so that it distributes evenly around the apples. Drizzle the tops of the apples with maple syrup and dust with cinnamon and ground star anise.

4. Put the skillet in the oven and cook for about 20 minutes, or until apples are soft. Drizzle with additional maple syrup if desired. Serve with vanilla ice cream or maple Greek yogurt.

Variation:
Use apple cider instead of water to make a nice apple-butter sauce, which you can simmer down after the apples are cooked to make a concentrated sauce. Fill the core with raisins or other dried fruits before baking. Substitute light brown sugar for maple syrup, sprinkling additional sugar on before serving.

Menu 2

Nothing will warm your bones and get you
through a cold winter night like a steaming bowl
of venison stew, alongside wheat loaf with
caramelized onions and black olives.

Venison Stew with vegetables

**Wheat Loaf with Caramelized
Onions & Black Olives**

**Chocolate Pudding Pie with
Graham Cracker Crust**

VENISON STEW

Makes 6 to 8 servings   Active Time: 30 minutes   Start to Finish: 6 to 8 hours

4 pounds venison shoulder

Salt and pepper to taste

4 to 6 slices bacon

¼ cup bacon drippings

2 onions, diced

1 carrot, peeled and diced

1 stalk celery, diced

¼ cup almond flour

12-oz. can diced tomatoes

½ cup mushrooms, sliced

2 cloves garlic, crushed

3 cups beef stock or broth

1 cup red wine

1 sprig thyme

1 spring rosemary

2 bay leaves

1. Season the venison with salt and pepper. In a heavy bottomed skillet, cook the bacon, reserving the cooked strips. In the bacon drippings, cook the venison so that it is browned on all sides. Put the venison in the slow cooker.

2. Into the skillet add the onions, carrots, and celery, and stir frequently until they have browned slightly. Add the almond flour and stir to combine. Put the mixture into the slow cooker with the venison.

3. In a large bowl, combine the tomatoes, mushrooms, garlic, beef stock or broth, red wine, thyme, rosemary, and bay leaves. Pour this over and around the venison.

4. Cook on Low for 6 to 8 hours or High for 5 to 7 hours.

WHEAT LOAF
with Caramelized Onions & Black Olives

Makes 8 servings   Active Time: 2 hours   Start to Finish: 12 to 14 hours

½ large white onion

3 tablespoons extra-virgin olive oil

1 cup black olives, pitted and halved

¼ teaspoon instant yeast

1½ cups water

2 cups whole-wheat flour

1 cup all-purpose flour

Fresh sea salt

1. On a large carving board, peel and chop off the ends of the onion, then slice the remaining onion into ¼-inch strips and set aside.

2. Place a medium cast-iron skillet over low heat and add 1 tablespoon olive oil to the pan. When hot, add the strips of onion and begin the caramelizing process. Sauté the onion strips for about 30 minutes, stirring about once per minute. Let the onions naturally stick to the pan so they become brown and extra tender. When finished, remove from the pan and let cool.

3. Mix the cooked caramelized onions with the black olives, and set aside.

4. In a large bowl, mix the water and yeast and let rest until the yeast has fully dissolved (about 5 minutes). Using your hands, stir in the flour and a pinch of sea salt. Mix thoroughly, then cover the bowl with a clean kitchen towel, transfer to a corner of the kitchen, and let rest overnight until the dough has risen significantly.

5. Dust a large carving board with a handful of flour and then transfer the dough from the bowl to the carving bowl. Carefully add the caramelized onions and olives from the dough and then, using a bread spatula, fold all four edges of the dough to the center and then flip the entire loaf upside down, so that the seams of the folded dough press onto the cutting board. Continue to do this until the dough begins to rise and take on a round shape.

6. Place the shaped dough inside a large bowl lined with a floured kitchen towel, seam side down. Let rest for 1 to 3 hours, until it rises significantly.

7. Place a large sheet pan in the oven and preheat the oven to 400 degrees F.

8. After the dough has risen, remove the hot sheet pan from the oven and carefully coat it with the remaining extra-virgin olive oil. Next, transfer the dough to the sheet pan and then to the oven. Bake for 30 to 45 minutes, until the loaf is golden brown.

9. Remove the loaf from the oven and let rest for about 15 minutes before slicing.

CHOCOLATE PUDDING PIE

Makes 6 to 8 servings   Active Time: 20 Minutes   Start to Finish: 90 Minutes

1 graham cracker crust

2 (3.5-oz.) boxes instant chocolate pudding (dark chocolate is preferable)

3 cups whole milk

2 cups whipped topping (Cool Whip or fresh whipped cream)

Whole fresh raspberries or sliced strawberries for garnish (if desired)

1. In a large bowl, combine the pudding mix and milk. Whisk until all the lumps are broken up, the pudding is smooth, and it has started to thicken, about 5 minutes.

2. Put the pudding in the graham cracker crust and cover with plastic wrap. Refrigerate for an hour or longer.

3. Before serving, top with the whipped topping and garnish with the fruit.

Graham Cracker Crust

Makes 1 10-inch crust   Active Time: 20 Minutes   Start to Finish: 90 Minutes

1½ cups graham cracker crumbs

2 tablespoons sugar

1 tablespoon maple syrup

5 tablespoons unsalted butter, melted, plus 1 tablespoon butter for greasing the skillet

1. Preheat the oven to 375 degrees F.

2. In a large bowl, combine graham cracker crumbs and sugar. Stir to combine. Add maple syrup and melted butter and stir to thoroughly combine.

3. Liberally grease the skillet with the butter. Pour the cracker crust dough into the skillet and lightly press into shape. Line with tin foil and fill with uncooked rice. Bake for 10 to 12 minutes until golden.

4. Allow to cool on a wire rack before filling.

Variations

• Chocolate Graham Cracker Crust—Use chocolate graham crackers instead of plain.

• Cinnamon Graham Cracker Crust—Use cinnamon graham crackers instead of plain or add ½ teaspoon ground cinnamon and ¼ teaspoon ground ginger to the basic graham cracker crust mix.

• Hint of Heat Graham Cracker Crust—Add ¼ to ½ teaspoon cayenne pepper to the graham crackers before adding sugar, syrup, and butter.

Menu 3

There's nothing an Italian "nonna" likes more than to feed her family (and everyone else in the neighborhood). Italian families across the country have argued for years about whose grandmother makes the best meatballs, and here's a menu featuring meatballs with a low-fat twist. Americans love Italian food, and this menu should become a favorite of your family's as well.

Garden Salad

Herbed Turkey Meatballs with Marinara Sauce

Spaghetti

Bread Pudding with Grand Marnier Sauce

GARDEN SALAD

Makes 6 Servings
Active Time: 15 Minutes
Start to Finish: 15 Minutes

---

3 heads iceberg lettuce

1 small red onion, sliced into ¼-inch rings

1 tomato, cut into wedges

1 cucumber

½ carrot, peeled

⅓ cup corn kernels

⅔ cup cheese

1. Rinse the heads of the lettuce and dry them thoroughly. Chop the lettuce and prepare the vegetables as desired.

2. In a medium bowl, combine all of the ingredients and serve.

HERBED TURKEY MEATBALLS

Makes 4 to 6 servings   Active Time: 15 minutes
Start to Finish: 30 minutes

---

1 large egg

2 tablespoons whole milk

½ cup plain breadcrumbs

¼ cup grated Monterey Jack cheese

1 Golden Delicious or Granny Smith apple, peeled, cored, and grated

3 tablespoons chopped fresh sage (or 1 tablespoon dried)

2 tablespoons chopped fresh parsley

1 tablespoon fresh thyme (or 1 teaspoon dried)

Pinch of ground allspice

1¼ pounds ground turkey

Salt and freshly ground black pepper to taste

Vegetable oil spray

Spaghetti

1. Preheat the oven to 450 degrees F. Line a rimmed baking sheet with heavy-duty aluminum foil, and spray the foil with vegetable oil spray.

2. Whisk egg and milk in a mixing bowl, and add breadcrumbs, cheese, apple, sage, parsley, thyme, and allspice, and mix well. Add turkey, season to taste with salt and pepper, and mix well again. Make mixture into 1½-inch meatballs, and arrange meatballs on the prepared pan. Spray tops of meatballs with vegetable oil spray.

3. Bake meatballs for 12 to 15 minutes, or until cooked through and no longer pink. Remove the pan from the oven, and serve immediately with cooked spaghetti and marinara sauce (recipe below).

Note: The meatball mixture can be prepared up to 1 day in advance and refrigerated, tightly covered. Also, the meatballs can be baked up to 2 days in advance and refrigerated, tightly covered. Reheat them in a 350 degrees F oven, covered, for 10 to 12 minutes, or until hot.

Variation:
- Make the meatballs with ground pork, ground veal, or some combination of the two.
- Fresh apple adds moisture as well as a slightly sweet flavor to these lean meatballs flavored with a variety of herbs and spices.

Marinara Sauce

Makes 4 cups   Active Time: 10 minutes   Start to Finish: 45 minutes

---

2 tablespoons olive oil

1 medium onion, finely chopped

¼ cup red lentils

4 garlic cloves, minced

2 tomatoes, quartered and crushed

1 cup water

½ teaspoon dried oregano

2 tablespoons chopped fresh basil

Salt and pepper to taste

1. Stovetop Pressure Cooker:
Place over medium heat. Add oil.

2. Electrical Pressure Cooker:
Select the Sauté function. Add oil.

3. Once hot, place the onion into the pressure cooker and cook for 3 minutes. Add the lentils and garlic and cook for another minute.

4. Add the tomatoes, water, basil, and oregano to the cooker, seal shut, select the High Pressure function, and let cook for 25 to 30 minutes.

5. Use the natural release method and slowly remove the lid once the pressure has left the cooker. Stir well and add salt and pepper to taste.

6. Place contents of the cooker into a food processor and blend until smooth.

GREEK SALAD

**Romaine lettuce or salad
greens mix**

2 tomatoes

1 yellow bell pepper

1 can black olives

Feta cheese for topping

1. Rip or cut the lettuce, dice
    the tomatoes, slice the
    pepper and olives and toss
    your salad.

2. Sprinkle with feta cheese,
    salt, and pepper, and serve
    with a vinaigrette.

MOUSSAKA

Makes 4 to 6 Servings   Active Time: 90 Minutes   Start to Finish: 2½ Hours

---

For the Filling

1 large eggplant, end trimmed and cut into cubes

¼ cup salt

4 cups cold water

⅓ cup olive oil

1 pound ground lamb

1 onion, diced

3 cloves garlic, minced

½ cup dry red wine

8-oz. can tomato sauce

2 tablespoons fresh parsley, chopped

1 teaspoon dried oregano

½ teaspoon cinnamon

Salt and pepper to taste

For the Crust

5 eggs

6 tablespoons butter

⅓ cup flour

2½ cups milk

⅔ cup grated Parmesan cheese

⅓ cup fresh dill, chopped (or substitute parsley)

1. Preheat the oven to 350 degrees F.

2. Prep the eggplant by putting the cold water in a bowl and adding the salt. When dissolved, add the eggplant cubes and stir. Cover the bowl with plastic wrap and let the cubes soak for about 20 minutes. After soaking, drain the water off in a colander and rinse with cold water. Squeeze the cubes in your hands to wring out the water, place them on a pile of paper towels, and blot them as dry as possible. Set aside.

3. While the eggplant is soaking, heat the skillet over medium-high heat. Add a tablespoon of oil to coat the bottom. Brown the ground lamb in the skillet until cooked, about 4 minutes. Use a slotted spoon to transfer the cooked meat to a bowl. Set aside.

4. Cook the prepared eggplant. Heat the skillet over medium-high heat again. Add ¼ cup of olive oil and add the cubes, stirring frequently, until they start to soften, about 5 minutes. Use the slotted spoon to add the cooked eggplant to the bowl with the lamb in it.

5. Put the skillet back on the heat and add the rest of the oil. Cook the onion and garlic together, stirring constantly, until the onion is translucent, about 3 minutes. Add the lamb and eggplant and stir to combine. Add the wine, tomato sauce, parsley, oregano, and cinnamon. Stir to combine, lower the heat to low, and cook, simmering, for about 15 minutes, stirring occasionally. Season with salt and pepper.

6. Next, make the topping. In a large bowl, beat the eggs lightly. Heat another skillet or saucepan over medium heat, melt the butter, lower the heat slightly, and add the flour, stirring to combine and form a paste. Slowly add the milk, stirring with a whisk. Bring to a boil over low heat, stirring constantly with the whisk. When the mixture reaches a boil, remove from the heat. Add about half the hot mix into the eggs and stir briskly, then pour the tempered eggs into the skillet and mix into the rest of the hot flour/milk mix. Add the cheese and dill (or parsley) and stir.

7. Smooth the topping over the lamb in the first skillet to even it out, then top with the flour/cheese mix. Put the skillet in the oven. Bake for 35 to 45 minutes until the topping is set and golden brown.

8. Allow to rest for about 5 minutes before serving.

Wild Rice Pilaf

Makes 4 to 6 servings   Active Time: 15 minutes   Start to Finish: 3 hours

3 tablespoons unsalted butter

1 large onion, chopped

1 carrot, chopped

1 cup wild rice, rinsed

¼ cup dried currants

3 cups Vegetable Stock (page 36), Chicken Stock (page 37), or purchased stock

Salt and freshly ground pepper to taste

1. Melt butter in a small skillet over medium heat. Add onion and carrot, and cook, stirring frequently, for 3 minutes, or until onion is translucent. Scrape mixture into a slow cooker.

2. Add wild rice, currants, and stock to the slow cooker, and stir well. Cook on Low for 7 to 8 hours or on High for 3 to 4 hours, or until rice is fluffed and tender and stock is absorbed.

3. Season to taste with salt and pepper, and serve hot.

GREEK-STYLE WALNUT PIE

Makes 8 to 10 servings   Active Time: 90 Minutes
Start to Finish: Several hours

---

1 flaky pastry crust recipe for a double crust (see page 107)

2½ cups finely chopped walnuts

¼ cup packed brown sugar

2 tablespoons granulated sugar

1½ teaspoons ground cinnamon

¾ cup butter, split into 3 (¼ cup) rations, melted, plus 1 tablespoon for greasing the skillet

¾ cup honey

1 tablespoon fresh squeezed lemon juice

1. Preheat the oven to 325 degrees F.

2. In a medium bowl, mix walnuts, brown sugar, granulated sugar, and the cinnamon.

3. Put the skillet over medium heat and melt the butter in it. Carefully remove pan from heat.

4. Place 1 of the piecrusts in the skillet. Pour ¼ cup of melted butter over the bottom of the pie crust. Spread the walnut mixture evenly over butter. Melt and drizzle another ¼ cup butter over the nut mixture and place the other crust over it, crimping the edges together. Cut large slits in the middle of the top crust and drizzle the remaining ¼ cup melted butter over it, brushing to distribute evenly.

5. Put the skillet in the oven and bake for about 20 minutes. Cover the outermost edge with aluminum foil in the last 10 minutes of baking to prevent it from burning. Bake an additional 30 to 35 minutes or until golden brown.

6. When pie is nearly finished, put honey and lemon in a small saucepan. Heat over medium heat, stir, and cook, stirring constantly, until mixture is almost watery in consistency.

7. Remove pie from the oven and slowly and carefully pour the honey-lemon mixture over the top, allowing it to penetrate and drizzle into the crust.

8. Allow pie to cool for several hours before serving.

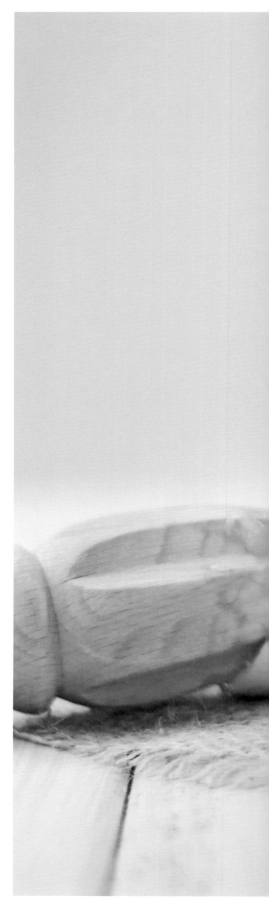

Menu 5

Here's a wholesome menu that reminds us of sturdier yet simpler times, when winter gales blew in from the ocean, leaving snow drifts as high as the windowsill. The fishermen on Cape Cod will tell you New England winters are never easy, but nothing is quite as cozy and warm as a wood stove and a bowl of hot chowder.

New England Chowder

Coleslaw (page 336)

Fried Clams with Tartar Sauce

Dutch Apple Baby

What we know as
New England chowder
dates from the mid-1800s.

NEW ENGLAND CHOWDER

Makes 4 to 6 servings   Active Time: 25 minutes   Start to Finish: 50 minutes

1 pint fresh chopped clams

4 tablespoons (½ stick) unsalted butter, divided

2 medium onions, diced

2 celery ribs, sliced

1 (8-oz.) bottle clam juice

2 medium red potatoes, cut into ½-inch dice

2 tablespoons chopped fresh parsley

1 bay leaf

1 tablespoon fresh thyme (or 1 teaspoon dried)

Salt and freshly ground black pepper to taste

3 tablespoons all-purpose flour

2 cups whole milk

1 cup heavy cream or half-and-half

Oyster crackers, for serving

1. For soup, drain clams in a sieve over a bowl, reserving juice in the bowl. Press down with the back of a spoon to extract as much liquid as possible from clams. Refrigerate clams until ready to use.

2. Melt 2 tablespoons butter in a large saucepan over medium heat. Add onions and celery, and cook, stirring frequently, for 3 minutes, or until onions are translucent. Add bottled clam juice and reserved clam juice to the pan, along with potatoes, parsley, bay leaf, and thyme. Bring to a boil, reduce the heat to low, and simmer, covered, for 12 minutes, or until potatoes are tender.

3. While mixture simmers, melt remaining 2 tablespoons butter in a small saucepan over low heat. Stir in flour and cook, stirring constantly, for 2 minutes. Raise the heat to medium and whisk in milk. Bring to a boil, whisking frequently, and simmer for 2 minutes. Stir thickened milk into the pot with vegetables, and add cream. Bring to a boil, reduce the heat to low, and simmer, uncovered, for 3 minutes. Remove and discard bay leaf, season to taste with salt and pepper, and keep hot.

4. To serve, ladle soups into bowls, and top each serving with oyster crackers.

Variations:

• Fry ½ pound bacon, cut into 1-inch lengths, in a skillet until crisp. Remove bacon from the pan with a slotted spoon, and discard all but 4 tablespoons of bacon fat. Cook vegetables in bacon fat rather than in button. Crumble cooked bacon, and add it to the soup along with the clam fritters.

• Add ½ cup cooked corn kernels to the soup, along with ¼ cup sautéed chopped red bell pepper.

Tip: One of the greatest convenience foods on the market is shucked and pre-minced quahog or cherrystone clams found in the seafood department.

FRIED CLAMS

Makes 2 to 4 Servings

1 cup all-purpose flour

½ teaspoon salt

½ teaspoon freshly ground black pepper

1 cup buttermilk or evaporated milk

1 pint shucked whole or strip clams, drained and well rinsed. Cherrystones, littlenecks, or Western littlenecks work best.

Canola or vegetable oil (for deep frying)

1. Prepare the dry ingredients in a large bowl and mix together thoroughly. In a separate bowl, have the buttermilk or evaporated milk poured out and carefully add your clams to avoid splashes.

2. Meanwhile, in a large saucepan or deep fryer begin heating your oil to about 360 degrees F. Additionally, preheat your oven to 200 degrees F and ready a rack over a baking sheet.

3. When the oil is nearly to heat, remove the clams from the milk a few at a time with either a fork or hands and coat them in the flour breading. If you want a thicker batter on your fried clams, dip the breaded clam back into the buttermilk and repeat the breading process. Don't do more than your fryer can fry in one batch, as these clams will be going directly from breading to the at-temp oil.

4. Fry the clams between 90 seconds to 2 minutes, until they are golden brown and to the crispiness of your preference. Move the finished clams to the rack in the oven to keep them warm and drip off any excess oil.

5. Repeat the process as many times as necessary, making sure the oil is to temp between batches.

Homemade Tartar Sauce

1 cup mayonnaise

1 tablespoon dill pickle relish

1 tablespoon minced white onion

2 tablespoons lemon juice

Salt and pepper to taste

In a bowl, mix together all ingredients. Season to taste with salt and pepper, and keep refrigerated until ready to serve.

DUTCH APPLE BABY

Makes 4 servings   Active Time: 45 Minutes   Start to Finish: 75 Minutes

2 firm, semi-tart apples, like Mutsu or Golden Delicious

4 tablespoons butter

¼ cup sugar

1 tablespoon cinnamon

¾ cup flour

¼ teaspoon salt

¾ cup milk

4 eggs

1 teaspoon vanilla or almond extract

Confectioner's sugar for dusting

The Dutch Apple Baby is attributed to early Pennsylvania Dutch settlers.

1. Preheat the oven to 425 degrees F and position a rack in the middle.

2. Peel and core the apples, and cut into slices. Heat a skillet over medium-high heat. Add the butter and apples and cook, stirring, for 3 to 4 minutes until the apples soften. Add the sugar and cinnamon and continue cooking for another 3 or 4 minutes. Distribute the apples evenly over the bottom of the skillet and remove from heat.

3. In a large bowl, mix the flour and salt. In a smaller bowl, whisk together the milk, eggs, and vanilla or almond extract. Add the wet ingredients to the dry ingredients and stir to combine. Pour the batter over the apples.

4. Put the skillet in the oven and bake for 15 to 20 minutes until the "baby" is puffed and browned on the top.

5. Remove from the oven and allow to cool for a few minutes. Run a knife along the edge of the skillet to loosen the dessert. Put a plate over the skillet and, using oven mitts or pot holders, flip the skillet over so the dessert is transferred to the plate. Serve warm with a dusting of confectioner's sugar.

79

Chinese New Year

In late January or early February, Asian kitchens across the country are getting ready for Chinese New Year. While the day itself changes from year to year, now is the time to gather the ingredients for one of the more festive holidays of the season. Here's a chance to treat your family to something fun and different, just like the holiday itself. Incidentally, Spring Rolls make tasty Super Bowl party snacks.

Citrus Spinach Salad

Spring Rolls

Szechuan Scallops in Black Bean Sauce

Almond Cookies

SPRING ROLLS

Yield: 18 rolls   Active time: 35 minutes   Start to finish: 55 minutes

5 large dried shiitake mushrooms

1 oz. bean thread noodles

½ pound ground pork

1 cup fresh bean sprouts, rinsed and cut into 1-inch lengths

½ cup shredded carrot

½ cup chopped scallions, white part and 4 inches of green tops

4 garlic cloves, minced

3 tablespoons fish sauce

2 large eggs, lightly beaten

½ cup granulated sugar, divided

Salt and freshly ground black pepper to taste

18 (8-inch) rice paper pancakes

Vegetable oil spray

Serve these, as well as other Asian finger food dishes, in a bamboo steamer. Line the steamer with plastic wrap and then with leaves of green or red head lettuce.

1. Soak dried mushrooms and bean thread noodles in separate bowls of very hot tap water for 30 minutes. Remove mushrooms, and squeeze well to extract as much water as possible. Discard stems, and finely chop mushrooms. Drain bean thread noodles. Place them on a cutting board in a long log shape, and cut into 1-inch pieces. Measure out ½ cup, and discard any additional liquid.

2. Preheat the oven to 400 degrees F. Cover a baking sheet with heavy-duty aluminum foil, and spray the foil with vegetable oil spray.

3. Place mushrooms and noodles in a mixing bowl, and add pork, bean sprouts, carrot, scallions, garlic, fish sauce, eggs, and 1 teaspoon sugar. Mix well, and season to taste with salt and pepper.

4. Fill a wide mixing bowl with very hot tap water, and stir in remaining sugar until dissolved. Place a damp tea towel in front of you on the counter. Place rice paper pancakes on a plate, and cover with a barely damp towel.

5. Fill 1 rice paper pancake at a time, keeping remainder covered. Totally immerse pancake in the hot water for 2 seconds. Remove it and place it on the damp tea towel; it will become pliable within a few seconds. Gently fold front edge of pancake one-third of the way to the top. Place about 2 tablespoons of filling on the folded up portion, and shape it into a log, leaving a 2-inch margin on each side. Lightly spray unfilled pancake with vegetable oil spray. Fold sides over filling, and roll tightly but gently, beginning with the filled side. Place roll on the baking sheet, and continue to fill remaining pancakes in the same manner.

6. Spray tops and sides of rolls with vegetable oil spray, and place them in the center of the preheated oven. Bake for 12 minutes, then turn rolls gently with tongs, and bake another 10–12 minutes, or until rolls are browned. Remove the pan from the oven, and blot rolls with paper towels. Slice each in half on the diagonal, and serve immediately.

Note: The filling can be prepared up to 1 day in advance and refrigerated, tightly covered. The rolls can be baked up to 2 days in advance. Reheat them in a 350 degrees F oven for 5 to 7 minutes, or until hot and crisp.

Variation:

• Substitute ground turkey or ground chicken for the pork.

• Substitute 2-3 tablespoons of lemon juice or ponzu for fish sauce to give the rolls a citrusy kick.

CITRUS SPINACH SALAD
with Toasted Almonds

Makes 4 servings   Active Time: 10 minutes   Total Time: 20 minutes

½ cup, plus 1 tablespoon olive oil

4 tablespoons white wine vinegar

½ small lime, juiced

¼ orange, juiced

1 small shallot, finely chopped

Coarsely ground black pepper

Fresh sea salt

4 cups baby spinach

½ to 1 cup cherry tomatoes, quartered

4 tablespoons currants

3 tablespoons sunflower seeds

2 tablespoons sesame seeds

½ cup almonds

1. Add the oil, vinegar, lime juice, orange juice, and shallot into a small jar, and season with pepper and salt.

2. In a large bowl, mix the spinach, tomatoes, currants, sunflower seeds, and sesame seeds and set aside.

3. In a small frying pan, heat 1 tablespoon of olive oil and then add the almonds. Toast until the almonds are brown. Remove from heat and mix into the spinach.

4. Combine the salad dressing and salad before serving.

SZECHUAN SCALLOPS
in Black Bean Sauce

Makes 4 to 6 servings   Active Time: 15 minutes   Start to Finish: 2 hours in a medium slow cooker

---

3 tablespoons Chinese fermented black beans, coarsely chopped but not rinsed

½ cup dry sherry

6 scallions, white parts + 4 inches of green tops, thinly sliced

2 tablespoons Asian sesame oil

4 garlic cloves, minced

3 tablespoons grated fresh ginger

½ pound bok choy, cut in ½-inch slices

2 cups seafood stock or vegetable stock

3 tablespoons soy sauce

3 tablespoons Chinese oyster sauce

2 tablespoons Chinese chile paste with garlic

1½ pounds bay scallops or sea scallops, cut into quarters

1 tablespoon cornstarch

Salt and freshly ground black pepper to taste

1. Stir black beans into sherry to plump for 10 minutes. Reserve 3 tablespoons scallions. Heat sesame oil in a small skillet over medium-high heat. Add remaining scallions, garlic, and ginger, and cook for 30 seconds, stirring constantly, or until fragrant. Scrape mixture into the slow cooker.

2. Add bok choy, sherry mixture, stock, soy sauce, oyster sauce, and chile paste to the slow cooker, and stir well. Cook on Low for 3 to 5 hours or on High for 1½ to 2 hours, or until vegetables are crisp-tender.

3. If cooking on Low, raise the heat to High. Stir in scallops, and cook for 15 to 30 minutes, or until scallops are cooked through. Mix cornstarch and 2 tablespoons cold water in a small cup, and stir cornstarch mixture into the slow cooker. Cook for an additional 5 to 10 minutes, or until juices are bubbling and slightly thickened.

4. Season to taste with salt and pepper. Sprinkle with remaining 3 tablespoons scallions, and serve hot.

Variation:

Substitute 1-inch cubes of cod, halibut, or any firm-fleshed white fish, or extra-large shrimp for the scallops.

Fermented black beans are small black soybeans with a pungent flavor that have been preserved in salt before being packed. Most supermarkets now carry them, if you don't have an Asian market nearby.

ALMOND COOKIES

Makes: 2 dozen   Active time: 15 minutes   Start to finish: 35 minutes

---

¾ cup amaranth flour

½ cup almond meal

¼ cup cornstarch

½ teaspoon xanthan gum

½ teaspoon baking soda

¼ teaspoon salt

½ cup smooth almond butter

4 tablespoons (½ stick) unsalted butter, softened

½ cup granulated sugar

½ cup firmly packed light brown sugar

1 large egg

1 teaspoon pure almond extract

24 blanched almonds

1. Preheat the oven to 350 degrees F. Line two baking sheets with parchment paper or silicon baking mats.

2. Combine amaranth flour, almond meal, cornstarch, xanthan gum, baking soda, and salt in a mixing bowl. Whisk well.

3. Combine almond butter, butter, granulated sugar, and brown sugar in another mixing bowl and beat at low speed with an electric mixer to combine. Increase the speed to high, and beat for 3 to 4 minutes, or until light and fluffy. Add egg and almond extract, and beat for 1 minute.

4. Slowly add dry ingredients to the butter mixture, and beat until stiff dough forms.

5. Form 1-tablespoon amounts of dough into balls, and transfer balls to the prepared baking sheets, leaving 2 inches of space between balls. Flatten balls with the bottom of a glass dipped into amaranth flour to a thickness of ⅓-inch. Press 1 almond into the center of each cookie.

6. Bake for 10 to 12 minutes, or until lightly brown. Cool cookies on the baking sheets for 2 minutes, and then transfer to a wire rack to cool completely.

Tip: For a traditional Chinese New Year twist, serve these cookies alongside orange slices.

Variation:

Substitute cashew butter for the almond butter, vanilla extract for the almond extract, and press cashews into the cookies before baking.

Menu 6

It's a well-known fact: Americans everywhere love meatloaf, and they love it with mashed potatoes. There's just something about its simplicity and its heartiness, not to mention its history: The use of surplus meats mixed with vegetables and spices extends as far back at the Ancient Romans and through the Middle Ages to today. Our comfort-food theme extends to making chocolate truffles—a large batch so you can share some for Valentine's Day.

Meatloaf

Mashed Potatoes

Roasted Cauliflower

Chocolate Truffles

MASHED POTATOES

Makes 6 Servings
Active Time: 30 Minutes
Start to Finish: 45 Minutes

3 pounds Yukon Gold potatoes, peeled and cut into quarters

1 cup half-and-half

½ cup (1 stick) unsalted butter, softened

Coarsely ground black pepper

Fresh sea salt

1. Place the potatoes in a large stockpot and fill with water so that it covers the potatoes by 1 inch.

2. Place the stockpot on the stove and bring to a boil. Cook for about 20 minutes, until you can pierce the potatoes with a fork. Remove from the pot from the heat and drain the water, leaving the potatoes in it.

3. Using a potato masher or fork (a little more work, but still a masher nonetheless), start mashing the potatoes so they break apart. Gradually beat in the half-and-half and butter, tasting the potatoes as you go along, until you arrive at the perfect blend of creamy, buttery, mashed potatoes. Season with the coarsely ground black pepper and fresh sea salt, and then serve warm.

Tip: Garlic makes a delicious addition to this dish - consider adding either minced or dried garlic to the potatoes as you mash them.

ROASTED CAULIFLOWER

Makes 4 to 6 servings   Active Time: ½ hour   Start to Finish: 1 hour

½ tablespoons olive oil

1 teaspoon salt

Freshly ground pepper

½ teaspoon ground cumin

½ teaspoon ground coriander

½ teaspoon turmeric

¼ teaspoon cayenne pepper

1 medium head cauliflower, stem and green leaves removed

Sour cream for serving (optional)

1. Preheat the oven to 425 degrees F.

2. In a bowl, combine oil, salt, pepper, and spices and whisk together.

3. Cut the cauliflower crosswise into ½-inch slices. Put the slices in the skillet and brush the tops liberally with oil mixture. Then turn the "steaks" over and brush the other side.

4. Put the skillet in the oven and roast for about 20 minutes, turning the pieces over after 10 minutes. A toothpick inserted in the flesh should go in easily to indicate the cauliflower is cooked through.

5. Serve the slices hot, with a side of sour cream if desired.

Variation:

This recipe can be made with cauliflower florets, too. Instead of slicing the cauliflower into cross sections, just pick off the florets. Put them in the bowl of seasoned oil to coat and then in the skillet to bake, shaking the pan halfway through to turn the pieces.

MEATLOAF

Makes 1 loaf   Active Time: 15 minutes   Start to Finish: 1 hour, 15 minutes

1½ pounds lean ground beef

¾ cup Quaker Oats (quick or old fashioned, uncooked)

¾ cup finely chopped onions (the finer the better)

½ cup ketchup

1 egg, lightly beaten

1 tablespoon Worcestershire sauce

2 cloves garlic, minced

½ teaspoon salt

½ teaspoon black pepper

1. Preheat the oven to 350 degrees F.

2. In a large bowl, mix all ingredients lightly but thoroughly.

3. Shape meat mixture into a loaf and place on a cookie sheet.

4. Bake 50 to 55 minutes.

To jazz up your meatloaf, consider adding any one of the following:

- Substitute salsa for the ketchup and add 2 tablespoons chopped fresh cilantro.
- Swap your favorite hot sauce for the Worcestershire sauce.
- Shred 2 carrots in a food processor, squeeze dry, and add to the meat mixture.
- Substitute spicy V8 juice for the ketchup.
- Add 1 jalapeno pepper, finely chopped.
- Add ½ green or red pepper, minced.

CHOCOLATE TRUFFLES

Makes 3 dozen   Active time: 20 minutes   Start to finish: 4 ½ hours, including 4 hours to chill.

1 pound good-quality
bittersweet chocolate

1¼ cups heavy cream

Pinch of salt

½ cup unsweetened cocoa
powder

Variations:

- Instead of cocoa powder, coat the
truffles in toasted coconut, finely
chopped nuts, or colored candy
sprinkles.

- Add 2 to 4 tablespoons liquor or
liqueur to the truffle mixture.

- Add 1 to 2 tablespoons instant
coffee powder or instant espresso
powder to make mocha truffles.

- Add 1 tablespoon grated orange
zest to the mixture.

- Form truffles around a small nut,
such as a hazelnut or a peanut.

1. Break chocolate into pieces no larger than a lima bean. Either chop chocolate in a food processor using on-and-off pulsing, or place it in a heavy resealable plastic bag, and smash it with the back of a heavy skillet.

2. Heat cream in a saucepan over medium heat, stirring frequently, until mixture comes to a simmer. Stir in salt, and add chocolate. Remove the pan from the heat, cover the pan, and allow chocolate to melt for 5 minutes. Whisk mixture until smooth, and transfer to a 9 x 9-inch baking pan. Chill mixture for at least 4 hours, or overnight.

3. Place cocoa powder in a shallow bowl. Using the large side of a melon baller, scoop out 2 teaspoons mixture, and gently form it into a ball. Roll balls in cocoa, and then refrigerate on a platter for 30 minutes to set cocoa.

4. Coat truffles in dark chocolate or white chocolate or some combination of the two. To do this, melt chopped chocolate in a mixing bowl set over simmering water, or place chopped chocolate in a microwave safe bowl and microwave on 100% (HIGH) for 20 seconds, stir, and repeat as necessary until chocolate is smooth and melted. Place a small amount of melted chocolate in the palm of your hand, and roll formed balls in the chocolate.

5. Note: The truffles can be made up to 1 week in advance, and refrigerated, tightly covered with plastic wrap or in an airtight container. (This is a great way to plan to give homemade Valentine's Day chocolates!) Allow refrigerated truffles to sit at room temperature for 1 hour before serving.

Tip: Shaping the truffles is easier with cold hands. Keep a bowl of ice water and a roll of paper towels handy while rolling the truffles. Submerge your hands in the water until they are very cold. Then dry them and roll some truffles, repeating as necessary.

91

Menu 7

Valentine's Day is about you and that special someone, but why not make the whole family happy? That's why this menu spreads the love around the whole dining room table, with a wedding soup everyone can enjoy, served with crostini (or "little toasts") for dipping, and a decadent red velvet cake with a classic cream cheese frosting. Wedding soup is an Italian-American creation. It is a mistranslation of minestra maritata which has nothing to do with nuptials but is a reference to the fact that green vegetables and meats go well together.
As does this meal...

Crostini

Italian Salad

Italian Wedding Soup
with Turkey Meatballs

Red Velvet Cake with
Cream Cheese Frosting

Tip: If you need to reheat these to crisp them up again, put them in a 350-degrees F oven for 3 to 4 minutes.

These crostini make a perfect base for bruschetta.

CROSTINI

Makes 20 pieces   Active Time: 10 minutes
Start to Finish: 20 minutes

---

20 slices thin Italian bread, ½-inch thick and 2x3 inches in size

½ cup olive oil

1 garlic clove, halved

1. Preheat the oven to 375 degrees F, and line a baking sheet with heavy-duty aluminum foil.

2. Brush both sides of bread slices with olive oil, and arrange bread on the prepared baking sheet. Bake until bread is beginning to brown, about 5 to 6 minutes.

3. Remove bread from the oven, and rub one side of toasts with cut surface of garlic clove.

Variation:
Use melted butter instead of olive oil.

ITALIAN SALAD

Makes 6 servings   Active Time: 15 minutes
Start to Finish: 20 minutes

---

2 bunches romaine, chopped

2 cups grape tomatoes, halved

1 small red onion, thinly sliced and separated into rings

8 pepperoncini

1 cup sliced black olives

¼ cup grated Parmesan cheese

½ cup fat-free Italian salad dressing

Croutons, as desired

1. In a large bowl, combine all the ingredients, except for the last two. When ready to serve, drizzle with salad dressing and toss the salad. Top with croutons and serve.

ITALIAN WEDDING SOUP
with Turkey Meatballs

Makes 6 to 8 servings   Active time: 20 minutes   Start to finish: 1 hour

---

Meatballs:

1 large egg

½ cup seasoned Italian breadcrumbs

¼ cup whole milk

1 small onion, grated

2 garlic cloves, minced

¼ cup chopped fresh Italian parsley

½ cup freshly grated Parmesan

1½ pounds ground turkey

Salt and freshly ground black
pepper to taste

Soup:

8 cups Chicken Stock (page 37) or purchased stock

1 pound curly endive, rinsed, cored, and coarsely chopped

2 large eggs

½ cup freshly grated Parmesan, divided

Salt and freshly ground black pepper to taste

1. Combine egg, breadcrumbs, milk, onion, garlic, parsley, and Parmesan, and mix well. Add turkey, season to taste with salt and pepper, and mix well into a paste.

2. Combine chicken stock and endive in a 3-quart saucepan, and bring to a boil over medium-high heat. Reduce the heat to low, and simmer soup, uncovered, for 10 minutes.

3. Using wet hands, form meatball mixture into 1-inch balls, and drop them into simmering soup. Cook for 7 to 10 minutes, or until cooked through and no longer pink.

4. Whisk eggs with 2 tablespoons cheese. Stir soup and gradually add egg mixture to form thin strands. Season to taste with salt and pepper, and serve immediately, passing remaining cheese separately.

Note: The soup can be made up to 2 days in advance and refrigerated, tightly covered.
Reheat it over low heat, covered.

Variations:
• Substitute baby spinach or escarole for the curly endive.
• Pork, or a combination of pork and veal, are equally delicious for the meatballs.
Add in vegetables and cooker pasta for a heartier soup!

Tip: Parmesan cheese is one of the distinctive and delectable ingredients in Italian cooking. Its flavor and aroma, however, dissipate quickly once the cheese is grated. That's why it's worth the effort to grate the real thing.

Brown sugar is granulated sugar mixed with molasses, and the darker the color, the more pronounced the molasses flavor. If a recipe calls for dark brown sugar, and you only have light brown sugar, add 2 tablespoons molasses per ½ cup sugar to replicate the taste.

RED VELVET CAKE
with Cream Cheese Frosting

Makes 8-10 servings   Active time: 30 minutes   Start to Finish: 90 minutes

For the cake:

1 cup butter, room temperature

1 ½ cups sugar

2 eggs, room temperature

1 cup buttermilk

2 tablespoons red food coloring

1 teaspoon white vinegar

1 teaspoon vanilla extract

2 ½ cups all-purpose flour

1 teaspoon baking soda

1 teaspoon salt

1 teaspoon cocoa powder

For the frosting:

½ cup butter, softened

1 package (8 ounces) cream cheese

3½ cups powdered sugar

1 teaspoon vanilla extract

1. Preheat oven to 350 degrees F. Liberally coat two circular 9-inch cake pans with butter or canola oil spray and lightly flour, tapping out the excess flour to create a thin, even coat.

2. In a stand mixer with a paddle attachment, cream together the butter and sugar until the mixture is light and fluffy. Once finished, add the eggs one at a time and beat until thoroughly incorporated, scraping down the sides of the bowl after each egg. Add red food coloring, white vinegar and vanilla extract.

3. In a separate medium mixing bowl, combine flour, baking soda, salt and cocoa powder.

4. Add ⅓ of the flour mixture to the stand mixer bowl with the butter-sugar mixture. Then add ⅓ of the buttermilk to the stand mixer bowl. Repeat this process, alternating between adding dry ingredients and buttermilk.

5. Transfer mixture to the prepared cake pans, distributing the batter evenly between the two pans.

6. Bake at 350 for 30-35 minutes, or until a toothpick comes out mostly clean.

7. While the cake is baking, prepare the frosting by beating the butter and cream cheese until blended, and then adding the powdered sugar and vanilla. Beat until frosting is thick and smooth.

8. Let the cake to rest in the pan for up to 30 minutes, then turn out of the pan and allow to completely cool on a wire cooling rack.

9. Once the cakes have cooled, spread a small amount of the cream cheese frosting on top of one cake, and then layer the second cake on top of it. Frost with the rest of the frosting and serve.

Menu 8

It's Mardi Gras time, and that means a hearty menu of down-home Cajun cooking: Shrimp Creole served over Cheesy Grits. And, for dessert, New Orleans Bread Pudding.

Shrimp Creole

Cheesy Grits

Creole Cabbage

New Orleans Bread Pudding

SHRIMP CREOLE

Makes 4 to 6 servings   Active Time: 30 minutes
Start to Finish: 3 to 6 hours, depending on slow cooker setting

3 tablespoons olive oil

6 scallions, white parts and 3 inches of green tops, chopped

2 celery ribs, sliced

½ green bell pepper, seeded and diced

3 cloves garlic, minced

1 tablespoon dried oregano

1 tablespoon paprika

1 teaspoon ground cumin

½ teaspoon dried basil

15-oz. can tomato sauce

½ cup white wine

2 bay leaves

1½ pounds extra-large shrimp, peeled and deveined

Salt and cayenne to taste

Jalepenos for garnish

A few fresh basil leaves for garnish

1. Heat oil in a medium skillet over medium-high heat. Add scallions, celery, bell pepper, and garlic. Cook, stirring frequently, for 3 minutes, or until scallions are translucent. Reduce the heat to low, and stir in oregano, paprika, cumin, and basil. Cook for about 1 minute, stirring constantly. Scrape mixture into the slow cooker.

2. Add tomato sauce, wine, and bay leaves to the slow cooker, and stir well. Cook on Low for 4 to 6 hours or on High for 2 to 3 hours, or until vegetables are soft.

3. If cooking on Low, raise the heat to High. Remove and discard bay leaves, and stir in shrimp. Cook for 15 to 30 minutes, or until shrimp are pink and cooked through. Season to taste with salt and cayenne. Serve over Cheesy Grits (see page 100) and top with fresh basil leaves and jalepenos for garnish.

Do not equate the words "fresh shrimp" with shrimp that have never been frozen. The truth is you probably would be unable to find never-frozen shrimp fresh from the ocean unless you net it yourself. Today, shrimp are harvested, cleaned, and flash-frozen on the boats before they ever reach the shore. But if you plan to freeze shrimp, ask the fishmonger to sell you some still frozen rather than thawed in the case.

CHEESY GRITS

Makes 4 to 6 servings   Active Time: 20 minutes   Start to Finish: 40 minutes

2 cups whole milk

2 cups water

1 cup grits

1 teaspoon salt

1 teaspoon pepper

2 cups grated cheddar cheese

1. Preheat the broiler to high. Bring the milk and water to a boil. Add the grits and stir, cooking constantly, until the grits are thickened and cooked, about 15 minutes. Add the salt and pepper and 1 cup cheese. Stir to combine.

2. Grease the skillet with some butter and add the grits. Sprinkle with the remaining cup of cheese.

3. Put the skillet in the oven and allow to toast under the broiler, about 2 minutes. Serve immediately.

Variation:

If you want spicier grits, use 1 cup Monterey Jack cheese as half of the cheese you include. Or try other hard cheeses like Swiss, mozzarella, or fresh Parmesan.

Creole Cabbage

Makes 4 servings   Active Time: 10 minutes   Start to Finish: 25 minutes

2 tablespoons butter

½ cup onions, chopped

½ cup green peppers, chopped

½ cup celery, chopped

2 cups cabbage, shredded

1 cup tomatoes, peeled and chopped

Salt and pepper to taste

1. Melt the butter in a sauté pan.

2. Add the other ingredients, cover, and simmer 5 to 7 minutes.

Tip: Keep things simple by buying shredded cabbage in a bag.

NEW ORLEANS BREAD PUDDING

Makes 6 to 8 servings   Active time: 15 minutes   Start to Finish: about 4 hours

½ cup raisins

½ cup bourbon

¼ cup chopped pecans

¼ cup sliced almonds

5 large eggs

1 cup granulated sugar

2 cups whole milk

6 tablespoons (¾ stick) unsalted butter, melted

1½ teaspoons pure vanilla extract

1 teaspoon ground cinnamon

Pinch of salt

½ pound loaf French or Italian bread, cut into ½-inch slices

½ to ¾ cup Marnier Sauce (page 67) or other caramel sauce

Vegetable oil spray

1. Preheat the oven to 350 degrees F. Combine the raisins and rum in a microwave-safe dish, and microwave on High for 40 seconds. Place pecans and almonds on a baking sheet and toast for 5 to 7 minutes, or until browned. Set aside.

2. Combine eggs, sugar, milk, melted butter, vanilla, cinnamon, and salt in a mixing bowl, and whisk well. Add bread slices to the mixing bowl, and press them down so that the bread absorbs the liquid. Stir in raisins, almonds, and pecans. Allow mixture to sit for 10 minutes.

3. Grease the inside of the slow cooker liberally with vegetable oil spray or melted butter. Spoon mixture into the slow cooker. Cook on High for 1 hour, then reduce the heat to Low and cook for 2 to 3 hours, or until puffed and an instant-read thermometer inserted in the center registers 165 degrees F.

4. Serve hot or at room temperature, topped with Marnier Sauce or caramel sauce.

Variations:

- Omit the sugar, cinnamon, and pecans, and add 1½ cups white chocolate, melted, to the bread mixture. Serve with chocolate sauce.

- Use maple syrup instead of sugar, reduce the cinnamon to ½ teaspoon, and use walnuts instead of pecans.

Menu 9

"Bubbes" in Jewish kitchens everywhere are getting ready for a Purim feast. Purim is one of the more festive of the Jewish holidays, commemorating the salvation of the Jewish people, and this menu reflects that spirit of celebration. These recipes have been passed down from generation to generation, and updated here for the modern kitchen.

Mujadara

White Beans & Diced Tomatoes

Grilled Artichokes with Garlic

Hamantaschen

MUJADARA

Makes about 6 to 8 servings   Active Time: 10 minutes
Start to Finish: 35 minutes

1 cup brown or green lentils

2 leeks, white and light green parts only, roots trimmed

2 teaspoons salt, more as needed

¼ cup extra virgin olive oil

2 garlic cloves, minced

¾ cup long-grain rice

1½ teaspoons ground cumin

½ teaspoon ground allspice

¼ teaspoon cayenne

4¼ cups water

1 bay leaf

1 cinnamon stick

4 cups trimmed and chopped spring greens (choice of chard leaves, spinach, kale, mustard or a combination)

Salt and pepper to taste

1. In a large bowl, soak your lentils in enough warm tap water to cover by 1 inch.

2. Meanwhile, halve leeks lengthwise and run them under warm water to clean before thinly slicing them crosswise.

3. Heat oil in a large pot over medium-high heat. Add your leeks and cook for 5 to 10 minutes, stirring occasionally, allowing them to crisp until golden brown. Remove half the leeks to a bowl on the side for later use as a garnish.

4. Add garlic and rice within the pot and sauté for about 2 minutes before adding the cumin, allspice, and cayenne.

5. Drain the lentils, and add them to the pot, then add 4¼ cups water, 2 teaspoons salt, a bay leaf, and a cinnamon stick. Bring the mixture to a simmer before covering and cook over low heat for 15 minutes.

6. Add in your greens and cover once more for 5 additional minutes. Rice and lentils should be tender and the greens wilted. Remove from the heat and let stand, covered, for 5 more minutes before serving. Sprinkle the finished dish with the crispy leeks originally set aside and add salt and pepper to taste.

WHITE BEANS & DICED TOMATOES

Makes 6 Servings   Active Time: 15 Minutes   Start to Finish: 15 Minutes

2 15-oz. cans cannellini beans, washed

1 pint cherry tomatoes, halved

½ cup fresh basil leaves, coarsely chopped

¼ cup flat-leaf parsley

3 tablespoons extra-virgin olive oil

½ medium lemon, juiced

2 garlic cloves, minced

1 tablespoon balsamic vinegar

¼ cup freshly grated Parmesan cheese

Coarsely ground black pepper

Fresh sea salt

1. In a large bowl, mix together the cannellini beans, tomatoes, basil, and parsley. Transfer to the refrigerator.

2. In a small cup, whisk together the extra-virgin olive oil, lemon juice, garlic, and balsamic vinegar. Set aside.

3. Remove the cannellini beans and tomatoes from the refrigerator, and then toss with the vinaigrette. Top with the freshly grated Parmesan cheese, and then season with the coarsely ground black pepper and fresh sea salt.

GRILLED ARTICHOKES
with Garlic

Makes 4 to 5 servings   Active Time: 25 minutes   Start to Finish: 45 minutes

½ large lemon, juiced

3 large artichokes, trimmed and halved lengthwise

5 large garlic cloves, finely chopped

½ olive oil

Coarsely ground black pepper

Fresh sea salt

1. Fill a medium stockpot with water and lemon juice, and then bring to boil over medium-high heat.

2. Prepare your gas or charcoal grill to medium-high heat.

3. When the lemon-water is boiling, add the trimmed artichokes to the water and boil until tender, about for about 15 minutes. Drain and mix in a small bowl with the garlic, olive oil, black pepper, and sea salt.

4. When the grill is ready, about 400 to 500 degrees F, put the artichokes on the grill and cook until lightly charred, about 6 minutes.

5. Remove from grill and serve warm.

HAMANTASCHEN

Makes about 24   Active Time: 10 minutes   Total Time: 60 minutes

1½ teaspoons baking powder

¾ teaspoon salt

4 cups all-purpose flour

1 cup (2 sticks) soft unsalted butter

1 cup sugar

3 large eggs

1½ cup jam or preserves of your choice. Date-Orange, Honey-Nut, or Poppy Seed Filling are traditional

1. Prepare the dry ingredients and whisk the baking powder, salt, and 4 cups of flour together in bowl.

2. In a separate large bowl, beat together the butter, sugar, and 2 eggs until there are no lumps.

3. Gradually add the dry ingredients and mix until a dough forms. Cover the dough, and put in the refrigerator to chill for at least 2 hours.

4. Remove one ball and allow it to soften to room temperature (about 30 minutes), then preheat your oven to 350 degrees F.

5. Roll out the dough on a flour-dusted surface until it is about ¼-inch thick. Cut out 3½-inch rounds with a cookie cutter, and transfer to a parchment-lined baking sheet. Gather up scraps, reroll, and cut out additional rounds, repeat as needed.

6. Lightly beat the remaining egg in a small bowl and brush the mix upon the edge of the rounds. Add about 1½ teaspoon of filling to the center. Fold up the sides of the circle to a triangular form and pinch the points to gently seal, leaving a small window to view the filling within.

7. Brush the sides of the dough with egg, and bake your cookies until the dough is golden brown (18 to 22 minutes). Allow them to cool on baking sheets when finished.

105

Menu 10

No matter how you slice it, Americans love pie. And while "Pi Day" is a new holiday (March 14 is 3.14 — get it?), American kitchens having been making pies since the earliest settlers landed. There's no better day to celebrate pie than on Pi Day, so here's a menu with pies as both the entrée and the dessert! Just leave room for seconds...

Chicken Pot Pie with a Flaky Pastry Crust

Arugula Salad with Tarragon-Shallot Vinaigrette

Tomato Pie

Salted Caramel Pecan Pie

FLAKY PASTRY CRUST

Makes two 9- to 12-inch crusts   Active Time: 30 Minutes
Start to Finish: 2 to 3 Hours

2½ cups flour

1 teaspoon salt

¼ cup vegetable shortening

½ cup (1 stick) butter, chilled and cut into small pieces (if using unsalted butter, increase salt to 1¼ teaspoons), plus 1 tablespoon butter for greasing the skillet

6 to 8 tablespoons cold water

1. In a large bowl, combine the flour and salt. Add the shortening, and using a fork, work it in until the mixture forms very coarse meal. Add the butter and work into the dough with a pastry blender or your fingers until the meal is just holding together. Don't overwork the dough; there can be chunks of butter in it. Add 4 tablespoons cold water to start, and using your hands or a fork, work the dough, adding additional tablespoons until it just holds together when you gather it in your hands.

2. Working on a lightly floured surface, gather the dough and place it on the work area, forming it into a solid ball. Separate into equal parts and form into disks. Wrap each tightly in plastic wrap and refrigerate for 30 to 60 minutes.

3. Take the dough out of the refrigerator to allow it to warm up a bit but work with it cold. Put the refrigerated dough on a lightly floured surface, and with a lightly dusted rolling pin, flatten the dough into 2 circles, working both sides to extend each to a 10- to 12-inch round.

4. Grease the cast iron skillet with 1 tablespoon of butter.

5. Carefully position the crust in the skillet so it is evenly distributed, pressing it in lightly and allowing the dough to extend over the side.

6. If making a single-crust pie, crimp the edges as desired. If filling and adding a top crust, leave the extra dough so it can be crimped with the top crust. Fill the pie as directed, and then roll out the top crust so it is just bigger than the diameter of the top of the skillet. For an extra flaky pastry crust, refrigerate the completed pie for about 30 minutes before baking.

7. When ready to bake, cut a slit or hole in the middle of the top crust for heat to escape. Brush the crust with milk, which will turn it a nice brown color. Bake as directed.

CHICKEN POT PIE

Makes 4 to 6 servings   Active Time: 1 hour   Start to Finish: 2 Hours

1 flaky pastry crust recipe for a single crust (see page 107)

2 tablespoons olive oil

½ yellow onion, diced

1 clove garlic, chopped

1 carrot, peeled and cut into thin rounds

2 tablespoons butter, cut into smaller slices

2 tablespoons flour

1¼ cup milk at room temperature

1½ cups cooked chicken, cut into bite-sized pieces

1 cup frozen peas

Salt and pepper to taste

½ teaspoon cayenne (optional)

1 tablespoon half-and-half

Tip:
This is a great recipe to pull out when you have leftover chicken.

1. Preheat the oven to 350 degrees F.

2. In a small skillet (not the cast-iron skillet), heat the olive oil. Add the onion and garlic and stir, cooking, for about 2 minutes. Add the carrot slices. Reduce the heat to low and cook, covered, stirring occasionally, until the carrots start to soften and the onions caramelize, about 5 minutes. Set aside.

3. Before starting to make the white sauce, be sure the milk is at room temperature. If it's not, microwave it so that it's just warm, about 15 to 20 seconds. Have the milk ready.

4. In the cast iron skillet, over medium heat, melt the butter. Sprinkle the flour over it and stir quickly yet gently to blend the flour in with the butter. Reduce the heat slightly so the butter doesn't burn. Stir until the butter and flour are combined, a minute or so. They will form a soft paste.

5. Add just a little of the warm milk and stir constantly to blend it in. Add more milk in small increments, working after each addition to stir it into the flour and butter mixture smoothly. Work this way until all the milk has been incorporated. Continue to stir the sauce, cooking over low heat, until it thickens, about 5 minutes.

6. Add the chicken pieces, peas, and vegetable mixture from the other skillet. Season with salt and pepper. If you want a hint of heat, add the cayenne pepper.

7. On a lightly floured surface, roll out the crust so it will fit over the filling. Lay it gently on top, push down slightly to secure, and cut 3 or 4 slits in the middle. Brush the crust with the half-and-half.

8. Put the skillet in the oven and bake for 30 to 40 minutes, until the crust is browned and the filling is bubbly.

9. Allow to cool slightly before serving.

ARUGULA SALAD
with Tarragon-Shallot Vinaigrette

Makes 6 Servings   Active Time: 10 Minutes   Start to Finish: 10 Minutes

1 pound Arugula, stemmed

1 shallot, minced

5 stalks tarragon, minced

¼ small lemon, juiced

1 teaspoon Dijon mustard

½ cup extra-virgin olive oil

3 tablespoons red wine vinegar

Coarsely ground black pepper

Fresh sea salt

1. Rinse the arugula and then dry thoroughly. Place in the refrigerator and set aside.

2. In a small bowl, whisk together the shallot, tarragon, lemon juice, and Dijon mustard, and then slowly add in the extra-virgin olive oil and red wine vinegar.

3. Season with the coarsely ground black pepper and fresh sea salt, and then pour over the arugula. Serve immediately.

TOMATO PIE

Makes 4 Servings   Active Time: 30 minutes   Start to Finish: 1 Hour

2 cups Bisquick

⅔ cup milk

4 or 5 tomatoes, peeled

½ tablespoon scallions, chopped

½ tablespoon basil, chopped

¼ cup Parmesan cheese

½ cup cheddar cheese

1 cup mayonnaise

Salt and pepper

1. Mix Bisquick with milk and roll out like a pie crust, and transfer dough to a 10-inch pie plate.

2. Submerge tomatoes in hot water to loosen the skins, then peel them. Cut into slices.

3. Arrange tomato slices evenly on the crust, just one layer to start. (Drain out the juice, if tomatoes are too juicy.) Then sprinkle with scallions, basil, salt and pepper, and Parmesan cheese.

4. Combine the cheddar cheese and mayonnaise, and spread this mixture over the tomato layer. Repeat, lasagna-style, ending with a cheese-mayonnaise spread.

5. Cover the edges of the crust with foil, and bake at 400 degrees F for 30 minutes. Remove from the oven with the pie top browns.

SALTED CARAMEL PECAN PIE

Makes 8 to 10 servings   Active Time: 45 Minutes   Start to Finish: 90 Minutes

1 flaky pastry crust recipe for a single crust (see page 107)

½ cup pecan pieces

1½ cups mixed salted nuts

1¾ cups granulated sugar

⅓ cup dark corn syrup

¼ cup water

2 tablespoons dark rum

¾ cup heavy cream

1 teaspoon salt

3 large eggs, beaten

1. Preheat the oven to 350 degrees F.

2. In a small bowl, combine the pecan pieces with the salted nuts and stir to combine. Set aside.

3. In a large, heavy-bottomed saucepan over medium heat, combine the sugar, corn syrup, and water. Cook, stirring constantly, until sugar is completely dissolved. Increase heat to medium-high and, while stirring, bring the mixture to a boil. Continue to stir as the mixture bubbles and begins to turn dark brown, about 10 minutes. Just before it starts to smoke, remove it from the heat.

4. Stand back from the saucepan and using a long-handled spoon, add the cream. The mixture will splatter. Stir until combined and settled. Return the saucepan to the heat. Add the rum and salt. Cook on medium-low until the mixture is smooth, another few minutes.

5. Ladle the mixture into a large bowl and allow to cool.

6. When cool, use a whisk and add the eggs. Pour the mixture into the pie crust. Sprinkle with the pecan/salted nut combination.

7. Put the skillet in the oven and bake for about 45 minutes or until a knife inserted toward the middle comes out clean.

8. Cool completely before serving. Serve with fresh whipped cream sprinkled with more salted nuts if desired.

Menu 11

Nearly 35 million Americans claim to have Irish ancestry, but we're all Irish on St. Patrick's Day! So put on the green, and gather your friends for a wee bit of "craic." This traditional menu is a favorite of families from the Emerald Isle, guaranteed to bring the luck of the Irish to your table as well. Chocolate salted pistachio pudding pie is a green favorite for all ages.

Corned Beef Dinner

Cabbage, Potatoes and Carrots

Irish Soda Bread

Chocolate Salted Pistachio Pudding Pie

CORNED BEEF

Serves 4 to 6
Active Time: 15 Minutes
Start to Finish: 9 Hours

---

4 large carrots, peeled and cut into matchstick pieces

10 baby red potatoes, cut in half

1 onion, peeled and cut into bite-sized pieces

⅛ teaspoon pepper

¾ cup water

1 (about 4 pounds) corned beef brisket

1 tablespoon Worcestershire sauce

½ head of cabbage, coarsely chopped

1. Place the potatoes, carrots, and onions at the bottom of your slow cooker.

2. Thoroughly rinse the brisket and place atop the vegetables. Sprinkle with pepper. Mix the water and Worcestershire sauce together before pouring over the beef.

3. Cover and cook on low heat for 8 hours, then add the cabbage and cook for an additional hour.

Tip: Serve corned beef with choice of vinegar or mustard.

IRISH SODA BREAD

Makes 6 to 8 Servings   Active Time: 30 Minutes   Start to Finish: 1 Hour

---

3½ cups flour

½ cup granulated sugar

1 teaspoon baking soda

2 teaspoons baking powder

1 teaspoon fresh sea salt

4 tablespoons (½ stick) unsalted butter

1¼ cups buttermilk, chilled

2 eggs

¾ cup raisins

1. Preheat the oven to 375 degrees F.

2. With an electric mixer, combine the flour, sugar, baking soda, baking powder, and salt. Slowly add the butter in 1-tablespoon pieces. Transfer the dough from the mixing bowl to a separate bowl.

3. With a wooden spatula, fold in the buttermilk and eggs, followed by the raisins.

4. Remove the dough from the bowl with your hands and form into a tight, round loaf. Place the loaf on a baking sheet lined with parchment paper, and then using the blunt edge of a knife, carve an X into the top of the loaf — this will allow for thorough baking.

5. Transfer the baking sheet to the oven and bake for 45 minutes, until you can pierce a knife through the bread's center and it comes out clean.

6. Remove from the oven and let rest for 10 minutes before slicing, allowing the crust to harden with the cool temperature.

CHOCOLATE SALTED-PISTACHIO PUDDING PIE

Makes 6 to 8 servings
Active Time: 60 Minutes
Start to Finish: 2 Hours

1 tablespoon butter

8 oz. chocolate wafer cookies, crushed

6 tablespoons butter, melted

2 oz. semisweet baking chocolate

¼ cup sweetened condensed milk

1 cup salted, shelled pistachio pieces, divided

2 (3.4-oz.) boxes instant pistachio pudding mix

2 cups milk

1 cup whipped topping (Cool Whip or fresh whipped cream)

1. Melt the tablespoon of butter in the cast iron skillet over low heat.

2. In a large bowl, mix the cookie crumbs with the 6 tablespoons butter until combined. Carefully remove the cast iron skillet from the heat and press the cookie mixture into the bottom of the pan to form a crust. Allow to cool and set.

3. In a small microwave-safe bowl, melt the chocolate in 15-second increments, stirring after each, until just melted. Stir in the sweetened condensed milk.

4. Pour the chocolate mixture over the pie crust. Sprinkle with the salted pistachio pieces. Refrigerate for about 30 minutes.

5. In a large bowl, whisk together the pudding mix and milk for about 3 minutes, until smooth and thickened. Put the pudding into the crust and spread evenly. Add a layer of whipped topping.

6. Cover with plastic wrap and refrigerate for at least 1 hour and up to 1 day. When ready to serve, remove plastic wrap and sprinkle with additional salted pistachio pieces.

Spring

Springtime ushers in a period of rebirth and renewal. Hummingbirds return, flowers bloom, and we begin to plant the gardens that will feed our tables for the year to come. This spirit of rebirth is reflected in the holidays of Easter and Passover, and it's a season of renewal in the kitchen as well.

Spring is a good time to take stock of your kitchen supplies. Give your refrigerator a good cleaning, and discard any old or outdated condiments. See what's left in your freezer after the long winter months, and make sure to use any frozen items that have overstayed their welcome. Likewise, update your spice rack by replacing any old seasonings, which may have lost their flavor and freshness.

It's also a good time to give the kitchen itself a good cleaning. Wipe, clean, and sanitize any surfaces and appliances, and clean and dust those hard-to-reach areas. And be sure to test your smoke detector and replace the batteries if necessary. You may even have the chance to open the kitchen window and let in a little fresh air.

The spring menus listed here reflect a lighter fare, as the heartier meals of winter give way to lighter, healthier meals. Fresh fruits and vegetables become more abundant, and as the weather warms up, there are even a few opportunities to head outside and use the grill.

Menu 12

Heaven knows it's been a long winter, and things are finally starting to thaw out. After all the shoveling, and the long, cold nights, now is a good time for some comfort food. Something simple and hearty to fill the stomach, lift your spirits, and get you ready for all the spring cleaning to come. Serve this one-pot mac-and-cheese with a house salad, followed up with a giant chocolate chip cookie. Yes, your cast-iron skillet is also a great baking sheet—just smaller, and with sides. So why not cook a giant cookie in it?

House Salad (page 56)

One-Pot Mac-and-Cheese

Baked Haddock with Seafood Stuffing

Giant Chocolate Chip Cookie

ONE-POT MAC-AND-CHEESE

Makes 6 to 8 servings   Active Time: 30 Minutes   Start to Finish: 60 Minutes

---

1 pound elbow macaroni
(uncooked)

1 tablespoon salt

3 tablespoons butter, room
temperature

3½ tablespoons flour

1½ cups milk, room
temperature or slightly
warmed

¼ cup sour cream

¾ pound sharp white cheddar,
grated

¼ pound Gruyère cheese,
grated

Salt and pepper to taste

Dash of cayenne pepper

1. Preheat the oven to 425 degrees F.

2. Put the macaroni in the skillet and add cold water so that it reaches ¼ inch below the top. Stir in the salt, turn the heat on to high, and cook the macaroni as the water boils for about 10 minutes. Test a piece after about 7 minutes. The pasta should be al dente — nearly cooked through but still a bit chewy. When it is cooked like this, drain it in a colander over a large mixing bowl so the water is retained.

3. Put your skillet back on the stove over medium heat, and add the butter. When it's melted, stir in the flour with a wooden spoon if possible, stirring constantly so no lumps form. When it is starting to bubble, start adding the milk, whisking constantly as you add it slowly. Add about a half cup at a time, being sure to whisk it thoroughly before continuing. When all the milk is stirred in, let the sauce simmer over low heat for about 10 minutes until thickened.

4. On low to medium heat, stir in the sour cream. When the mix is warm again, stir in the cheeses, stirring gently as they melt. Season with the salt, pepper, and cayenne.

5. Finally, add the macaroni gently into the cheese sauce. If it seems too thick, add some of the pasta water. The consistency should be like a thick stew. When the noodles are hot, transfer the skillet to the oven.

6. Bake in the oven for about 15 minutes, then take a peek. The dish should be bubbling and the cheese on the top starting to brown. This takes somewhere between 15 and 25 minutes. Be careful not to let it burn. Let the macaroni cool slightly before serving.

Variations:

- Lightly steam some broccoli and add it the macaroni and cheese before you pop it in the oven.

- Add chopped fresh kale before baking.

- Add chopped green onions before baking.

- Sprinkle bread crumbs on top before baking.

- Serve with crumbled bacon on top.

- Serve with chopped tomatoes or canned stewed tomatoes warmed up.

- Try using different pasta shapes and different cheeses (though they should be cheeses that melt, which are typically hard cheeses or aged cheeses).

BAKED HADDOCK
with Seafood Stuffing

Makes 4 to 6 servings   Active Time: 15 minutes   Start to Finish: 1 hour

3 tablespoons olive oil

1 celery stalk, finely chopped

3 green onions, finely chopped

1 teaspoon minced garlic

1 (6 oz.) can lump crabmeat, drained

3 slices dry white bread, crusts removed and cut to cubes

¼ teaspoon salt

¼ teaspoon ground black pepper

1 egg, beaten

½ cup grated Romano cheese

2 tablespoons lemon juice

1 tomato, diced

5 tablespoons butter, melted

6 (4 oz.) haddock fillets

¼ cup parsley, chopped (optional garnish)

1. Preheat your oven to 375 degrees F. Lightly grease a 9x13-inch baking dish.

2. In a skillet over medium heat, heat olive oil and add the celery, green onion, and garlic. Cook until the onions are translucent and remove from heat. Within the mixture, add in the crabmeat, bread cubes, egg, cheese, lemon juice, and diced tomato. Season to taste with salt and freshly ground pepper until the mixture is well blended.

3. Lay the haddock fillets in the prepared baking dish. Brush each fillet with some melted butter before placing a heaping tablespoon of the crab mixture onto half of each fillet. Fold over the other half of the fillet and secure with a toothpick.

4. Cover the dish with a lid or aluminum foil, and bake for 20 minutes in the preheated oven. Remove the cover and continue to bake until the top has browned and the fish flakes easily (about 10 minutes).

5. Lightly sprinkle chopped parsley atop as garnish and serve.

GIANT CHOCOLATE CHIP COOKIE

Makes 1 large cookie   Active Time: 20 Minutes   Start to Finish: 45 Minutes

---

1 cup (2 sticks) butter, softened

½ cup white sugar

1 cup brown sugar

2 eggs

2 teaspoons vanilla extract

1 teaspoon baking soda

2 teaspoons hot water

½ teaspoon salt

2½ cups flour

2 cups semisweet
chocolate chips

1. Preheat the oven to 375 degrees F. Heat the skillet in the oven while making the batter.

2. In a large bowl, cream together the butter and sugars. Add the eggs one at a time, being sure to combine thoroughly before proceeding. Stir in the vanilla.

3. Dissolve the baking soda in the hot water and add to the batter along with the salt. Stir in the flour and chocolate chips.

4. Remove the skillet from the oven and put the batter in it, smoothing the top with a spatula.

5. Put the skillet in the oven and cook until golden, about 15 minutes.

6. Slice into wedges and serve with ice cream.

Variation: Mix in ½ cup walnut or almond pieces when adding the flour and chocolate chips.

Easter

Easter is one of America's favorite holidays, when the whole family gathers around the table for one of the biggest meals of the season. With the children dressed in their Sunday best, and the baskets of chocolate and Easter eggs, it's a day to celebrate. And it's a day for this classic Easter menu, whether it's a casual brunch or a more formal Easter dinner (this menu gives you a little bit of both!). Enjoy!

Ham and Cheddar Quiche

Blueberry Scones

Potato Pancakes

Sticky Buns

Green Bean Casserole

Holiday Ham

Lamb Chops with Parsley Mint Sauce

Cosmic Carrot Cake

HAM AND CHEDDAR QUICHE

Makes 6 to 8 servings
Active Time: 40 minutes
Start to Finish: 1½ hours

---

1 baked flaky pastry crust (see page 107)

2 tablespoons brown mustard

1 cup diced fully cooked ham

1 cup shredded sharp cheddar cheese

4 eggs

1½ cups whole milk or half-and-half

1 teaspoon salt

1 teaspoon ground pepper

Paprika (optional)

1. Preheat the oven to 350 degrees F.

2. With the crust in the skillet, use a pastry brush or the back of a spoon to spread the mustard on the bottom and sides.

3. Sprinkle the ham pieces and shredded cheddar evenly over the bottom of the pie.

4. In a medium bowl, whisk the eggs until thoroughly combined. Add the milk, salt, and pepper and whisk to combine.

5. Pour the egg mixture over the meat and cheese, shaking the pan gently to distribute evenly and settle the liquid. If desired, sprinkle the top with paprika.

6. Put the skillet in the oven and bake for 35 to 40 minutes or until the quiche is puffy and golden brown and the eggs are set.

7. Allow to sit for 10 minutes before slicing and serving.

BLUEBERRY SCONES

Makes 4 to 6 servings   Active Time: 30 Minutes
Start to Finish: 50 Minutes

---

3 cups flour

⅓ cup sugar

2½ teaspoons baking powder

½ teaspoon baking soda

1 teaspoon salt

¾ cup (1½ sticks) unsalted butter, chilled and cut into pieces

1 tablespoon orange zest

1 cup milk or half-and-half

1 cup fresh blueberries

1. Preheat the oven to 400 degrees F. Position a rack in the middle of the oven.

2. In a large bowl, whisk together the flour, sugar, baking powder, baking soda, and salt. Add the butter pieces and mix with an electric mixer until just blended, or mix with a fork so that the dough is somewhat crumbly.

3. Stir in the orange zest and milk, and gently fold in the blueberries, being careful not to overmix.

4. With flour on your hands, transfer the dough to a lightly floured surface. Form the dough into a circle about ½-inch thick. With a long knife, cut the dough into 12 wedges.

5. Butter the skillet, and put the scone wedges in a circle in it, leaving some space between the pieces. Bake for 20 to 25 minutes, or until golden.

6. If desired, sprinkle with some additional sugar when just out of the oven.

POTATO PANCAKES

Makes 6 servings   Active Time: 1½ hours   Start to Finish: 2 hours

---

6 large russet potatoes, washed and peeled

1 large onion

3 eggs, beaten

¼ to ½ cup bread crumbs

Salt and freshly ground pepper

1 cup canola or vegetable oil

Variations

• Serve with chunky unsweetened applesauce and a small dollop of sour cream.

• Serve as you would French fries—with salt and vinegar, with ketchup, with gravy, or with salsa.

• For a non-traditional taco, top potato pancakes with chili and cheese.

1. Using a hand grater or a food processor with a shredding attachment, grate the potatoes onto a large baking dish, and then transfer to a colander in the sink.

2. Grate the onion or use a knife to process into a very fine dice. Put the grated onion into a bowl.

3. Squeeze as much liquid out of the potatoes as possible. Take half of the grated potatoes, mix them with the onions, and process the mixture in a food processor or blender to create a rough puree. Don't overblend or chop, as the mix will get too starchy.

4. Put the puree in a separate colander so that it can drain. Let both colanders drain for another 20 to 30 minutes. Push down on both to release more liquid and squeeze them again before continuing with the recipe.

5. Combine the two batches into a large bowl, and add the eggs and bread crumbs. Stir to thoroughly combine. Season with salt and pepper.

6. Heat the skillet over medium-high heat and add the oil. Be careful making the pancakes, as the oil can splatter. Take spoonfuls of the potato mix and place them in the oil. Cook for about 3 minutes a side. The pancakes should be golden brown on the outside, and cooked through on the inside. You may need to adjust the temperature of the oil to get the right cooking temperature, especially if you have more than three in the skillet at one time.

7. When cooked, transfer with a slotted spoon to a plate lined with paper towels. Keep warm until ready to eat. Season with additional salt and pepper.

Tip: The way to make the best-tasting potato pancakes is to get as much liquid out of the grated potatoes and onions as possible.

STICKY BUNS

Makes 6 servings   Active Time: 1½ hours   Start to Finish: 2 hours

1 (26.4-oz.) package frozen biscuits

All-purpose flour for dusting

½ cup chopped pecans, toasted

1 teaspoon ground cinnamon

¼ teaspoon nutmeg

4 tablespoons butter, softened

¾ cup firmly packed light brown sugar

1 cup confectioner's sugar

3 tablespoons half-and-half

½ teaspoon vanilla extract

Variations

· Substitute toasted walnut or almond pieces instead of the pecans for a nuttier, earthier flavor.

· Substitute dark brown sugar instead of the light brown sugar if you want more of a molasses flavor.

1. Preheat the oven to 375 degrees F.

2. Lightly dust a flat surface with flour. Spread the frozen biscuit dough out in rows of 4 biscuits each. Cover with a dish cloth and let sit for about 30 minutes until the dough is thawed but still cool.

3. While dough is thawing, toast the pecans. Spread the pieces on a cookie sheet and bake for about 5 minutes, stirring the pieces with a spatula about halfway through. Be sure not to overcook. Allow to cool. Put the pieces in a bowl and add the cinnamon and nutmeg, stirring to coat the nuts with the spices.

4. Sprinkle flour over the top of the biscuit dough, and fold the dough in half, then press it out to form a large rectangle (approximately 10 inches by 12 inches). Spread the softened butter over the dough.

5. Sprinkle the brown sugar over the butter, then the seasoned nuts. Roll the dough with the butter, sugar, and nuts in it, starting with a long side. Cut into 1-inch slices and place in a lightly greased skillet.

6. Bake at 375 degrees F for about 35 minutes, until rolls in the center are cooked through. Remove from the oven and allow to cool.

7. Make the glaze by mixing the confectioner's sugar, half-and-half, and vanilla. Drizzle over the warm rolls and serve.

LAMB CHOPS
with Parsley Mint Sauce

Makes 4 servings.   Active Time: 30 minutes
Start to Finish: 1 hour and 30 minutes

Lamb Ingredients

2 garlic cloves

2 tablespoons rosemary, finely chopped

2 tablespoons olive oil

4 lamb chops, about 1¼ inches thick

Coarsely ground black pepper

Fresh sea salt

Sauce Ingredients

1 garlic clove, finely chopped

1 cup flat-leaf parsley, finely chopped

¼ cup mint leaves, finely chopped

2 anchovies, finely chopped (optional)

¼ small lemon, juiced

1 chili pepper, seeded and chopped (optional)

½ cup olive oil

Coarsely ground black pepper

Fresh sea salt

1. In a small bowl, combine the garlic, rosemary, and olive oil. Pour the contents of the bowl onto the lamb chops and then let rest at room temperature for 1 hour.

2. A half hour before grilling, prepare your gas or charcoal grill to medium-high heat.

3. While waiting, in a small bowl, mix together the garlic, parsley, mint, anchovies (optional), 1 chili pepper, seeded and chopped (optional) and lemon juice. Gradually whisk in the olive oil, and then season with coarsely ground black pepper and fresh sea salt. Transfer to the refrigerator.

4. When the grill is ready, at about 400 to 450 degrees F with the coals lightly covered with ash, season one side of the chops with coarsely ground pepper and sea salt. Place the seasoned-sides of the chops on the grill at medium heat. Wait 3 minutes until they are slightly charred. A minute before flipping, season the uncooked sides of the chops with the remaining pepper and sea salt. Turn the chops and grill for another 3 minutes for medium-rare, and about 4 minutes for medium. The chops should feel slightly firm if poked in the center.

5. Remove the lamb chops from the grill and transfer to a large cutting board. Let stand for 10 minutes, allowing the lamb to properly store its juices and flavor. Serve warm on a bed of greens alongside chilled parsley-mint sauce.

GREEN BEAN CASSEROLE

Makes 6 servings   Active Time: 30 minutes   Start to Finish: 40 minutes.

6 slices thick bacon

1 large shallot, finely chopped

2 pounds green beans, ends trimmed

2 tablespoons unsalted butter

2 garlic cloves, finely chopped

½ cup breadcrumbs

¼ cup freshly grated Parmesan cheese

Coarsely ground black pepper

Fresh sea salt

1. Place a large cast-iron skillet on the stove over low-medium heat. When hot, add the bacon and shallots and cook until the bacon is crisp and the shallots are translucent, about 6 to 8 minutes. Transfer to a rack lined with paper towels.

2. Increase the heat to medium. Some of the oils from the bacon should remain in the bottom of the skillet. Add the green beans and sear until lightly browned, about 6 minutes. Add the bacon and shallots and toss well. Remove from the skillet and transfer to a large bowl.

3. In the same skillet, add the butter, followed by the garlic. Sear about 2 minutes, until the garlic is golden brown, and then remove from the heat. While the pan is still hot, stir in the breadcrumbs and sear lightly so that they absorb the flavors from the pan.

4. Pour the breadcrumbs from the pan onto the green beans and toss so they are evenly distributed. Garnish with the Parmesan cheese, and then season with the coarsely ground black pepper and fresh sea salt. Serve warm.

Holiday Ham

Makes 10 to 12 servings

1 6- to 8-pound cooked, spiral-sliced ham

1 8-oz can crushed pineapple

½ cup honey

¼ cup firmly packed brown sugar

¼ cup Dijon mustard

2 tablespoons orange juice

Nonstick cooking spray

1. Spray the bottom of the slow cooker generously with the cooking spray.

2. Place the ham flat side down in the slow cooker. Pour the pineapple over the ham.

3. In a bowl, combine the honey, brown sugar, orange juice and mustard, and stir to thoroughly combine. Pour the sauce over the ham.

4. Cover and cook on Low for 6 to 8 hours or on High for 3 to 4 hours, finishing with a final 30-60 minutes on Low.

If you want to decorate your ham for the table, you'll need pineapple rings and maraschino cherries. Drain the water from a large can of sliced pineapple rings. Pat the slices dry with some paper towels. Heat a small skillet over medium, and saute the slices until just browned on both sides, about 3 minutes a side. Remove maraschino cherries one by one from their jar, and with a long toothpick, secure the cherry on the ham, and put a pineapple ring over it. Start at the top of the ham and work down around the sides.

COSMIC CARROT CAKE

Makes 8 servings   Active Time: 20 Minutes   Start to Finish: 60 Minutes

8 tablespoons (1 stick) butter

1 cup julienned carrots, chopped fine

1 cup fresh chopped pineapple chunks (if using canned, drain juice)

1 (15.25-oz.) box of carrot cake mix

¾ cup water

⅔ cup vegetable oil

6 oz. unsweetened applesauce

4 eggs

1 cup unsweetened coconut flakes

1. Preheat the oven to 350 degrees F.

2. In the skillet, melt the butter over medium heat. When it's melted, add the carrots. Allow the carrots to simmer in the butter over low to medium heat until the butter is bubbling. Add the pineapple pieces and let them simmer with the carrots on low heat.

3. In a large bowl, combine the cake mix, water, oil, applesauce, eggs, and coconut. Stir to combine.

4. When the butter in the skillet is bubbling, turn off the heat and pour the batter over the carrot/pineapple mix.

5. Bake 35 to 40 minutes until browned on the top and sides and a toothpick inserted in the middle comes out clean.

6. Allow to cool for about 10 minutes. The skillet will still be hot. Put a large serving plate on the counter and, working quickly and deliberately, flip the skillet so the cake is inverted onto the plate.

Menu 13

Now that the days are getting longer and the sun is setting later, it's starting to feel like spring is really here. And to compliment the brighter days and warmer temperatures, here's a meal that's lighter and fresher. This seafood paella is a Spanish rice dish chock full of everything good: chorizo sausage, calamari, shrimp, and mussels. Polenta cakes with greens are a good complement. And we round out the dinner with light and spring-like key lime chiffon pie.

Seafood Paella

Polenta Cakes with Greens

Biscuits

Key Lime Chiffon Pie

SEAFOOD PAELLA

Makes 4 to 6 servings   Active Time: 1½ hours
Start to Finish: 2 hours

4 cups chicken broth

2 tablespoons olive oil, as needed

1 onion, diced

4 cloves garlic, minced

1 teaspoon smoked paprika

½ teaspoon saffron threads, crushed

2½ cups short-grain rice (Arborio or paella)

2 ripe tomatoes, seeded and chopped

1 cup dry white wine

1 teaspoon salt

Freshly ground black pepper

1 cup frozen peas

½ pound calamari, cut into 1-inch pieces

8 oz. Spanish chorizo, cut into ¼-inch rounds

½ pound unpeeled jumbo shrimp, deveined

16 mussels, scrubbed and debearded

1. Preheat the oven to 425 degrees F.

2. In a saucepan, bring the chicken broth to a simmer over medium heat.

3. Heat the skillet over medium high heat. Add the olive oil, onion, and garlic, and cook, stirring occasionally, until the onion is translucent, about 3 minutes. Add the paprika and saffron, and cook, stirring, for another minute.

4. Add the rice, stirring to coat, then stir in the tomatoes and wine. Bring to a boil, cooking until the liquid is reduced by half, about 2 minutes. Add the hot chicken broth and peas, stir, then bring to a boil and cook for 5 minutes. Season with salt and pepper.

5. Add the peas, calamari, and chorizo and stir to combine. Put the skillet in the oven and bake for about 30 minutes, until the calamari are soft. Scatter the shrimp and mussels over the top of the paella and return to the oven. Cook until the shrimp are opaque and the mussels have opened, 5 to 10 minutes.

6. Keep an eye on the dish so the seafood on top doesn't overcook.

7. Remove from the oven, discard any mussel shells that didn't open, let rest for about 5 minutes, and serve.

POLENTA CAKES
with Greens

Makes 4 to 6 servings.   Active Time: 1/2 hour
Start to Finish: 1 hour

Olive oil for preparing skillet

1 cup coarse-grind or medium-grind polenta

3 cups water

Salt and freshly ground black pepper

1 pound bitter greens such as kale, chard, escarole, or dandelion, tough stems removed

3 tablespoons extra-virgin olive oil

3 cloves garlic, chopped

Red pepper flakes

Grated Romano for topping

1. Preheat the oven to 400 degrees F.

2. Liberally oil the skillet and put it in the oven for a few minutes to heat.

3. In a heavy saucepan, whisk together the polenta and water. Heat over medium and bring to a boil, whisking to prevent lumps from forming. When bubbling, reduce the heat to low and simmer, uncovered, for a couple of minutes or until smooth. Season with salt and black pepper.

4. Pour the polenta into the skillet. Put in the oven and bake for about 30 minutes, until it is lightly golden and coming away from the edges of the pan.

5. While it's baking, make the greens. Bring a large pot of salted water to a boil, add the greens, and boil until very tender, 15 to 20 minutes. Drain in a colander and squeeze to remove excess moisture. Cut the greens into pieces. Heat the olive oil in a pan, add the garlic and cook, stirring, until fragrant, about 2 minutes. Add the red pepper flakes, stir, then add the greens. Cook until heated through. Season with salt and pepper. Keep warm until polenta is cooked.

6. Cut the polenta into wedges, top with greens, and sprinkle on the grated cheese.

Polenta is cornmeal cooked into porridge and then baked or fried.

BISCUITS

Makes 4 to 6 servings   Active Time: 20 minutes
Start to Finish: 40 minutes

---

2 cups flour

1 teaspoon sugar

1 teaspoon salt

1 tablespoon baking powder

8 tablespoons butter, cut into pieces

½ cup + 2 tablespoons buttermilk

1. Preheat oven to 450 degrees F.

2. In a large bowl, combine the flour, sugar, salt, and baking powder.

3. Using a fork, blend in 6 tablespoons of the butter to form crumbly dough. Form a well in the middle and add ½ cup buttermilk. Stir to combine and form a stiff dough. Using your fingers works best! If it seems too dry, add another tablespoon of buttermilk.

4. Put 2 tablespoons butter in the skillet and put it in the oven to melt while the skillet heats.

5. Put the dough on a lightly floured surface and press out to a thickness of about 1 inch. Press out biscuits using an inverted water glass. Place the biscuits in the skillet and bake for about 10 minutes, until golden on the bottom.

For fluffy biscuits, work with a very hot skillet—and carefully! The golden-brown crust on the bottom is as much of a delight as the airy, warm dough.

KEY LIME CHIFFON PIE

Makes 6 to 8 servings   Active Time: 30 Minutes   Start to Finish: 2 Hours

---

1 graham cracker crust (see page 62)

2 cups heavy cream

¼ cup sugar

⅓ cup fresh squeezed lime juice

1 envelope (about 1 tablespoon) unflavored gelatin

½ cup sweetened condensed milk

Whipped cream and lime zest or wheels for garnish

1. In a large bowl, beat the cream on high until peaks just start to form. Add the sugar and continue to beat on high until stiff peaks form.

2. In a small saucepan, combine the lime juice, zest, and gelatin, and stir until gelatin is dissolved. Turn the heat on to medium and cook the mixture until it begins to thicken, stirring constantly, about 3 to 5 minutes. Do not let it boil or burn. Remove from heat and allow to cool slightly. Stir in the sweetened condensed milk.

3. Fold this mixture into the whipped cream until combined and smooth. Don't overwork it.

4. Pour the filling into the crust. Cover with plastic wrap and refrigerate until set, about 45 minutes (or refrigerate for up to a day).

Menu 14

There's nothing like a good steak, and here's an American classic with a French twist. And if the weather is right, this might be a good opportunity to get outside to use your grill for the first time this season. But if April showers have come your way, no worries: this menu is as easily prepared in the kitchen.

Steak au Poivre

Grilled Asparagus

Charred Sweet Potatoes

Skillet Brownies

STEAK AU POIVRE

Makes 2 to 3 Servings   Active Time: 25 Minutes

Start to Finish: 1 Hour and 15 Minutes

Steak Ingredients

2 New York strip steaks, about 1½ inches thick

2 tablespoons olive oil

6 tablespoons black peppercorns

Fresh sea salt

Sauce Ingredients

3 tablespoons clarified butter

1 shallot, minced

½ cup Cognac

½ cup heavy cream

2 tablespoons parsley, finely chopped

Fresh sea salt

1. Rub both sides of the steaks with olive oil and let rest at room temperature for about 1 hour.

2. A half hour before cooking, prepare your gas or charcoal grill to medium-high heat.

3. Seal the peppercorns in a small, sealable plastic bag and crush with the bottom of a cast- iron skillet.

4. When the grill is ready, at about 400 to 450 degrees F when the coals are lightly covered with ash, press the peppercorns and sea salt firmly into both sides of the steak. Place the seasoned-sides of the steaks on the grill at medium heat and cook for 4 to 5 minutes until they are slightly charred. Turn the steaks and grill for another 3 to 4 minutes for medium-rare, and 4 to 5 minutes for medium. The steaks should feel slightly firm if poked in the center.

5. Remove the steaks from the grill and transfer to a large cutting board. Let rest for 10 minutes, allowing the steaks to properly store their juices and flavor.

6. While the steaks rest, heat the clarified butter in a small saucepan over medium heat. Add the minced shallot, stirring occasionally until softened, about 1 to 2 minutes.

7. Carefully add the Cognac, and if it flames, shake the pan and wait for the flame to burn out. Boil until it has reduced by half.

8. Next, mix in the heavy cream until the sauce has slightly thickened, about 2 to 3 minutes, and then add the parsley and salt.

9. Place the steaks onto warmed plates and spoon the sauce on top of the steaks.

GRILLED ASPARAGUS

Makes 4 servings   Active Time: 10 minutes
Start to Finish: 30 minutes

1 to 1½ pounds fresh asparagus, washed

3 tablespoons olive oil

Coarsely ground black pepper

Fresh sea salt

1. Prepare your grill to medium-high heat.
2. Drizzle the olive oil over the asparagus and then season with coarsely ground black pepper and fresh sea salt.
3. Next, when the grill is ready, about 400 to 500 degrees F, add the asparagus onto the grill. Turn the asparagus and grill until the asparagus are brown. Transfer to a large carving board and let rest for 5 minutes before serving.

Variation

Wrap the asparagus in bundles of three with a thick piece of bacon.

Charred Sweet Potatoes

Makes 4 servings   Active Time: 45 minutes   Start to Finish: 1 hour

4 large sweet potatoes

2 tablespoons olive oil

Ground black pepper

Sea salt

Butter for serving

1. Rub the sweet potatoes with olive oil and season with ground black pepper and sea salt.

2. Prepare your gas or charcoal grill to medium-high heat.

3. When the grill is ready, about 400 to 500 degrees F, add the sweet potatoes over direct heat and grill for 45 minutes, turning every 15 minutes until finished—a fork should easily pierce through.

4. Remove from the grill and serve with butter.

SKILLET BROWNIES

Makes 6 to 8 servings   Active Time: 40 Minutes   Start to Finish: 90 minutes

10 tablespoons unsalted butter

8 oz. semisweet chocolate, coarsely chopped

1 cup sugar

3 eggs at room temperature

1 teaspoon vanilla extract

½ cup + 2 tablespoons all-purpose flour

2 tablespoons unsweetened cocoa powder

¼ teaspoon salt

1 cup semisweet chocolate chips

1. Preheat the oven to 350 degrees F.

2. In a microwave-safe bowl, melt the butter and chocolate pieces together, cooking in 15-second increments and stirring after each increment. The butter and chocolate should be just melted together and smooth.

3. In a large bowl, whisk the sugar in with the eggs. Add the vanilla and stir to combine. Working in batches, start mixing the melted chocolate into the sugar/egg mixture, stirring vigorously to combine after each addition. In a small bowl, mix the flour, cocoa powder, and salt. Gently fold the dry ingredients into the chocolate mix. Next, fold in the chocolate chips.

4. Over medium heat, melt 1 tablespoon butter in the skillet. When melted, pour in the batter. Bake for about 30 minutes or until a toothpick inserted in the center comes out with a few moist crumbs. It may need a couple more minutes, but be careful not to overbake this or you'll lose the great gooiness. When it's ready, remove from the oven and allow to cool about 10 minutes.

5. Dig right in, or scoop into bowls and serve with your favorite ice cream.

Tip: When shopping for the ingredients, remember that the better quality the chocolate, the better the taste and texture of the brownie.

Menu 15

This meal is perfect for a vegetarian, springtime dinner—or for a meatless Friday during Lent. You can start the potatoes in the slow cooker, use one skillet each for the blacked tilapia and the Black Forest cake, and assemble the spinach-strawberry salad in a jiffy.

Cheesy Potato Casserole

Blackened Tilapia

Spinach-Strawberry Salad

Black Forest Cake

CHEESY POTATO CASSEROLE

Makes 4 to 6 servings   Active Time: 20 minutes

Start to Finish: 4 Hours

---

6 to 8 golden potatoes

7 tablespoons butter

1 tablespoon flour

1 cup milk, warmed to room temp

2 cups grated sharp cheddar

Crumbled bacon (optional)

Dried herbs (optional)

1. Peel potatoes and cut into thick slices. Rinse them off and pat them dry. Put them in the slow cooker and dot with 6 tablespoons butter. Cover and cook on Low for about 4 hours, until tender.

2. To make the cheese sauce: melt 1 tablespoon of butter in a skillet over low to medium heat. When melted, add the flour and stir. Have the milk handy while you're cooking the flour. After about a minute, start gradually adding the milk. Stir quickly to mix without causing clumps. As the milk is incorporated, raise the heat slightly and continue to add milk. The sauce will thicken. When the milk is added, turn the heat to Low and stir in the grated cheese, 1 cup at a time. Get the sauce to the thickness and cheesiness you want by adding more milk or cheese.

3. Pour the cheese sauce into the potatoes and stir to combine. Serve with crumbled bacon, if desired, or even more cheese.

*Tip: To get a cheesy crust,
broil the casserole in the oven for a
few minutes before serving.*

BLACKENED TILAPIA

Makes 4 servings   Active Time: 40 minutes   Start to Finish: 1½ hours

1 stick melted butter

4 boneless tilapia fillets, about
4 oz. each

1 lemon, cut into 4 wedges

Blackened Seasoning:

2 tablespoons paprika

1 tablespoon onion powder

3 tablespoons garlic powder

2 tablespoons cayenne pepper

1 tablespoon white pepper

1½ tablespoons finely ground
black pepper

1 tablespoon dried thyme

1 tablespoon dried oregano

1 tablespoon ground chipotle chile

1. In a bowl, combine all the spices for your blackened seasoning and set aside.

2. Heat the skillet over high heat for about 10 minutes until very hot. While the skillet heats, rinse the fillets and then pat dry with paper towels. Dip the fish fillets in the melted butter, covering both sides, and then press the blackened seasoning generously into both sides.

3. Put the fish in the skillet and cook for about 3 minutes a side, placing a bit of butter on the tops while the bottoms cook. Serve with lemon.

Tip: Tilapia is a wonderful fish for blackening, but you can also use catfish, tuna, grouper. Halibut, trout, or shrimp. The blackening process creates a lot of smoke, so turn on the oven fan and open the windows.

Spinach-Strawberry Salad

Makes 4 servings   Active Time: 5 minutes   Total Time: 5 minutes

1 pound baby spinach, washed

½ pound strawberries, washed
and sliced

¼ cup pine nuts

1. This is as simple as 1, 2, 3: spinach, strawberries, and pine nuts.

2. Serve with vinaigrette.

BLACK FOREST CAKE

Makes 8 servings   Active Time: 20 Minutes
Start to Finish: 1 hour

---

1 (15-oz.) can pitted dark cherries in heavy syrup

1 cup water/syrup combination

8 tablespoons (1 stick) butter

2 tablespoons dark brown sugar

1 (15.25-oz.) box of chocolate fudge cake mix

2 tablespoons unsweetened cocoa powder

½ cup vegetable oil

6 oz. unsweetened applesauce

4 eggs

1 (14 oz.) can of whipped cream

1 (4 oz.) bar good quality milk chocolate, finely chopped or grated

Fresh cherries

1. Preheat the oven to 350 degrees F.

2. Drain the syrup from the cherries into a measuring cup. Top with water to yield 1 cup of liquid. Chop the cherries into halves or quarters.

3. In the skillet, melt the butter over medium heat. When it's melted, sprinkle the brown sugar over it. Allow the sugar to melt in the butter over low heat. No need to stir, but don't let the butter get too hot.

4. In a large bowl, combine the cake mix, cocoa powder, chopped cherries, syrup/water, oil, applesauce, and eggs. Mix thoroughly.

5. Pour the batter into the skillet. The butter/sugar mixture will come up over the sides of the batter. It's all part of the magic.

6. Bake 25 to 30 minutes until browned on the top and sides and a toothpick inserted in the middle comes out clean.

7. Allow to cool for about 10 minutes. The skillet will still be hot. Put a large serving plate on the counter and, working quickly and deliberately, flip the skillet so the cake is inverted onto the plate. Allow to cool completely before decorating.

8. Decorate with whipped cream, chocolate shavings and fresh cherries. That's it!

Menu 16

There's something to be said about resourcefulness, and after that big Easter meal, there's bound to be some leftover ham to put to good use in this grilled split-pea soup and chef salad. Cherry clafouti—essentially full-flavored cherries baked in a custard—closes out dinner in style.

Grilled Split Pea Soup with Ham

Chef Salad with Homemade Croutons

Garlic-Rosemary Rolls

Cherry Clafouti

153

Homemade Croutons

Active time: 15 minutes
Start to Finish: about 4 hours

½ cup olive oil

4 cloves garlic, finely minced

1 (8 oz) loaf French bread baguette, cut into ½ inch cubes

½ cup finely grated Parmigiano-Reggiano cheese, divided

½ teaspoon Italian seasoning or 1 tablespoon fresh chopped herbs

½ teaspoon paprika

½ teaspoon ground pepper

½ teaspoon salt

1 pinch cayenne pepper

1. Stir together olive oil and garlic in a bowl. Allow this to sit until the flavors are well infused (about 3 hours).

2. Preheat your oven to 300 degrees F.

3. With the bread cubes in a separate large bowl or large ziplock bag, pour the garlic oil through a strainer and onto the bread. Add the cheese and seasonings and toss until the bread is evenly coated with everything.

4. Spread out upon a cookie sheet and bake for 20 minutes, stir the croutons, then bake for 20 more minutes until the cubes are crisp and crunchy.

CHEF SALAD

Serves 4   Active time: 45 minutes   Start to Finish: 45 minutes

---

1½ lbs your choice of lettuce, or a mixture of greens

½ cup your choice of dressing

4 oz. Swiss cheese

4 oz. leftover ham

4 oz. smoked turkey

4 oz. roast beef

2 hard-boiled eggs

1 ripe Hass avocado

16 ripe cherry tomatoes, halved

1 medium cucumber, sliced

1 cup toasted croutons

Salt and pepper to taste

1. Tear or cut the lettuce into bite-sized pieces and put into a large mixing bowl. Add your choice of dressing and toss to evenly coat the lettuce, then either lay out upon a large serving platter for the whole family or set up four individual serving bowls.

2. Arrange cheese and meat atop. You may either cut these into matchstick pieces, or roll together and cut into decorative pinwheels. Cut the hard-boiled eggs in halves or quarters and add. Slice up the avocado, tomatoes, and cucumber, and scatter on top. Season with salt and pepper to taste.

GRILLED SPLIT PEA SOUP
with Ham

Makes 6 Servings   Active Time: 1½ Hours   Start to Finish: 2½ Hours

1 tablespoon olive oil

1 cup carrots, chopped into ¼-inch segments

1 medium yellow onion, finely chopped

3 garlic cloves, minced

1 pound dried split peas

¼ teaspoon red pepper flakes

1 ready-to-eat ham, about 4 pounds

6 cups water

2 sprigs thyme, leaves removed

Coarsely ground black pepper

Fresh sea salt

1. Place a large Dutch oven on your gas or charcoal grill and prepare to medium heat. Leave the grill covered while heating, as it will add a faint smoky flavor to the skillet.

2. When the grill is ready, at about 400 degrees F with the coals lightly covered with ash, add the olive oil into the Dutch oven, followed by the carrots and yellow onion. Cook for about 5 to 7 minutes until the carrots are tender and the onion is translucent. Stir in the garlic and cook for another minute.

3. Add the split peas, red pepper flakes, and ham into the Dutch oven, and then submerge with the 6 cups of water (you may need more or less depending on the size of the Dutch oven and ham). Cover and cook until the peas have fully cooked into the water, about 1½ to 2 hours. Be sure to restock the grill while cooking.

4. Add the thyme and cook for a few more minutes before removing from grill. Let the soup rest for about 15 minutes so that the soup can thicken, and then season with coarsely ground black pepper and fresh sea salt. Serve hot.

GARLIC-ROSEMARY ROLLS

Makes 6 to 8 Servings (8 Rolls)
Active Time: 1½ Hours   Start to Finish: 3 Hours

---

1 package active dry yeast

1 cup water (110 to 115 degrees F)

1 tablespoon sugar

1 tablespoon butter, melted

1 teaspoon salt

2 cloves garlic, minced

4 cups flour

1 teaspoon fresh rosemary leaves, chopped, or 2 teaspoons dried, crushed rosemary

1 tablespoon butter

1 egg, lightly beaten

Sea salt

1. In a large bowl, mix the yeast, water, and sugar and let the yeast proof for about 10 minutes, until foamy.

2. Next add the sugar, melted butter, salt, garlic, and half the flour. Mix until the dough forms a sticky dough. Continue to add flour, mixing to form a soft dough. Add the rosemary with the last addition of flour.

3. Form into a ball, cover the bowl with plastic wrap or a tea towel, put in a warm, draft-free place, and let rise until doubled in size, about 1 hour.

4. Put the skillet in the oven and preheat the oven to 400 degrees F.

5. Transfer the dough to a lightly floured surface. Divide into 8 pieces and form into balls.

6. Remove the skillet from the oven and melt the butter in it. Place the rolls in the skillet, turning to cover them with butter. Wash the rolls with the beaten egg and sprinkle with sea salt.

7. Bake in the oven until golden and set, about 40 minutes.

Make cheesy garlic-rosemary rolls by sprinkling Parmesan or pecorino romano cheese on the tops after washing with the beaten egg. Skip the sea salt.

CHERRY CLAFOUTI

Makes 4 to 6 servings   Active Time: 20 Minutes   Start to Finish: 45 Minutes

---

8 tablespoons (1 stick) butter, melted

½ cup sugar

⅔ cup flour

½ teaspoon salt

1 teaspoon vanilla extract

3 eggs, beaten

1 cup milk

2 tablespoons unsalted butter

3 cups ripe cherries (pits in)

½ cup + 2 teaspoons sugar

Confectioner's sugar for garnish

1. Preheat the oven to 400 degrees F.

2. In a large bowl, mix together 6 tablespoons of the butter, sugar, flour, salt, vanilla, eggs, and milk until all ingredients are blended and smooth. Set aside.

3. Put 2 tablespoons of butter in the skillet and put it in the oven to heat up.

4. Transfer the skillet to the stovetop and add the additional butter. When it is melted, put the sugar in the skillet and shake it so it distributes evenly. Add the cherries. Pour the batter over the cherries, sprinkle with the last teaspoons of sugar, and put the skillet back in the oven. Bake for about 30 minutes, or until the topping is golden brown and set in the center.

5. Sprinkle with confectioner's sugar, if you'd like. Serve warm—and be sure to let diners know that the cherries contain their pits.

There is some debate about whether the pits should be removed from the cherries before baking, but even Julia Child left them in, going with the belief that the pits add flavor.

Menu 17

The late April weather means it's just about time that the herb garden gets planted. That means there's no better time for a classic Italian feast, one that reminds one of the familiar fragrances and warmer climes of the Mediterranean.

Classic Antipasti

Grilled Meatballs in Marinara Sauce

Cheesy Garlic Bread

Butter Pecan Bread Pudding

CLASSIC ANTIPASTI

Makes 4 Servings
Active Time: 15 Minutes
Start to Finish: 1 Hour

---

12 cherry tomatoes

½ cup, plus 4 tablespoons olive oil

½ cup assorted olives

½ teaspoon garlic, chopped

1 sprig thyme, leaves removed

¼ cup walnuts

¼ cup almonds

½ pound fresh prosciutto, shaved

8 to 10 thick slices hard salami

Coarsely ground black pepper

1. Stem the cherry tomatoes and place in a small bowl. Submerge in a high-quality olive oil and let marinate for 30 minutes to 1 hour.

2. In a small bowl, mix the assorted olives, garlic, thyme, and remaining 2 tablespoons of olive oil and let marinate for 30 minutes to 1 hour.

3. Take a small frying pan and place it over medium-high heat. Add in 2 tablespoons of olive oil. When hot, stir in the walnuts and almonds and toast for about 2 minutes. Remove and set aside.

4. Arrange the prosciutto and hard salami on a large platter and garnish/season lightly with coarsely cracked black pepper.

5. Arrange the almonds, tomatoes, and olives on the platter as well. Serve immediately.

GRILLED MEATBALLS
in Marinara Sauce

Makes 4 Servings   Active Time: 1 Hour   Start to Finish: 1 Hour and 35 Minutes

---

Meatball Ingredients

1 pound ground beef

1 pound ground veal

1 large yellow onion, finely chopped

¼ cup almond flour

3 garlic cloves, minced

2 large eggs, beaten

¼ cup tablespoons flat-leaf parsley, minced

2 tablespoons basil leaves, minced

1 tablespoon red pepper flakes

Fresh sea salt

Sauce Ingredients

¼ cup olive oil, plus 2 tablespoons

4 garlic cloves, minced

2 pounds plum tomatoes, crushed by hand

1 sprig oregano

1 sprig rosemary

1 sprig thyme

¼ cup dry white wine

½ cup basil, finely chopped

1 teaspoon coarsely ground black pepper

1 teaspoon fresh sea salt

1. In a large bowl, combine with your hands the beef, veal, and onion, and then slowly add in the almond flour. Let rest for 5 minutes and then add in the rest of the ingredients. Let stand at room temperature for 30 minutes.

2. A half hour before cooking, place a cast-iron skillet on your gas or charcoal grill and prepare the grill to medium-high heat. Leave covered while heating, as it will add a faint, smoky flavor to the skillet.

3. Using your hands, firmly form the meat into balls 1½ to 2 inches wide. Place on a plate and set alongside grill.

4. When the grill is ready, at about 400 degrees F and lightly covered with ash, add the 2 tablespoons of olive oil into the skillet. When hot, add the meatballs one by one and sear on all sides for about 8 minutes, or until all sides are browned. Remove from skillet and set aside.

5. Next, add the remaining ¼ cup of olive oil to the skillet, scraping off brown bits from the bottom. When the oil is hot, add the garlic and cook until golden, about 30 seconds to 1 minute: Do not let brown. Add the tomatoes, oregano, rosemary, thyme, and the seared meatballs. Simmer for 15 minutes. Add the wine, basil, pepper, and salt and simmer for 20 more minutes, until the meatballs are cooked through.

6. Remove the cast-iron skillet from the grill and spoon the meatballs and sauce into warmed bowls.

CHEESY GARLIC BREAD

Makes 8 Servings   Active Time: 20 Minutes   Start to Finish: 35 Minutes

1 loaf Country Sourdough (page 54), or any artisanal sourdough

6 garlic cloves, minced

1 tablespoon flat-leaf parsley, finely chopped

1 tablespoon fresh rosemary, finely chopped

½ cup (1 stick) unsalted butter, softened

1 cup 50/50 blend mozzarella and Parmesan cheeses

Coarsely ground black pepper

Fresh sea salt

1. Preheat your oven to 375 degrees F. Cut the bread into ¼- to ½-inch slices.

2. In a small bowl, combine the garlic, parsley, and rosemary with the softened butter and mix thoroughly.

3. Using the back of a spoon, thoroughly press and apply the garlic and herb butter to the slices of sourdough. Transfer the slices of bread to a baking sheet lined with aluminum foil, and then to the oven. Bake for about 15 minutes, until crisp, and then remove from the oven.

4. Bring the oven to 450 degrees F.

5. Distribute the cheese onto the slices of garlic bread, and then season with a little coarsely ground black pepper and fresh sea salt. Transfer back into the oven and cook for another 10 minutes or so, until the cheese has melted thoroughly over the bread.

6. Remove from the oven and serve immediately.

BUTTER PECAN BREAD PUDDING

Makes 4 to 6 Servings   Active Time: 45 Minutes   Start to Finish: 2 Hours

½ cup chopped pecans

4 tablespoons butter

4 cups cubed bread from a day-old loaf of French or Italian bread

2 eggs

¼ cup rum

1 gallon butter pecan ice cream, left out to soften (high-quality so that it is as rich as possible)

1. Place the skillet over medium-high heat. When hot, add the chopped pecans. Using pot holders or oven mitts, shake the pecans in the skillet while they cook. You want them to toast but not brown or burn. This should take just a few minutes.

2. When toasted, transfer the pecans to a plate and allow to cool.

3. Add the butter to the skillet and, over low heat, let it melt. Add the bread pieces to the skillet and distribute evenly. Sprinkle the pecan pieces over the bread cubes.

4. In a bowl, whisk the eggs with the rum. Add the softened or melted ice cream and stir just enough to combine. Pour the egg/ice cream mixture over the bread and nuts. Shake the skillet gently to distribute the liquid evenly.

5. Cover with plastic wrap, put in a cool place, and allow the mixture to rest for about 30 minutes so that the bread cubes are saturated with the ice cream.

6. Preheat the oven to 350 degrees F.

7. Bake for 40 to 45 minutes until the cream mixture is set and it is slightly brown around the edges. Use pot holders or oven mitts to take the skillet out of the oven. Allow to cool for 5 to 10 minutes before inverting onto a serving dish. Serve immediately. No need for additional ice cream.

Menu 18

Feliz Cinco De Mayo! There's no better way to celebrate then by heading into the cocina to make a delicious Mexican meal the whole family will enjoy. Here's a menu of simple Mexican-inspired recipes that are sure to be crowd pleasers.

Chicken Fajitas with Homemade Tortillas

Cilantro Lime Rice

Corn Salsa

Mexican Wedding Cookies

CORN SALSA

Makes 4 servings   Active time: 5 minutes
Start to Finish: 10 minutes

1 ear corn, shucked

1 pint cherry tomatoes

½ diced red onion

1 serrano pepper

½ cup cilantro, chopped

1. Preheat grill to medium-high heat. Place corn directly on the grill. Turn the corn and grill for about 8 minutes, or until corn becomes lightly charred and kernels have browned. Let these cool for a bit and then cut the kernels from the cob into a large bowl.

2. Place the tomatoes, red onions and pepper into a food processor and puree. Add mixture to the bowl of grilled corn and mix. Stir in the cilantro and serve.

CHICKEN FAJITAS

Makes 6 to 8 Servings   Active Time: 30 Minutes
Start to Finish: 60 Minutes

For the Chicken

½ cup orange juice

1 lime, squeezed (about 3 tablespoons juice)

4 cloves garlic, minced

1 jalapeno pepper, ribs and seeds removed, diced

2 tablespoons fresh cilantro, chopped

1 teaspoon cumin

1 teaspoon dried oregano

Salt and pepper

3 tablespoons olive oil

3 to 4 boneless, skinless chicken breasts, cut into strips

For the Vegetables

2 tablespoons olive oil

1 red onion, thinly sliced

1 red bell pepper, ribs and seeds removed, thinly sliced

1 green bell pepper, ribs and seeds removed, thinly sliced

1 yellow bell pepper, ribs and seeds removed, thinly sliced

2 jalapeno peppers or serrano chiles, ribs and seeds removed, sliced thin

3 cloves garlic, minced

¼ cup fresh-squeezed lime juice

½ cup fresh cilantro, chopped

Salt and pepper to taste

1. In a bowl, combine orange juice, lime juice, garlic, jalapeno, cilantro, cumin, oregano, and salt and pepper. When thoroughly combined, add the olive oil. Put the chicken pieces in the mix, stir, cover with plastic wrap and refrigerate for about 4 hours.

2. About an hour before you want to eat, get the sides prepared so you'll have them on hand when the dish is sizzling.

3. Heat the skillet over medium-high heat. Remove the chicken from the marinade with a slotted spoon and put it in the skillet, stirring and turning the pieces so they brown on all sides. Cook thoroughly, about 8 to 10 minutes. Transfer the cooked chicken to a platter and cover loosely with foil to keep warm.

4. Reduce the heat to medium, add the oil, and then add the onion, peppers, jalapeno, and garlic. Cook, stirring, for 3 to 5 minutes until vegetables soften. Add the lime juice and cilantro and cook for a few minutes more. Season with salt and pepper.

5. While vegetables are still sizzling, push them to one side of the pan and put the chicken on the other side. Serve immediately.

Variation: You can use the same ingredients to make steak fajitas, but substitute 1 pound of flank steak for the chicken, and marinate it in the mix overnight. Don't slice the steak until it's been cooked.

The trick is to bring this dish to the table while the meat and veggies are still sizzling. You'll want to be sure you have all the sides prepped ahead of time so you can go straight from stove to table with this.
You'll want tortillas, guacamole, salsa, jalapenos, sliced black olives, and sour cream.

These flatbreads are even simpler to make than the ones that involve yeast. There's no need to let the dough rise for tortillas—simply mix, knead, and shape—all with your hands, which is really fun. Then cook. Oh, and eat!

Tortillas

Makes 12 large tortillas   Active Time: 30 minutes
Start to Finish: 50 to 60 minutes

---

3 cups flour

1 teaspoon salt

2 teaspoons baking powder

3 tablespoons Crisco shortening (or 4 tablespoons chilled butter)

1½ cups water at room temperature

1. Put the flour in a large bowl. Mix in the salt and baking powder.

2. Add the shortening (or butter), and using your fingers, blend it into the flour mix until you have a crumbly dough. Add 1 cup of the water and work it in, then portions of the additional half cup, working it in with your hands, so that you create a dough that's not too sticky.

3. Lightly flour a work surface and turn out the dough. Knead it for about 10 minutes until it's soft and elastic. Divide it into 12 equal pieces.

4. Using a lightly floured rolling pin, roll each piece out to almost the size of the bottom of the skillet.

5. Heat the skillet over high heat. Add a tortilla. Cook for just 15 seconds a side, flipping to cook both sides. Keep the cooked tortillas warm by putting them on a plate covered with a damp tea towel. Serve warm.

CILANTRO LIME RICE

Makes 4 servings   Active Time: 5 minutes
Start to Finish: 15 minutes

---

2 cups long-grain white rice

2½ cups water

¼ cup vegetable oil

1½ teaspoons salt

2 tablespoons fresh lime juice

⅓ cup fresh cilantro, chopped

1. Add the rice, water and oil into the pressure cooker, seal shut, select the High Pressure function and let cook for 8 minutes.

2. Use a quick release method and slowly remove the lid once the valve has dropped. Fluff the rice.

3. In a separate bowl, combine the remaining ingredients and mix well. Add the rice, stir to combine and serve warm.

MEXICAN WEDDING COOKIES

Makes 3 dozen   Active Time: 20 minutes
Start to Finish: 45 minutes

½ pound (2 sticks) unsalted butter, softened

1¾ cups confectioners' sugar, divided

1 cup cake flour

1 cup self-rising flour

1 cup blanched almonds, very finely chopped

½ teaspoon pure vanilla extract

1. Preheat the oven to 350 degrees F. Grease 2 baking sheets with butter.

2. Place butter in a mixing bowl with 1¼ cups sugar, and beat well at medium speed with an electric mixer until light and fluffy. Add cake flour, self-rising flour, almonds, and vanilla to the bowl, and mix briefly until just combined. The dough will be very stiff; add a few drops of hot water, if necessary, to make it pliable.

3. Form dough into ¾-inch balls, and place them 1 inch apart on the prepared baking sheets. Bake for 15 to 18 minutes, or until firm. Remove the pans from the oven.

4. Sift remaining sugar into a low bowl, and add a few cookies at a time, rolling them around in the sugar to coat them well. Transfer cookies to a rack to cool completely. The cookies can be stored in an airtight container at room temperature up to 3 days, or they can be frozen up to 3 months.

Tip: If your butter is too cold to work into dough, don't soften it in the microwave. A few seconds too long and you've got a melted mess. Grate cold butter on the large holes of a box grater. It will soften in a matter of minutes.

Sometimes called polvarones, these rich and buttery cookies are like shortbread. Here we replace the more traditional lard with unsalted butter.

169

Menu 19

If you haven't already used the grill this spring, now is the time. There's nothing like cooking over an open flame, and almost everything on this menu can be grilled outdoors—including dessert! So get out the folding chairs, light up the grill, and enjoy the sunny days ahead.

Grilled Beef Short Ribs with Red Wine & Basil Marinade

Grilled Eggplant with Herbs

Corny-Spicy Bread

Grilled Peaches with Coconut Cream

GRILLED EGGPLANT
with Herbs

Makes 4 to 5 servings
Active Time: 30 minutes
Start to Finish: 45 minutes

½ **small white onion, finely chopped**

½ **cup olive oil**

¼ **cup parsley leaves, chopped**

1 **medium eggplant, sliced in half lengthwise**

Coarsely ground black pepper

Fresh sea salt

1. Combine the onion, olive oil, and parsley into a roasting pan and mix thoroughly. Next, add the eggplant halves into the mix and let stand at room temperature while you prepare the grill.

2. Prepare your gas or charcoal grill to medium-high heat. Designate two sections of the grill, one for direct-heat and the other for indirect; you will want to cook the eggplant over indirect-heat.

3. When the grill is ready, about 400 to 500 degrees F, remove the eggplant halves from the roasting pan and place them down over indirect heat. Cover the grill and cook for about 15 to 25 minutes until softened.

4. Remove from grill and serve warm.

GRILLED BEEF SHORT RIBS
with Red Wine & Basil Marinade

Makes 4 to 5 Servings   Active Time: 1 Hour   Start to Finish: 8 Hours

Short Rib Ingredients

3 to 4 pounds beef short ribs, meaty and cut into 3 to 5 inches

Coarsely ground black pepper

Fresh sea salt

Red Wine & Basil Marinade Ingredients

2 cups basil leaves, finely chopped

2 large carrots, finely chopped

2 large onions, finely chopped

2 garlic cloves, finely chopped

1 scallion, finely chopped

2 sprigs thyme, leaves removed

2 sprigs rosemary, leaves removed

2 sprigs oregano, leaves removed

3 tablespoons olive oil

1 bottle dry red wine

1. The night before you plan on grilling, combine all the ingredients for the marinade except for the wine in a large bowl or roasting pan. Add the short ribs and pour in the wine. Move the bowl to the refrigerator and let rest for 4 to 6 hours.

2. Transfer the ribs from the marinade to a large cutting board or plate and let stand at room temperature for 1 hour. Season one side of the ribs with half of the pepper and salt.

3. A half hour before cooking, prepare your gas or charcoal grill to medium-high heat.

4. When the grill is ready, at about 400 to 450 degrees F with the coals lightly covered with ash, place the seasoned-sides of the ribs on the grill and cook for about 4 minutes. Season the tops of the ribs while waiting. When the steaks are charred, flip and cook for 4 more minutes.

5. Transfer the ribs to a cutting board and let rest for 5 to 10 minutes. Serve warm.

CORNY-SPICY BREAD

Makes 4 to 6 Servings   Active Time: 1 Hour
Start to Finish: 3 to 4 Hours

---

4 cups finely ground yellow cornmeal

½ cup sugar

1 tablespoon salt

4 cups boiling water

1 cup flour

2 tablespoon butter, melted

1 (4-oz.) can sweet corn kernels

1 jalapeno pepper, ribs and seeds removed, chopped fine

2 eggs, lightly beaten

2 teaspoons baking powder

1 teaspoon baking soda

1 cup milk

1 teaspoon butter

1. In a large bowl, combine cornmeal, sugar, salt, and boiling water. Stir to combine and let sit for several hours in a cool, dark place or overnight in the refrigerator. Stir occasionally while batter rests.

2. When ready to make, preheat the oven to 450 degrees F.

3. Add flour, melted butter, corn, jalapenos, eggs, baking powder, baking soda, and milk. Stir to thoroughly combine.

4. Heat the skillet over medium-high heat and melt the teaspoon of butter in it. Add the batter. Transfer the skillet to the oven and cook for 15 minutes. Reduce the heat to 250 degrees F and cook another 40 minutes or until golden brown on the top and set in the center.

5. When the cornbread is fresh out of the oven, melt a tablespoon or two of butter over the top.

This corn bread has whole corn kernels and jalapenos for some kick!

GRILLED PEACHES
with Coconut Cream

Makes 3 to 6 Servings.   Active Time: 30 Minutes
Start to Finish: 35 Minutes

For the Coconut Cream:

1 13.5-oz. can whole (or full-fat) organic coconut milk, refrigerated overnight

2 teaspoons raw honey (preferably organic), or pure maple syrup

1 teaspoon pure vanilla extract (or one vanilla bean)

For the Grilled Peaches:

Extra-virgin coconut oil, to brush the grill rack

3 large peaches (preferably organic)

3 tablespoons raw honey (preferably organic), or pure maple syrup

2 tablespoons clarified butter or coconut oil

1 teaspoon pure vanilla extract (or one vanilla bean)

½ teaspoon sea salt

2 tablespoons toasted chopped pecans (optional)

Mint leaves, for garnish

Variations:

· Use nectarines for a slightly tangier version!

· Top with any variety of toasted nuts, or even toasted coconut flakes!

To Make the Coconut Cream:

1. Remove the can of whole coconut milk from the refrigerator and open the can. The liquid should have risen to the surface, separating from the thicker, heavier cream.

2. Pour the liquid out of the can (and save it in a separate bowl—use it for a paleo soup or smoothie!).

3. Scoop the remaining cream into a bowl and whip it with a whisk until it reaches a whipped-cream-like consistency and texture.

4. Whip in the honey and vanilla; add more to achieve desired sweetness.

5. Put the bowl of prepared coconut cream in the refrigerator until the grilled peaches are ready.

To Make the Grilled Peaches:

1. Start by washing your peaches and slice them in half, removing the pits.

2. In a small saucepan, combine the honey, clarified butter, vanilla, and salt over low heat and stir until the butter has melted and the ingredients have combined to form a light sauce, about five minutes. When the sauce starts to bubble, remove from heat and set aside.

3. Brush your clean grill rack lightly with coconut oil.

4. Bring your grill to medium heat. Place your peach halves face-down on the grill and drizzle with about a third of your sauce.

5. Flip the peaches after about ten minutes (or until grill marks appear on the flesh), and brush the surface with another third of your sauce. Allow to grill for another five to ten minutes, or until peaches are tender.

6. Serve warm, topped with chopped pecans (if desired), a dab of coconut cream, and a drizzle of your remaining sauce.

Grilling peaches enhances their tangy sweetness by allowing the natural sugars to caramelize, and the rich and silky coconut cream, plus a drizzle of honey and sprinkle of chopped nuts, makes for the perfect topping.

Mother's Day

Attention grandfathers, husbands, and children!
Today is a day that the women in your life are not allowed to
cook! It's Mother's Day, and that means grandmothers
and mothers of all kinds deserve a break and a bit of
relaxation. Now, that doesn't mean they won't offer a
little help or advice, but remember—it's their day! Show that
someone special just how much she really means.

Crab Cakes

Skillet Eggplant Parmesan

Dinner Rolls

Masala Rice with Peas and Tomatoes

Sautéed Kale with Prosciutto

Citrus Angel Food Cake

Chocolate Nut Torte

CRAB CAKES

Makes 6 Cakes   Active Time: 1 Hour
Start to Finish: 1½ Hours

---

1 pound lump crab meat

¼ cup onion, minced

½ cup bread crumbs

1 teaspoon Worcestershire sauce

1 teaspoon Old Bay seasoning

1 teaspoon dried parsley flakes

1 tablespoon mayonnaise

1 tablespoon milk

1 large egg, lightly beaten

Salt and freshly ground pepper to taste

¼ cup oil (preferably peanut, but olive is fine)

Lemon wedges

1. In a large bowl combine crab meat, onion, bread crumbs, Worcestershire sauce, Old Bay seasoning, parsley flakes, and mayonnaise. Mix the milk into the egg and add to the crab mix, blending gently but thoroughly. Season with salt and pepper. If mix seems dry, add some more mayonnaise.

2. Heat the skillet over medium-high heat. Add the oil. It should be about ¼-inch deep. When oil is hot, add 3 or 4 individual heaping spoons full of crab mix to the skillet, pressing down on the tops of each to form a patty (cake). Brown the cakes on each side for about 3 minutes. Try to turn the cakes over just once. If you're worried about them being cooked through, put a lid on the skillet for a minute or so after they've browned on each side.

3. Transfer the cakes to a plate and cover with foil to keep them warm while you cook the next batch. Serve on a platter with lemon wedges.

For great flavor, go for top-quality crab meat—the kind that's in the refrigerated section of your store's fish department. Don't buy crab meat that's canned like tuna. It has neither the flavor nor the consistency needed for these cakes.

DINNER ROLLS

Makes about a dozen rolls   Active Time: 60 Minutes
Start to Finish: 3 Hours

1¼ cups whole milk, heated to 110 degrees F

3 tablespoons sugar

1 tablespoon active dry yeast

8 tablespoons (1 stick) unsalted butter

¾ teaspoon salt

2 eggs at room temperature, lightly beaten

3½ cups cake or bread flour (not all-purpose flour)

1. In a small bowl, combine ½ cup warm milk and the sugar. Sprinkle the yeast over it, stir, and set aside so the yeast can proof (about 10 minutes).

2. While the yeast is proofing, melt the butter in the skillet over low to medium heat, and remove from heat when melted.

3. When the yeast mix is frothy, stir in 3 tablespoons of the melted butter, the remaining milk, the salt, and the eggs. Then stir in the flour, mixing until all ingredients are incorporated. Transfer to a lightly floured surface and knead the dough for 5 to 10 minutes until it is soft and springy and elastic.

4. Coat the bottom and sides of a large mixing bowl (ceramic is best) with butter. Place the ball of dough in the bowl, cover loosely with plastic wrap, put it in a naturally warm, draft-free location, and let it rise until doubled in size, about 45 minutes to 1 hour.

5. Prepare a lightly floured surface to work on. Punch down the dough in the bowl and transfer it to the floured surface. Warm the skillet with the butter so that it is melted again.

6. Break off pieces of the dough to form into rolls, shaping them into 2-inch balls with your hands. Roll the balls in the butter in the skillet, and leave them in the skillet as they're made and buttered.

7. Cover the skillet loosely with a clean dish towel, put it in the warm, draft-free spot, and let the rolls rise until doubled in size, about 30 minutes. While they're rising, preheat the oven to 350 degrees F.

8. When the rolls have risen and the oven is ready, cover the skillet with aluminum foil and bake in the oven for 20 minutes. Remove the foil and finish cooking, another 15 minutes or so, until the rolls are golden on top and light and springy. Serve warm.

SKILLET EGGPLANT PARMESAN

Makes 4 Servings   Active Time: 20 Minutes
Start to Finish: 1 Hour

1 large eggplant

Salt for sprinkling on eggplant

2 tablespoons olive oil

1 cup Italian seasoned breadcrumbs

2 tablespoons grated Parmesan cheese

1 egg, beaten

Prepared spaghetti sauce (no sugar or meat added)

2 cloves garlic, pressed through a garlic press

8 oz. mozzarella cheese, shredded

Fresh basil, for garnish

1. Preheat the oven to 350 degrees F. Trim the top and bottom off the eggplant and slice into ¼-inch slices. Put the slices on paper towels in a single layer, sprinkle salt over them, and leave them for about 15 minutes. Turn the slices over, salt this side, and let sit for another 15 minutes. Rinse the salt from all the pieces and dry with clean paper towels.

2. Drizzle oil over a baking sheet in preparation for the eggplant.

3. In a shallow bowl, combine the breadcrumbs and Parmesan cheese. Put the beaten egg in another shallow bowl. Dip the slices of eggplant in egg, then breadcrumbs, coating both sides. Put them on the baking sheet.

4. Bake in the oven for about 10 minutes, turn them over, and bake another 10 minutes. Remove the sheet from the oven.

5. Put a layer of spaghetti sauce in the cast iron skillet and stir in the pressed garlic. Lay the eggplant slices in the sauce, layering to fit. Top with the shredded mozzarella.

6. Put the skillet in the oven and bake for about 30 minutes, until the sauce is bubbling and the cheese is golden. Allow to cool for about 10 minutes, then serve with extra sauce and fresh basil if desired.

MASALA RICE
with Peas and Tomatoes

Makes 6 servings   Active Time: 35 minutes   Start to Finish: 1½ hours

2 tablespoons extra-virgin olive oil

1 medium white onion, finely chopped

2 teaspoons minced fresh ginger

3 garlic cloves, minced

2 plum tomatoes, chopped into ¼-inch cubes

½ cup fresh peas

2 teaspoons curry powder

2 cups chicken broth

1½ cups uncooked jasmine rice

1 tablespoon coarsely ground black pepper

1 tablespoon fresh sea salt

1. Preheat the oven to 400 degrees F, positioning the rack in the center.

2. Add the olive oil to a medium oven-safe saucepan and place over medium heat. When hot, add the onion and ginger and cook for about 7 minutes, until the onions are translucent. Stir in the garlic and cook for another 2 minutes, until golden.

3. Stir in the tomatoes, pea, curry powder, and broth and bring to a boil. Remove from the heat when the broth begins to boil.

4. Add the peas, pepper, and salt to the saucepan and transfer to the oven. Cook for about 1 hour, until the rice is soft and cooked through. Remove from the oven and serve warm.

Tip: Replace the chicken broth with vegetable broth for a vegetarian alternative.

Indian-inspired flavors give just enough spice to this rice dish.

Sautéed Kale with Prosciutto

Makes 5 to 6 servings   Active Time: 15 minutes   Start to Finish: 30 minutes

8 to 10 slices prosciutto

2 tablespoons extra-virgin olive oil

2 garlic cloves, minced

2 pounds kale, coarsely chopped

2 tablespoons red wine vinegar

Coarsely ground black pepper

Fresh sea salt

1. Preheat the oven to 375 degrees F.

2. Lay the prosciutto evenly on a baking sheet. Transfer the baking sheet to the oven and cook until the prosciutto is browned and crisp, about 15 minutes. Remove from the oven and place on a plate lined with paper towels. When cool, chop the prosciutto into medium-sized pieces.

3. Add the extra-virgin olive oil into a sauté pan with a lid and place over medium-high heat.

4. When hot, add the garlic and cook for about 2 minutes, until golden but not browned. Add the chopped kale and sauté, covered, for 7 minutes, until softened.

5. Remove the lid and cook for 2 more minutes. Add the prosciutto and red wine vinegar and then remove from the heat. Season with ground black pepper and fresh sea salt, and serve warm.

You can boil, bake, or steam kale, but sautéeing not only cooks it quickly but allows the kale to keep its texture and taste.

CHOCOLATE NUT TORTE

Makes 8 Servings   Active Time: 15 Minutes   Start to Finish: 1½ Hours, Including 1 Hour For Chilling

---

10 oz. bittersweet chocolate, chopped and divided

2 cups pecan or walnut halves, toasted in a 350 degree oven for 5 minutes

2 tablespoons plus ½ cup granulated sugar

1 cup (2 sticks) unsalted butter, softened and divided

3 large eggs, at room temperature

1 tablespoon rum

Variations:

• Add 1 tablespoon of instant espresso powder to the batter.

• Substitute triple sec or Grand Marnier for the rum, and add 2 teaspoons of grated orange zest to the batter.

• Substitute blanched almonds for the pecans or walnuts, substitute amaretto for the rum, and add 1/2 teaspoon of pure almond extract to the batter.

1. Preheat the oven to 375 degrees F and grease an 8-inch round cake pan. Cut out a circle of wax or parchment paper, fit into the bottom of the pan, and then grease the paper.

2. Melt 4 oz. of the chocolate in a microwave oven or over simmering water in a double boiler. Cool slightly.

3. Reserve 12 nut halves and chop the remaining nuts with 2 tablespoons of the sugar in a food processor fitted with a steel blade, using on-and-off pulsing. Scrape the nuts into a bowl.

4. Beat ½ cup (1 stick) of the butter and the remaining sugar in the food processor until light and fluffy. Add melted chocolate, then eggs, 1 at a time. Beat well between each addition, and scrape the sides of the work bowl with a rubber spatula. Add rum, then fold the chocolate mixture into the ground nuts.

5. Scrape batter into the prepared pan and bake for 25 minutes. Cake will be soft but firm up as it cools. Remove the cake from the oven and cool for 20 minutes on a wire cooling rack. Invert cake onto a plate, remove the paper, and cool completely.

6. To make the glaze, combine the remaining 6 oz. of chocolate and remaining ½ cup (1 stick) of butter in a small saucepan. Melt over low heat and beat until shiny and smooth.

7. Place the cake on a wire rack over a sheet of wax paper. Pour the glaze over the center of the cake, and rotate the rack at an angle so the glaze runs down sides of the cake. Top with the 12 reserved nut halves, and allow to rest in a cool place until the chocolate hardens.

Tip: If you find that the parchment paper sticks to the top of the cake, brush the paper with a little warm water. After ten seconds the paper should peel right off.

This cake can serve as the base for many mixed fruit salads, as well as being delicious all alone.

CITRUS ANGEL FOOD CAKE

Makes 8 servings   Active Time: 25 minutes
Start to Finish: 2½ hours

¾ cup orange juice

2 tablespoons finely grated orange zest

2 tablespoons finely grated lemon zest

⅓ cup potato starch

⅓ cup white rice flour

¼ cup tapioca flour

½ teaspoon xanthan gum

¾ cup granulated sugar, divided

10 large egg whites, at room temperature

1 teaspoon cream of tartar

1. Preheat the oven to 350 degrees F. Rinse a tube pan and shake it over the sink to remove excess moisture, but do not wipe it dry.

2. Combine orange juice, orange zest, and lemon zest in a small heavy saucepan and bring to a boil over medium heat. Reduce by three-quarters, pour mixture into a soup bowl, and refrigerate until cool. Sift potato starch, white rice flour, tapioca flour, and xanthan gum with ¼ cup of sugar; set aside.

3. Place egg whites in a grease-free mixing bowl and beat at medium speed with an electric mixer until frothy. Add cream of tartar, raise the speed to high, and beat until soft peaks form. Add remaining sugar, 1 tablespoon at a time, and continue to beat until stiff peaks form and meringue is glossy. Lower the speed to Low and beat in cooled orange juice mixture. Gently fold flour mixture into meringue and scrape batter into the tube pan.

4. Bake in the center of the oven for 40 to 45 minutes, then remove cake from the oven and invert cake onto the neck of a tall bottle for at least 1½ hours, or until cool. Run a knife or spatula around the outside of the pan to loosen cake and invert cake onto a serving plate.

Variation:
Substitute lime zest for the lemon zest.

A Proper Breakfast in Bed for Mother's Day

On a typical morning, your mother will be running around trying to start the day; ma king breakfast, getting the kids off to school, and getting herself off to work. That's why breakfast in bed on Mother's Day is such a treat. It's one time when she can relax and enjoy the morning without all the fuss, and a chance for you to do for her what she does for you all too often. Here's a few tips on how to make it a perfect Mother's Day breakfast in bed.

- Most of all, don't disturb Mom while you're making breakfast. Try to keep down the noise while she rests. Let her sleep in on her special day.

- Do some prep work ahead of time, especially if it's a surprise. Get sneaky, and ask Mom about her favorite breakfast earlier in the week. Then make anything you can when Mom's not around. That way you'll limit the amount of time spent in the kitchen, and lessen the chances of Mom catching on to your plans.

- Keep it simple. When kids are involved, things tend to get chaotic. There's no need to make things overly complicated and create too much of a mess—no one wants a bed covered in her favorite food. Make sure the tray you use is big enough and sturdy enough, and use dishes and glassware that are well-balanced and won't easily spill.

- Do something special. Buy Mom her favorite magazine to read in bed, or scones from her favorite bakery. Make a smiley face with the bacon and eggs, or use syrup to write a message on the pancakes. Put a flower in a vase. And be sure to write a note wishing your mother a happy Mother's Day.

- Know what Mom likes. If your Mom like sweets, focus on a sweet breakfast like pancakes or waffles with fruit, syrup, and whipped cream. Or maybe she likes savory dishes, where an Eggs Benedict with Poached Eggs will do the trick. Is she a bacon lover, or is she vegetarian? Remember, it's her special day. Here's a simple starter menu, depending on what your mother likes:

Toast with Butter and Jam

Fresh Eggs
(see "How to Cook Eggs," page 34)

Pancakes or Waffles with Maple Syrup

Crispy Bacon

Orange Juice

Coffee or Tea

Mom's favorite dessert sweet
(tarts, cookies, donuts, scones, etc.)

- Lastly, you — not Mom — is responsible for clean-up. Be sure to clean all the dishes and pots and pans, and make sure the kitchen is tidy and clean. Mom will be very proud.

Menu 20

Who says you can't roast a whole chicken on a grill while enjoying the outdoors? That's what we do here. Feel free to throw some potatoes on the coals as well. Still in the mood for picnic food? Chocolate cheesecake brownies to the rescue.

Grilled Lemon and Garlic Chicken

Spinach and Tomato Side Salad

Classic Baked Potato

Chocolate Cheesecake Brownies
with Cream Cheese Batter

189

GRILLED LEMON AND GARLIC CHICKEN

Makes 4 to 5 servings   Active Time: 1 hour and 15 minutes   Start to Finish: 1 hour and 30 minutes

1 to 2 feet butcher's twine

A 4- to 5-pound chicken

Coarsely ground black pepper

Fresh sea salt

3 lemons, halved

1 garlic head, halved

1 bunch thyme

1 bunch rosemary

5 tablespoons olive oil

Tip: Before filling the chicken's cavity with the garlic, thyme, and rosemary, heavily rinse the cavity with a couple cups of orange juice and salt—an easy way to up the flavor and wow your guests!

1. Prepare your gas or charcoal grill to medium heat.

2. Place the chicken into a large roasting pan. Season its cavity generously with coarsely ground black pepper and fresh sea salt. Take 5 of the lemon halves and fill them into the cavity, gently juicing them while doing so. Then, grab the remaining lemon half and rub it across the chicken, squeezing it lightly so that its juices seep into the chicken. Discard this half. Fill the cavity with the 2 halves of the garlic head and the thyme and rosemary, and tie the legs together with the butcher's twine. Let rest for 15 minutes.

3. Take 4 tablespoons of olive oil and massage it over the chicken's skin. Season the outside with additional pepper and salt.

4. When the grill is ready, at about 400 degrees F with the coals lightly covered with ash, place the chicken on the grill, skin side up. Cover the grill and cook for about 40 minutes. Before flipping, brush the top of the chicken with the remaining tablespoon of olive oil. Turn and cook for about 15 more minutes until the skin is crisp and a meat thermometer, inserted into the thickest part of the thigh, reads 165 degrees F.

5. Remove from grill and place on a large carving board. Let the chicken rest at room temperature for 10 minutes before carving. Serve warm.

Spinach and Tomato Side Salad

Makes 4 servings   Active Time: 10 minutes   Start to Finish: 10 minutes

4 yellow tomatoes, cut into wedges

8 oz. grape tomatoes, halved

8 oz. baby spinach leaves

¼ cup toasted pine nuts or almond slivers

¼ cup fresh basil, coarsely chopped

¼ cup extra-virgin olive oil

2 tablespoons balsamic vinegar

Salt and pepper to taste

1. Combine the tomatoes, basil, spinach, and nuts in a large bowl.

2. Drizzle atop the olive oil and balsamic vinegar as dressing, toss gently to combine, and add salt and pepper to taste.

CLASSIC BAKED POTATO

Makes 6 servings   Active Time: 10 minutes   Start to Finish: 50 minutes

6 russet potatoes, washed & scrubbed

2 tablespoons extra-virgin olive oil

Coarsely ground black pepper

Fresh sea salt

¼ cup chopped chives, optional for toppings

¼ cup fresh sour cream, optional for toppings

¼ cup aged Parmesan cheese, optional for toppings

1 stick softened, unsalted butter, optional for toppings

1. Prepare your oven to 400 degrees F with an oven rack at medium position.

2. While the oven heats, pierce your russet potatoes with a fork and then rub lightly with olive oil. Season the potatoes generously with the coarsely ground black pepper and fresh sea salt, and then set aside.

3. When the oven is ready, place the potatoes directly on the oven-rack and bake for about 45 minutes until the skins are crisp and the potatoes can be easily pierced with a fork.

4. Remove the potatoes from the oven and serve immediately along with several classic toppings found in the ingredients above.

For this brownie,
a swirl of cheesecake batter
adds an extra creamy goodness.

CHOCOLATE CHEESECAKE BROWNIES

Makes 6 to 8 servings   Active Time: 40 minutes   Start to Finish: 1½ hours

8 tablespoons (1 stick) butter

¼ cup unsweetened cocoa powder

1 cup sugar

½ cup flour

½ teaspoon salt

2 large eggs, lightly beaten

1 teaspoon vanilla extract

1 cup semisweet chocolate chips

Cream Cheese Batter

4 oz. cream cheese, softened

¼ cup sugar

1 egg

1 teaspoon vanilla extract

1. Preheat the oven to 325 degrees F.

2. Prepare the cream cheese batter by combining the cream cheese, sugar, egg, and vanilla in a bowl. Set aside.

3. Melt butter in the skillet over medium-low heat.

4. Put the cocoa powder in a medium-sized bowl. When the butter is melted, pour it over the cocoa powder, leaving a film of butter on the skillet. Whisk the butter into the chocolate, then add the sugar, stirring to combine. Combine the flour and salt, and stir this into the batter. Add the eggs, vanilla, and chocolate chips and stir to blend.

5. Put the batter into the cast iron skillet. Drop the cream cheese batter in spoonfuls onto the brownie, distributing evenly. Use a small knife to gently swirl the cream cheese into the chocolate.

6. Put the skillet in the oven and bake for 30 to 35 minutes until the edges start to brown and a toothpick inserted in the middle comes out clean. Use pot holders or oven mitts to remove the hot skillet. Let it cool for about 10 minutes.

Menu 21

Here's a meal of restaurant classics to impress the family, with three dishes you'll find in brasseries and steakhouses across the country. While this menu has all the hallmarks of fine dining, there's no need to have graduated from culinary school. Here's the dirty little secret: these recipes really aren't that difficult at all.

Chicken Cordon Bleu

Mashed Potatoes (page 87)

Braised Fennel

Orange Cake

CHICKEN CORDON BLEU

Makes 4 to 6 servings   Active Time: 30 minutes
Start to Finish: 2 to 3 hours on High

6 medium sized skinless and boneless chicken breasts

1 pound Swiss cheese, cut into slices

1 pound cooked ham from the deli, sliced thin

3 tablespoons flour

1 teaspoon paprika

6 tablespoons butter

½ cup dry white wine

1 chicken bouillon cube

1 tablespoon arrowroot

1 cup heavy cream

½ cup chopped fresh parsley, for garnish

1. If you're starting with thick chicken breasts, place them between sheets of wax paper and pound them to about ¼-inch thickness with a wooden mallet or rolling pin. Lay the breasts flat, and place slices of cheese and ham on them, distributing evenly. Fold breasts over and secure ends with toothpicks.

2. In a shallow soup bowl, combine flour and paprika and blend well. Dip chicken pieces in flour/spice mixture to coat on both sides.

3. Heat butter in a large skillet over medium high heat, and cook the chicken pieces in the butter until browned on both sides, about 3 minutes a side. Transfer the chicken pieces with a slotted spoon to the slow cooker. In the butter and juices in the skillet, add the wine and bouillon cube and stir until cube is dissolved. Pour the mixture over the chicken in the slow cooker.

4. Cover and cook on Low for 5 to 7 hours or on High for 2 to 3 hours. Chicken should be cooked through and tender. Transfer chicken to a warm plate and cover with foil while you make the sauce.

5. Turn the slow cooker on High to heat up the juices. In a measuring cup, mix the arrowroot and heavy cream until blended. Add a large spoonful of the hot juice to the cream mixture and stir, then pour the cream mixture into the slow cooker. Stir thoroughly and continue to stir while sauce thickens, about 5 minutes. Serve the sauce over the chicken.

Braised Fennel

Makes 4 to 6 servings
Active Time: 15 minutes
Start to Finish: 2½ to 6 hours,
depending on setting

**2 medium fennel bulbs, about
1 pound each**

2 tablespoons butter

½ small onion, thinly sliced

1 clove garlic, minced

1 cup vegetable broth

**1 teaspoon fresh thyme, or
¼ teaspoon minced**

Salt and pepper to taste

1. Cut stalks off fennel bulb, trim root end, and cut bulb in half through the root. Trim out core, then slice fennel into 1-inch-thick slices across the bulb. Arrange slices in the slow cooker, and repeat with the second bulb.

2. Heat butter in a small skillet over medium heat. Add onion and garlic and cook, stirring frequently, for 3 minutes, or until onion is translucent. Scrape mixture into the slow cooker.

3. Add broth and thyme to the slow cooker. Cook on Low for 4 to 6 hours or on High for 2 to 3 hours, or until fennel is tender. Top with cracked pepper and serve in a dish.

Although the celery-like stalks are trimmed off the fennel bulb for this dish, don't throw them out. They add a wonderful anise flavor as well as a crisp texture and are used in place of celery in salads and other raw dishes.

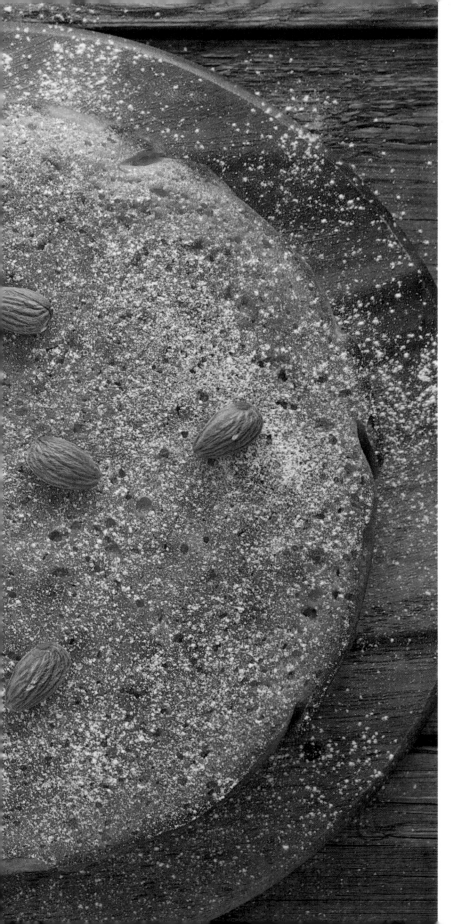

ORANGE CAKE

Makes 6 to 8 servings
Active Time: 40 minutes
Start to Finish: 1½ hours

¾ cup sugar

Zest of two oranges (about 2 tablespoons)

8 tablespoons (1 stick) butter, cut in pieces

3 eggs

1½ cups flour

1 teaspoon baking powder

½ cup orange juice (preferably fresh-squeezed)

1. Preheat the oven to 350 degrees F. Put a cast iron skillet in the oven to get it hot.

2. In a large bowl, combine the sugar and orange zest, working them together so the zest penetrates the sugar. Add the butter, and cream the butter and lemon-sugar together until light. Add the eggs one at a time, combining thoroughly after each addition.

3. In the measuring cup you use for the flour, add the baking powder and mix the dry ingredients together. Alternately add the flour mix and the orange juice to the butter-sugar mix until thoroughly combined.

4. Remove the skillet from the oven using pot holders or oven mitts. Pour the cake batter into it.

5. Put in the oven and bake for about 30 to 35 minutes, until the top is golden and the cake springs to the touch and a toothpick inserted in the middle comes out clean. Cool and cut into wedges. Serve with fresh whipped cream.

199

Memorial Day

Best. Burgers. Ever.

Juicy Turkey Burgers

Black Bean Burgers

Spicy Grilled Corn on the Cob

Coleslaw (page 336)

Memorial Day is the year's first great American holiday, a day that celebrates American heroes and signifies the start to the summer. It's also a day for family, and now that the weather has warmed up, it's a great opportunity to gather everyone outdoors for a picnic of some classic American dishes, prepared on the grill. When you think of "American" food, this is the meal you picture.

Home-Style
Baked Beans
(page 46)

Classic Potato
Salad

Strawberry-
blueberry
parfait

Chocolate
Walnut
Brownies

BEST. BURGERS. EVER.

Makes 4 to 6 Burgers   Active Time: 30 Minutes   Start to Finish: 30 Minutes

1 pound ground beef

Salt and pepper for seasoning

Hamburger buns (not too bready)

Slices of cheese (optional)

Lettuce, tomato, and onion (optional)

Ketchup, mustard, pickles, mayonnaise (optional)

The kind of meat you use matters. The meat-to-fat ratio should be about 80-20. Most ground beef found in the grocery store is 85-15 or 90-10. If you have to go with one of these, choose the fattier proportion. The best thing to do, though, is ask the meat department to grind the meat for you. You want a chuck cut with a good amount of fat in it. The fat should show up as almost chunky in the meat, not pulverized into the grind to look like pale red "mush."
Trust me on this one.

1. Refrigerate the hamburger meat until ready to use.

2. When it's time to make the burgers, first brush your skillet with a thin sheen of oil, and heat it over medium-high heat. Take the meat out of the fridge and form the patties. Don't overhandle the meat, simply take a handful of it (about 3 oz.), and gently form into a patty. Make 3 or 4, depending on how many will fit in the skillet.

3. Put the patties in the skillet and don't touch them. Let them start to cook on the medium-high heat. They'll spatter and sizzle. That's fine. Sprinkle some salt on them, and grind some pepper over them (but not too much). Let them cook on one side for about 3 minutes.

4. When you flip the burgers, if you want cheese on one or all of them, put it on now. The cheese should blanket the meat, not be an afterthought.

5. Leave the burgers to cook on this side just as you did the other side. The skillet takes care of even distribution of the heat. Wait 3 or 4 minutes. Scoop the burger off the skillet with the spatula, slide it onto a bun, top with whatever you like, and dig in. Best. Burgers. Ever.

BLACK BEAN BURGERS

Makes 4 Servings   Active Time: 90 Minutes   Start to Finish: 2 Hours

---

1 (15-oz.) can black beans, drained and rinsed

⅓ cup scallions

¼ cup chopped roasted red peppers

¼ cup cooked corn

¼ cup breadcrumbs (plain)

1 egg, lightly beaten

2 tablespoons cilantro, chopped

½ teaspoon cumin

½ teaspoon cayenne pepper

½ teaspoon freshly ground black pepper

1 teaspoon fresh-squeezed lime juice

1 tablespoon olive oil

Hamburger buns

Tomato slices

Avocado slices

Spinach leaves

Onion slices

1. In a food processor or blender, combine half the beans with the scallions and roasted red peppers. Pulse to blend until you have a thick paste. Transfer to a large bowl.

2. Add the corn, breadcrumbs, egg, cilantro, cumin, cayenne, pepper, and lime juice. Stir to blend. Add the remaining beans and stir vigorously to get all ingredients to stick together. Cover bowl with plastic wrap and let sit at room temperature for about 30 minutes.

3. Heat skillet over medium-high heat. Form mixture into 4 to 6 patties. Add oil to skillet and, when hot, add the patties. Cook, covered, about 5 minutes per side.

4. Serve immediately on hamburger buns with topping options, including tomato slices, avocado slices, spinach, and onion slices.

Variation: Replace the avocado slices with guacamole (and put out lots of napkins!).

Tip: For even healthier burgers, reduce the black beans to 1 cup, and add 1/2 cup cooked quinoa and 1/2 cup wild or brown rice.

JUICY TURKEY BURGERS

Serves 4   Active time: 20 minutes   Total time: 35 minutes

---

1 small onion, finely chopped

1½ pounds lean ground turkey

1 tablespoon Worcestershire sauce

2½ tablespoon ketchup

Salt and pepper to taste

1. Mix with your hands the ground turkey, Worcestershire sauce, and ketchup in a large bowl. With your hands, form the meat into 4 patties about ⅓ to ½ inch thick, and season with salt and pepper.

2. Prepare your grill to medium-high heat.

3. Place the burgers on the grill and cook for 3 to 4 minutes each side.

4. Serve burgers warm on buns with lettuce, tomato, and red onion.

CLASSIC POTATO SALAD

Makes 8 Servings   Active time: 10 minutes   Prep time: 30 minutes

8 medium potatoes, cooked and diced

1½ cups mayonnaise

2 tablespoons cider vinegar

2 tablespoons sugar

1 tablespoon mustard

1 teaspoon salt

1 teaspoon garlic powder

½ teaspoon pepper

2 celery ribs, chopped

1 cup onion, minced

5 hard-boiled eggs

Paprika

1. Boil the potatoes, then cool. Dice the potatoes and set aside.

2. In another bowl, combine the mayonnaise, vinegar, and spices. Then add in the potatoes, celery and onions.

3. Stir in the eggs and dust with paprika on top.

Spicy Grilled Corn on the Cob

Makes 4 servings   Active time: 10 minutes   Start to Finish: 20 minutes

2 teaspoons cumin

2 teaspoons coriander

1 teaspoon salt

1 teaspoon rosemary, finely chopped

½ teaspoon ground ginger

¼ teaspoon pepper

¼ teaspoon cinnamon

2 tablespoons olive oil

4 ears of corn, shucked

1. In a small bowl, mix all the ingredients other than the olive oil and corn.

2. Brush the olive oil on the corn to help the coating stick.

3. Sprinkle the mixture over the corn and place each ear in a large piece of foil. Fold the foil over and crimp edges to create a tightly sealed packet.

4. Preheat grill to medium heat and cook for 10 to 12 minutes, making sure to turn the packet occasionally. When the corn is tender and charred, remove from heat and serve.

CHOCOLATE WALNUT BROWNIES

Yield: 2 dozen   Active time: 15 minutes   Start to finish: 1 hour

---

1 tablespoon egg replacement powder, such as Ener-G

1 cup coarsely chopped walnuts, divided

⅔ cup (10 tablespoons) soy margarine, sliced

1 cup granulated sugar

¼ cup firmly packed light brown sugar

1 cup unsweetened cocoa powder (natural or Dutch-process)

¼ teaspoon salt

½ teaspoon pure vanilla extract

½ cup whole-wheat pastry flour

1. Preheat the oven to 350 degrees F. Line the bottom and sides of an 8x8-inch baking pan with parchment paper or foil, allowing the paper to extend 2 inches over the top of the pan. Grease the paper.

2. Toast ½ cup walnuts for 5 to 7 minutes, or until browned. Remove nuts from the oven, and reduce the oven temperature to 325 degrees F.

3. Combine margarine, granulated sugar, brown sugar, cocoa, and salt in a medium heatproof bowl and set the bowl in a wide skillet of barely simmering water. Whisk it from time to time until margarine melts and mixture is smooth and hot. Remove the bowl from the skillet and set aside briefly until the mixture is only warm, not hot.

4. Stir in vanilla and egg replacement mixture, and whisk until it looks thick and shiny. Add flour, and whisk until incorporated, and then beat for 1 minute with a spoon. Stir in toasted nuts, and spread batter evenly in the prepared pan. Top with untoasted nuts.

5. Bake in the center of the oven for 20 to 25 minutes, or until a toothpick inserted into the center comes out with just a few crumbs attached. Cool completely on a wire rack. Lift up the ends of the parchment or foil liner, transfer brownies to a cutting board, and cut into pieces.

Note: The brownies can be made up to 3 days in advance and kept at room temperature in an airtight container.

Variations:

• Substitute pure orange oil for the vanilla, and add 2 tablespoons grated orange zest to the batter.

• For mocha brownies, stir 1 tablespoon instant espresso powder to the egg replacement mixture.

Strawberry-Blueberry Parfait

Serves 2

½ cup strawberries, sliced

½ cup blueberries

1 cup heavy cream

1. Put the sliced strawberries and blueberries in a bowl and stir to combine

2. In a separate bowl, beat the heavy cream on high until it forms stiff peaks. Distribute the berries between 2 bowls and top with whipped cream.

Variation:

Thicken the whipped cream by beating in 2 tablespoons cream cheese, and flavor it with a splash of vanilla extract or unsweetened rum extract. Garnish with fresh mint.

O say can you see, by the dawn's early light,
What so proudly we hailed at the twilight's last gleaming,
Whose broad stripes and bright stars through the perilous fight,
O'er the ramparts we watched, were so gallantly streaming?
And the rockets' red glare, the bombs bursting in air,
Gave proof through the night that our flag was still there;
O say does that star-spangled banner yet wave
O'er the land of the free and the home of the brave?

On the shore dimly seen through the mists of the deep,
Where the foe's haughty host in dread silence reposes,
What is that which the breeze, o'er the towering steep,
As it fitfully blows, half conceals, half discloses?
Now it catches the gleam of the morning's first beam,
In full glory reflected now shines in the stream:
'Tis the star-spangled banner, O long may it wave
O'er the land of the free and the home of the brave.

The Star-Spangled Banner

And where is that band who so vauntingly swore
That the havoc of war and the battle's confusion,
A home and a country, should leave us no more?
Their blood has washed out their foul footsteps' pollution.
No refuge could save the hireling and slave
From the terror of flight, or the gloom of the grave:
And the star-spangled banner in triumph doth wave,
O'er the land of the free and the home of the brave.

O thus be it ever, when freemen shall stand
Between their loved homes and the war's desolation.
Blest with vict'ry and peace, may the Heav'n rescued land
Praise the Power that hath made and preserved us a nation!
Then conquer we must, when our cause it is just,
And this be our motto: 'In God is our trust.'
And the star-spangled banner in triumph shall wave
O'er the land of the free and the home of the brave!

—Francis Scott Key, September 20, 1814

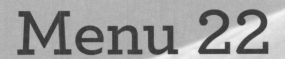

Menu 22

Roast pork is an American favorite and sweet pineapple is the perfect complement. Combined with delicious veggies and a brown sugar cake, this meal will become one of your family's favorites!

Grilled Roast Pineapple Pork Loin

Fingerling Potatoes with Herbs

Roasted Cauliflower (page 88)

Coconut Brown Sugar Cake

GRILLED ROAST PINEAPPLE PORK LOIN

Makes 5 to 6 Servings   Active Time: 1 Hour and 30 Minutes
Start to Finish: 2 Hours and 15 Minutes

5 tablespoons olive oil

1 or 2 sprigs fresh rosemary

1 cup crushed pineapple

¼ cup honey

¼ cup water

1 teaspoon fresh ground or grated ginger

2¼ pounds pork loin

Sea salt

Fresh cracked pepper

1. Fire up your grill and allow the coals to settle into a temperature of about 350 degrees F.

2. While the grill is heating, slowly sauté the olive oil and rosemary in a cast-iron or All-Clad style high heat friendly pan. Be sure the pan is oven-friendly, as you will be placing this pan directly onto your grill.

3. After the oil and rosemary have been thoroughly heated and the flavors of the sprigs are infused throughout the oil, add in a ½ cup of crushed pineapple, honey, water, and ginger. Stir thoroughly, and bring the mixture to a soft boil.

4. Rub your pork loin with salt and pepper to your desired seasoning, and place the pork loin into the pan, turning it so the entire loin is covered with the basting sauce for 5 to 10 minutes at a medium heat until the loin begins to brown. Once your grill has reached the desired temperature, move the entire pan to your grill grate.

5. Cover your grill and allow the pork to cook for 45 minutes, turning and basting the pork occasionally so all sides are browned from the heat of the hot pan.

6. After about 45 minutes, remove the pork loin from the pan and place directly on the grate. Use the remaining ½ cup of crushed pineapple to baste the loin thoroughly creating a golden-brown glaze as you turn the loin for another 15 minutes.

7. Remove from fire and let the loin rest for 10 to 12 minutes. Carve and serve with sides of your choice.

FINGERLING POTATOES
with Herbs

Makes 6 to 8 servings   Active Time: 15 Minutes
Start to Finish: 40 Minutes

---

4 pounds fingerling potatoes, halved lengthwise

2 tablespoons extra-virgin olive oil

2 tablespoons fresh rosemary, finely chopped

2 tablespoons fresh thyme, finely chopped

Coarsely ground black pepper

Fresh sea salt

1. Preheat the oven to 400 degrees F, placing the rack in the center of the oven.

2. In a large bowl, toss the potatoes with oil, rosemary, and thyme, and then season generously with pepper and salt.

3. Spread the potatoes evenly across a large baking sheet and transfer to the oven. Bake for 30 to 35 minutes, until the potatoes are browned and can be easily pierced with a fork.

4. Remove from the oven and serve immediately.

COCONUT
BROWN SUGAR CAKE

Makes 8 servings
Active Time: 20 minutes
Start to Finish: 1 hour

---

8 tablespoons (1 stick) butter

2 tablespoons dark brown sugar

1 (15.25 oz.) box of white cake mix

1 cup unsweetened coconut flakes

1/2 cup unsweetened shredded coconut

1¼ cups water

⅓ cup vegetable oil

6 oz. unsweetened applesauce

4 eggs

1. Preheat the oven to 350 degrees F.

2. In the cast iron skillet, melt the butter over medium heat, then sprinkle brown sugar over it. Allow the sugar to melt in the butter over low heat. No need to stir, but don't let the butter get too hot.

3. In a large bowl, combine the cake mix, coconut flakes, shredded coconut, water, oil, applesauce, and eggs. Stir to combine.

4. Pour the batter into the skillet. The butter-sugar mixture will come up over the sides of the batter. This is part of the magic.

5. Bake 25 to 30 minutes until browned on the top and sides and a toothpick inserted in the middle comes out clean.

6. Allow to cool for about 10 minutes. The skillet will still be hot. Put a large serving plate on the counter and, working quickly and deliberately, flip the skillet so the cake is inverted onto the plate. Allow to cool an additional 15 to 20 minutes before slicing and serving.

Tip: Dress up this cake by serving it with a scoop of vanilla or chocolate ice cream and a drizzle of chocolate sauce.

Menu 23

This time of year means bathing suit weather is here again. And after all the hot dogs and hamburgers on Memorial Day, it's time for some lighter fare. Summer goes hand in hand with seafood and citrus, and with a little help from this menu, you'll be ready for the beach in no time.

Grilled Swordfish Steaks with Citrus Salsa

Charred Sweet Potatoes (page 144)

Grilled Shishito Peppers

Lemon Cake

GRILLED SWORDFISH STEAKS
with Citrus Salsa

Makes 4 to 6 servings   Active time: 20 minutes
Total Time: 40 minutes

Swordfish

½ lemon, juiced

¼ cup fresh basil leaves

1 garlic clove, minced

½ cup olive oil, plus extra for the grill

4 swordfish steaks, 1¼ to 1¾ inches thick

Coarsely ground black pepper

Fresh sea salt

Citrus Salsa

1 cup ripe pineapple, diced

¼ cup fresh cucumber, diced

¼ cup ripe mango, diced

1 small shallot, chopped

2 tablespoons red bell pepper, diced

1 tablespoon fresh cilantro, finely chopped

¼ small lime, juiced

½ teaspoon Tabasco sauce

Coarsely ground black pepper

Fresh sea salt

1. In a medium bowl, combine the lemon juice, fresh basil leaves, and garlic. Whisk in the olive oil and then let the marinade infuse for 1 hour. Next, rub the oil over the swordfish steaks and then season with coarsely ground black pepper and sea salt. Let stand at room temperature while you prepare the grill and citrus salsa.

2. Prepare your gas or charcoal grill to high heat.

3. While the grill heats, combine the pineapple, cucumber, mango, shallot, red bell pepper and cilantro in a large bowl. Stir in the lime juice and Tabasco sauce and then season with coarsely ground black pepper and sea salt. Transfer the bowl to the refrigerator and let chill.

4. When the grill is ready, about 450 to 500 degrees F and the coals are lightly covered with ash, brush the grate with a little olive oil. Place the swordfish steaks on the grill and then grill for about 3 to 4 minutes per side, until the fish is opaque.

5. Remove the steaks from the grill and place on a large carving board. Let stand for 5 to 10 minutes, and then serve with a side of citrus salsa.

GRILLED SHISHITO PEPPERS

Makes 4 servings
Active Time: 10 minutes
Start to Finish: 30 minutes

2 to 3 cups whole shishito peppers

2 tablespoons olive oil

Coarsely ground black pepper

Fresh sea salt

1. In a cast-iron skillet, combine the shishito peppers and olive oil, and then season with coarsely ground black pepper and sea salt.

2. Prepare your gas or charcoal grill to medium-high heat.

3. When the grill is ready, about 400 to 500 degrees F, place the cast-iron skillet on the grill and cook the shishito peppers in the skillet until blistered, about 8 to 10 minutes.

4. Remove from the grill and serve while hot.

*Tip:
About one
out of every
ten or so
shishito peppers
is spicy!*

LEMON CAKE

Makes 6 to 8 servings   Active Time: 40 minutes
Start to Finish: 90 minutes

¾ cup sugar

Zest of two lemons (about 1 tablespoon)

6 tablespoons butter, cut in pieces

2 eggs

1 cup flour

1 teaspoon baking powder

½ cup milk

1. Preheat the oven to 350 degrees F.

2. In a large bowl, combine the sugar and lemon zest, working them together so the zest penetrates the sugar. Add the butter, and cream the butter and lemon-sugar together until light. Add the eggs one at a time, combining thoroughly after each addition.

3. In the measuring cup you use for the flour, add the baking powder and mix the dry ingredients together. Alternately add the flour mix and the milk to the butter-sugar mix until thoroughly combined.

4. Grease the cast iron skillet with some butter and add the cake batter.

5. Put in the oven and bake for about 30 to 35 minutes, until the top is golden and the cake springs to the touch and a toothpick inserted in the middle comes out clean. Cool and cut into wedges.

Variations

This cake is delicious on its own, but it can be topped with all kinds of treats. Consider these:

• Fresh-squeezed lemon juice and granulated sugar

• Whipped cream

• Fresh fruit like raspberries, strawberries, blueberries, blackberries or a combination of berries

• Ice cream

• Pecans sautéed in butter and brown sugar.

Menu 24

"Home on the Range" means more than just the time spent on our stovetops—it's evocative of old American West. Here's a meal for the cowpoke in all of us. So rustle up a seat at the campfire, because we're about the ring the chow bell. Here we've got cowboy steaks, bone marrow mashed potatoes, cabbage, and strawberry-rhubarb pie. Come and get it, pardners!

Cowboy Steaks

Bone Marrow Mashed Potatoes

Crazy-Good Cabbage

Strawberry-Rhubarb Pie

COWBOY STEAKS

Makes 2 to 3 Servings
Active Time: 15 Minutes
Start to Finish: 1 Hour and 30 Minutes

---

2 bone-in rib eye steaks, about 1¼ to 1½ inches thick, cut from rib roast

2 tablespoons extra-virgin olive oil

Coarsely ground black pepper

Fresh sea salt

1. Rub both sides of the steaks with the extra-virgin olive oil and let rest at room temperature for about 1 hour.

2. 30 minutes before cooking, prepare the gas or charcoal grill to medium-high heat.

3. When the grill is ready, about 400 to 450 degrees F with the coals lightly covered with ash, season one side of the steaks with half of the coarsely ground pepper and sea salt. Place the seasoned-sides of the steaks on the grill and cook for about 6 to 7 minutes, until blood begins to rise from the tops. Season the tops of the steaks while you wait.

4. When the steaks are charred, flip and cook for 4 to 5 more minutes for medium-rare and 5 to 6 more minutes for medium. The steaks should feel slightly firm if poked in the center. (I recommend cooking the rib eye to medium; medium-rare will be very chewy and tough. For a boneless rib eye, cook for 2 to 4 minutes less.)

5. Remove the steaks from the grill and transfer to a large cutting board. Let stand for 5 to 10 minutes, allowing the steaks to properly store their juices and flavor.

BONE MARROW MASHED POTATOES

Makes 6 to 8 Servings   Active Time: 25 Minutes   Start to Finish: 1 Hour

---

8 Yukon Gold potatoes, peeled and cut into quarters

4 to 6 large beef marrow bones, halved lengthwise

½ cup half-and-half

½ cup (1 stick) unsalted butter, softened

1 teaspoon fresh rosemary, finely chopped

Coarsely ground black pepper

Fresh sea salt

1. Preheat the oven to 375 degrees F, placing the rack in the center of the oven.

2. Place the marrow bones on a baking sheet, transfer to the oven, and then cook for about 15 minutes, until the marrow is nicely browned. Remove from the oven and let stand.

3. While the marrow bones are roasting, place the potatoes in a large stockpot and fill with water so that it covers the potatoes by 1 inch.

4. Place the stockpot on the stove and bring to a boil. Cook the potatoes by boiling for about 20 minutes, until you can pierce the potatoes with a fork. Remove the pot from heat and drain the water, leaving the potatoes in it.

5. Using a potato masher or fork, start mashing the potatoes so they begin to break apart. Gradually mash in the half-and-half and butter, tasting the potatoes as you go along, until arrive at the perfect blend of creamy, buttery, mashed potatoes.

6. Scoop the marrow from the bones and add to the potatoes, along with the rosemary. Mix thoroughly, and then season with the coarsely ground black pepper and fresh sea salt. Serve warm.

Crazy-Good Cabbage

Makes 4 to 6 servings   Active Time: 30 minutes   Start to Finish: 1 hour

---

2 tablespoons olive oil

1 medium head cabbage, cored and shredded

1 green pepper, seeds and ribs removed, diced

1 medium onion, diced

3 cups fresh tomatoes, seeds removed, chopped

1 ear corn, kernels removed

8 oz. of canned corn, drained

1 teaspoon cayenne pepper

Salt and pepper to taste

1. Heat a skillet over medium-high heat and add the oil. Add cabbage, peppers, and onions and stir, cooking, until onions become translucent, about 3 minutes. Add the tomatoes, corn, and cayenne and stir. Season with salt and pepper.

2. Cover, reduce the heat to low, and simmer until the cabbage is cooked through, about 30 minutes. Stir occasionally. Serve hot with extra cayenne on the side.

STRAWBERRY-RHUBARB PIE

Makes 6 to 8 servings
Active Time: 45 Minutes
Start to Finish: 2 hours

---

1 flaky pastry crust recipe for a double crust (see page 107)

4-5 stalks rhubarb, cleaned and cut into 1-inch pieces (use about 1½ pounds frozen rhubarb, thawed, if fresh isn't available)

1 quart fresh strawberries, washed and tops trimmed, and sliced in half or quarters (use ½ pound frozen strawberries, thawed, if fresh aren't available)

¾ cup sugar

⅓ cup flour

1 tablespoon butter

1 egg white

1. Preheat the oven to 375 degrees F.

2. In a large bowl, toss rhubarb and strawberries with sugar and flour.

3. Place 1 of the piecrusts in the bottom of a glass pie plate. Fill with rhubarb/strawberry mix, and place the other crust over the fruit, crimping the edges together.

4. Brush the top crust with the egg white. Cut 4 or 5 slits in the middle.

5. Put the pie plate in the oven and bake for about 45 to 55 minutes until golden brown and bubbly. Cover the outermost edge with aluminum foil in the last 10 minutes of baking to prevent it from burning.

6. Allow to cool before serving. Serve with whipped cream.

Father's Day

They say the way to a man's heart is through his stomach, and there's no better way to prove this theory than on Father's Day. Here's a hearty home-cooked meal any father will appreciate; one that rivals a night at his favorite steakhouse. You don't need to be a father to enjoy this meal, but you might loosen your belt later nonetheless!

Tomatoes and Mozzarella

Filet Mignon

Lamb Chops with Rosemary and Lemon

Braised Vidalia Onions & Mushrooms

Corn Fritters

Beer Brownies

TOMATOES AND MOZZARELLA

Makes 4 to 6 Servings   Active Time: 10 Minutes
Start to Finish: 10 Minutes

---

1 package of cherry tomatoes

1 pack fresh mozzarella cheese, sliced into ¼-inch pieces

½ cup fresh basil leaves

1 tablespoon extra-virgin olive oil

1 tablespoon balsamic vinegar

Coarsely ground black pepper

Fresh sea salt

1. Place the tomatoes, mozarella, and basil leaves in a platter.

2. In a small glass, combine the extra-virgin olive oil and balsamic vinegar, and then drizzle it evenly across the tomatoes and mozzarella.

3. Season with the coarsely ground black pepper and fresh sea salt, and then serve immediately.

FILET MIGNON

Makes 2 to 3 Servings.   Active Time: 20 Minutes
Start to Finish: 1 Hour And 30 Minutes

---

2 filet mignon steaks, about 2 to 2½ inches thick

3 tablespoons olive oil

Coarsely ground black pepper

Fresh sea salt

1 to 2 feet of butcher's string

1. Tie the butcher's string tightly around each steak. Then rub both sides of the steaks with the 2 tablespoons olive oil and let rest at room temperature for about 1 hour.

2. A half hour before cooking, place the cast-iron skillet on the grate and prepare your gas or charcoal grill to medium-high heat. Leave the grill covered while heating, as it will add a faint, smoky flavor to the skillet.

3. When the coals are ready, about 400 degrees F with the coals lightly covered with ash, season one side of the steaks with half of the coarsely ground pepper and sea salt.

4. Spread the remaining tablespoon of olive oil in the skillet, and then place the steaks, seasoned sides down, into the cast-iron skillet. Wait 2 to 3 minutes until they are slightly charred, seasoning the uncooked sides of the steaks with the remaining pepper and sea salt while waiting. Turn the steaks and sear for another 2 to 3 minutes. Remove from the skillet and let rest, uncovered, for 30 minutes.

5. Preheat the oven to 400 degrees F.

6. Put the steaks back into the cast-iron skillet and place in the oven. For medium-rare, cook for 11 to 13 minutes, and for medium, cook for 14 to 15.

7. Remove the steaks from the oven and transfer to a large cutting board. Let stand for 10 minutes. Detach the butcher's string from the steaks and serve warm.

LAMB CHOPS
with Rosemary and Lemon

Makes 4 Servings   Active Time: 15 Minutes
Start to Finish: 30 Minutes

---

4 tablespoons fresh-squeezed lemon juice (no seeds)

2 tablespoons fresh rosemary leaves, chopped

2 cloves garlic, pressed

Salt and pepper to taste

8 lamb chops

1. Preheat the broiler on high. Position a rack to be about 5 to 7 inches away from the heat. Put the skillet in the oven so it gets hot.

2. In a bowl, combine the lemon juice and rosemary. Press the garlic into the mix and season with salt and pepper. Using your hands, rub the chops in the mix, being sure to coat both sides and distribute evenly. Put the chops on a platter.

3. When the skillet is hot, take it out and position the chops in it so they fit. Return to the rack under the broiler and cook for about 5 minutes. Since the skillet is already hot, the lamb is cooking on both sides at once.

4. Remove from the oven, let rest for a minute, and serve.

BRAISED VIDALIA ONIONS & MUSHROOMS

Makes 6 Servings
Active Time: 15 Minutes
Start to Finish: 20 Minutes

3 tablespoons extra-virgin olive oil

1 large Vidalia onion, peeled and chopped into ¼-inch slices

1 pint Portobello mushrooms, sliced

Coarsely ground black pepper

Fresh sea salt

1. Heat the extra-virgin olive oil in a medium cast-iron skillet over low-medium heat.

2. When hot, add the Vidalia onions and Portobello mushrooms to the skillet and cook until tender, about 10 to 15 minutes.

3. Remove the skillet from the heat and serve immediately.

CORN FRITTERS

Active Time: 40 Minutes
Start to Finish: 1 Hour and 45 Minutes

1 egg, well beaten

1 teaspoon sugar

½ teaspoon salt

1 tablespoon butter, melted

2 teaspoons baking powder

1 cup flour

⅔ cup milk

2 cups cooked corn, cooled

1 tablespoon canola oil

1. In a large bowl, combine egg, sugar, salt, butter, baking powder, flour, and milk and stir thoroughly. Add the corn and mix.

2. Heat the skillet over medium-high heat and add the oil. Drop spoonfuls of batter into the skillet. Brown on both sides, about 3 minutes per side. Scoop out with a slotted spoon and put on a plate lined with paper towels to drain. Keep fritters warm while making more. Serve warm.

The best corn to use for this is leftover cooked corn on the cob that's been in the refrigerator overnight. Otherwise, you can take frozen corn and thaw the kernels, drying them before putting them in the batter. If you use canned corn, be sure all water is drained from it, and choose a high-quality brand so the kernels are firm and sweet, not mushy.

BEER BROWNIES

Makes 6 to 8 servings   Active Time: 30 minutes
Start to Finish: 1 hour and 30 minutes

---

8 tablespoons (1 stick) unsalted butter

½ cup dark chocolate morsels or 4 oz. 60% dark chocolate broken into pieces

½ cup stout (chocolate or coffee)

2 eggs

⅔ cup sugar

½ cup flour

2 tablespoons unsweetened cocoa powder

1 tablespoon espresso powder

¼ teaspoon salt

1. Preheat the oven to 350 degrees F.

2. Melt the butter in a cast-iron skillet over medium heat. Add the chocolate pieces and stir until melted. Add the beer, stir to combine, and remove from the heat.

3. In a bowl, whisk together the eggs and sugar until combined. In a separate bowl, stir together the flour, cocoa powder, espresso powder, and salt. Add to the egg/sugar mix, whisking until just combined. Pour this batter over the chocolate in the skillet and stir gently until just combined.

4. Bake for 25 to 30 minutes, until the top has set and a toothpick inserted in the middle comes out with just some crumbs. Be careful not to overbake.

5. Remove from the oven and allow to cool 10 to 15 minutes before serving.

Happy Father's Day to every dad!

Thank you for all you do and did for us!

Menu 25

American kitchens are greatly influenced by the diversity of our immigrant population, and what was once considered "exotic" is now familiar, including a few of the recipes included here. Nowadays, Americans everywhere have been introduced to South Asian cooking, and it's become a staple in homes across the country. The smoked ginger chicken is perfect when served with the almond dipping sauce, a strong substitute to the classic peanut sauce.

**Smoked Ginger Chicken Satay
with Almond Dipping Sauce**

Cucumber Salad

Naan

Flourless Peanut Butter Cookies

FLOURLESS PEANUT BUTTER COOKIES

Makes 12 cookies, depending on size
Active time: 15 minutes   Total time: 25 minutes

1 cup natural peanut butter

1 egg

2/3 cup white sugar

1/3 cup brown sugar

1 teaspoon baking powder

¼ cup white sugar, set aside in a bowl for rolling

1. Preheat oven to 350 degrees and line a baking sheet with parchment paper.

2. In a large bowl, combine all the ingredients except the ¼ cup white sugar for rolling.

3. Shape the dough into rounded tablespoonfuls, roll in the white sugar, and place on the parchment-lined baking sheet, at least 1 inch apart.

4. Crosshatch the top of each cookie by pressing a fork down into the dough horizontally and then vertically.

5. Bake the cookies for 10 minutes, until they start to slightly brown on the edges.

6. Remove from the oven and let cool on a wire cooling rack.

Variation:
Add ¼ cup mini chocolate chips to the dough.

Summer

Summer is the season to get outdoors, and holidays like Memorial Day and the Fourth of July mean one thing: grilling. Menus for this season include those that take the kitchen outside, whether it's a picnic in the park, grilling in the backyard, or even cooking over a campfire.

Before your first cookout of the season, be certain your grill is clean and properly maintained. Clean the grates and any cooktops, and check that all the hoses and fittings are in place, and any propane tank is safely connected. Likewise, make sure your grilling tools—forks, tongs, grill—have been freshly cleaned after months of storage.

Check for rust or cracks, and check for loose wheels that can tip your grill over. Make sure your grill is on a flat surface, and located at a safe distance from your home and any flammable sources. Also, be sure to have a fire extinguisher nearby. Never use a grill indoors or in an enclosed area.

Summer is a perfect time to visit your local farmer's market or farm stand. This season's recipes use a wealth of fruits and vegetables, and fresh produce from the farm stand (and fresh herbs from your herb garden) will only heighten the flavors of the summer.

Menu 26

Summer means camping out and cooking over an open flame. Whether you're exploring the great outdoors, or just roughing it in the backyard, here's a few different options from the mess tent that you can prepare over the fire or simply on the grill. Start the meal with smoked mussels and end with delicious scout sundaes. Okay, troops, time for KP duty!

Smoked Mussels

Grilled Trout

Summer Vegetable Packet

Scout Sundaes

SMOKED MUSSELS

Makes 4 to 6 servings   Active Time: 30 minutes
Total Time: 1 hour 10 minutes

---

2 to 3 pounds mussels, cleaned and debearded

4 tablespoons flat-leaf parsley, chopped

8 garlic cloves, 4 minced

4 tablespoons olive oil

1 lemon, halved

Coarsely ground black pepper

Fresh sea salt

1 medium yellow onion, quartered

1. In a large bowl, combine the cleaned mussels, parsley, 4 minced garlic cloves, and olive oil and toss evenly. Next, squeeze the lemon halves over the mussels and then season with coarsely ground black pepper and sea salt.

2. An hour before grilling, add the yellow onion and 4 remaining garlic cloves into a bowl of water, and let soak.

3. Preheat your gas or charcoal grill to medium-high heat.

4. When the grill is ready, at about 450 to 500 degrees F with the coals lightly covered with ash, toss the soaked onion and garlic cloves over the coals, or into the smoking box. Wait 5 minutes for the smoke to develop. Add the mussels into a grill basket (a sheet of aluminum foil will do) and place onto the grill. Cover the grill and cook for about 10 minutes until the mussels open.

5. Remove mussels when opened; for any that don't open, try cooking them a bit longer and throw them out if they still don't open. Transfer the mussels into a large bowl and let rest, uncovered, for 5 to 10 minutes before serving.

GRILLED TROUT

Makes 4 servings   Active Time: 35 minutes
Start to Finish: 70 minutes

½ cup olive oil

4 garlic cloves, finely chopped

2 tablespoons white wine vinegar

¼ small lemon, juiced

2 teaspoons fresh rosemary

1 teaspoon fresh sage

½ teaspoon fresh thyme

8 trout fillets, about 2 pounds, or 4 rainbow trout

Coarsely ground black pepper

Fresh sea salt

1. Add olive oil to a small saucepan over medium-high heat. When hot, stir in the garlic and cook until golden, about 2 minutes. Stir in the white wine vinegar, lemon juice, rosemary, sage, and thyme into a small bowl and simmer for 1 minute. Remove and let infuse for 30 minutes.

2. Place the trout fillets into a large baking dish and cover with the garlic and herb oil. (If the mixture doesn't cover the fillets, flip the fish halfway through the marinating time.) Transfer the dish to the refrigerator and let the fillets rest in the oil for 30 to 45 minutes.

3. Prepare your gas or charcoal grill to medium-high heat.

4. When the grill is ready, at about 400 to 500 degrees F with the coals lightly covered with ash, remove the fillets from the marinade and season with pepper and salt. Place the fillets on the grill, skin side down, and cook for about 2 to 3 minutes per side. Transfer the steaks from the grill to a large carving board and let rest for 10 minutes. Serve warm.

SUMMER VEGETABLE PACKET

Makes 4 servings   Active Time: 10 minutes   Start to finish: 30 minutes

4 ears corn, shucked

2 bell peppers, diced

2 zucchini, cut into ½-inch slices

½ red onion, diced

½ teaspoon oregano

½ teaspoon garlic powder

½ teaspoon basil

½ teaspoon parsley

Salt and pepper, to taste

4 tablespoons olive oil

Feta cheese, for sprinkling

1. Begin by removing kernels from the cob into a medium bowl. Add bell pepper, zucchini slices and diced onions and mix together.

2. Sprinkle oregano, garlic powder, basil, parsley and a pinch of salt and pepper over the vegetables, making sure to mix thoroughly. Add the olive oil and toss to coat evenly.

3. Prepare two large pieces of foil and distribute the vegetables evenly between the two. Fold the foil into a packet and crimp the edges to seal.

4. Preheat grill to medium-high heat and place the packets on the grill. Let these cook for 15 to 20 minutes. Once vegetables are tender, remove from heat, sprinkle feta over each packet and serve.

Scout Sundaes

Makes 1 sundae   Active time: 8 minutes   Start to finish: 20 minutes

Square of tinfoil

1 banana with peel

⅓ cup chocolate chips or chocolate chunks

¼ cup miniature marshmallows (optional)

¼ cup chopped walnuts (optional)

1. Prepare your tinfoil into a bowl-like form large enough for the length of sliced banana.

2. Carefully cut your banana to slice through the fruit, but not through to the other side of the peel, and spread the cut to fill.

3. Place the chocolate chunks and marshmallows in the middle, then fold the foil boat until closed to roast on the campfire for a few minutes (about 5) until the chocolate is melted and the fruit is warm.

4. Carefully remove and allow the foil to cool before unwrapping, then sprinkle the chopped walnuts over the melted goodness. Eat with a spoon straight from the peel boat, using the foil as additional support to try and prevent mess.

Americans eat more marshmallows than any other country, maybe because the modern manufacturing of them was established in the Chicago area in the early 1950s by Duomak.

The Fourth of July

The Fourth of July is our most patriotic
of days, and a great reason to get the whole family
together to celebrate. This Independence Day
menu includes a number of star-spangled recipes
that are uniquely American, plus some
picnic classics that have become synonymous with
the holiday. And if you're looking to make some burgers,
don't forget to look back in the Memorial Day menu,
where you'll find a variety of
hamburger recipes.

Bacon Deviled Eggs

New York Strip Steaks

Fried Chicken

Coleslaw (page 336)

Home-Style Baked Beans (page 46)

Broccoli Salad

Potato Salad (page 206)

Strawberry Pie

Red, White and Blue Bread Pudding

BACON DEVILED EGGS

Makes 6 Servings   Active Time: 15 Minutes   Start to Finish: 30 Minutes

2 egg yolks, room temperature

¼ medium lemon, juiced

1 cup light olive oil

10 large eggs

6 thick strips of bacon

2 tablespoons Dijon mustard

2 tablespoons fresh parsley, finely chopped

Coarsely ground black pepper

Fresh sea salt

1 teaspoon paprika (optional)

3 chives, finely chopped (optional)

1. In a small food processor, add the 2 raw egg yolks and the lemon juice and puree for 30 seconds. Very gradually, add in the light olive oil until you reach a thick, mayonnaise-like consistency. Add the light olive oil slowly to the processor slowly; if you go too quickly, you will not reach the desired constancy.

2. Fill a medium saucepan with water. Carefully add the 10 eggs and then place the saucepan over medium heat. When the water reaches a boil, pull the eggs from the water and place under cool water. Let rest for a few minutes, and then peel back the shells.

3. Slice the eggs into halves. Using a fork, transfer the egg yolks from the eggs and place in a small bowl. Whisk in the mayonnaise mixture, Dijon mustard, and parsley, and then season with coarsely ground black pepper and fresh sea salt. Set aside.

4. Place a medium frying pan over medium-high heat. Add the thick strips of bacon to the pan and cook until crispy, a few minutes on each side. (If you would like to add a smoked flavor to the bacon, consider smoking the bacon on the grill.) Transfer the bacon to a carving board and chop into bits. Whisk into the mixture.

5. Spoon the mixture from the small bowl back into the egg whites. If you would like, garnish with paprika and chopped chives. Serve chilled.

Tip: Consider doubling or tripling this recipe for a larger gathering.

FRIED CHICKEN

Makes 4 servings   Active Time: 1 hour   Start to Finish: 1½ hours

---

3 chicken legs (drums and
thighs together, cut to make
3 drumsticks and 3 thighs)

¼ cup flour

Salt and pepper

1 cup milk

1 tablespoon white vinegar

2 eggs, lightly beaten

1½ cups corn flakes, finely
crushed

½ cup plain breadcrumbs

1 teaspoon paprika

1 cup vegetable oil

1. Preheat the oven to 400 degrees F. Place a cast-iron skillet in the oven to get it hot.

2. Rinse and dry the chicken pieces.

3. In a shallow bowl or cake pan, whisk together the flour with some salt and pepper. In the measuring cup of milk, add the vinegar and let the combination sit for 10 minutes (to create buttermilk). When ready, mix the milk in a bowl with the beaten eggs. In another large bowl, combine the corn flakes, breadcrumbs, paprika, and 2 tablespoons of the vegetable oil.

4. Coat the chicken pieces one at a time by dipping each in the flour, then the milk mixture, then the crumb mixture, being sure to coat all sides. When coated, put the pieces on a plate, cover with plastic wrap, and refrigerate for about 15 minutes.

5. Remembering how hot it's going to be (wear oven mitts!), take the skillet out of the oven and put the oil in it. Heat it on low until hot. Add the cold chicken pieces and turn in the hot oil so both sides are coated with oil.

6. Put the skillet back in the oven and bake for about 30 minutes, turning the pieces after 15 minutes. The chicken is done when the juices run clear when pierced with a knife. Serve immediately.

NEW YORK STRIP STEAK

Makes 2 to 3 Servings   Active Time: 15 Minutes
Start to Finish: 1 Hour and 30 Minutes

---

2 New York strip steaks, about 1½ inches thick

2 tablespoons olive oil

Coarsely ground black pepper

Fresh sea salt

Rosemary for garnish, if desired

1. Remove the steaks from the refrigerator and rub with the olive oil and let rest at room temperature for 1 hour.

2. A half hour before cooking, prepare your gas or charcoal grill to medium-high heat.

3. When the grill is ready, about 400 to 450 degrees F with the coals lightly covered with ash, season one side of the steaks with half of the coarsely ground pepper and sea salt.

4. Place the seasoned-sides of the steaks on the grill at medium heat. Wait 3 to 5 minutes until they are slightly charred. One minute before flipping, season the uncooked sides of the steaks with the remaining pepper and sea salt. Turn the steaks and grill for another 3 to 4 minutes for medium-rare, and 4 to 5 minutes for medium. The steaks should feel slightly firm if poked in the center.

5. Remove the steaks from the grill and transfer to a large cutting board. Let stand for 10 minutes, allowing the steaks to properly store their juices and flavor. Serve warm, and if desired, garnish with a little rosemary.

Tip: Letting the steak rest at room temperature for an hour is not necessary, so if you are in a rush please feel free to skip it. However, if you do have the time, definitely let the steaks absorb the oil so that they are grizzled and tender when pulled from the grill.

You can sear the steak in a cast iron skillet, too!

BROCCOLI SALAD

Makes 6 to 8 servings   Active time: 15 minutes   Total time: 20 minutes

---

1 head of broccoli

6 to 8 slices cooked bacon, crumbled

½ cup red onion, finely chopped

½ cup raisins

8 oz. sharp cheddar, cut into small cubes or grated

1 cup mayonnaise

2 tablespoons white vinegar

¼ cup sugar

Salt and pepper to taste

1. Cut the broccoli head into bite-sized pieces and place into a large bowl.

2. Add in the crumbled bacon, onion, raisins, and cheese.

3. In a separate small bowl, mix together the remaining ingredients as a dressing. Add to the broccoli mixture and toss gently to evenly coat. Add salt and pepper as needed to taste.

RED, WHITE AND BLUE BREAD PUDDING

Makes 4 to 6 servings   Active Time: 45 minutes   Start to Finish: 2 hours

---

4 tablespoons butter

4 cups cubed bread from a day-old loaf of French or Italian bread

1 cup fresh or frozen blueberries

2 eggs

1 gallon strawberry ice cream, left out to soften (high-quality so that it is as rich as possible)

1. Place the cast-iron skillet over low heat. Melt the butter in the skillet. Add the bread pieces to the skillet and distribute evenly. Sprinkle the blueberries over the bread pieces.

2. In a bowl, whisk the eggs. Add the softened or melted ice cream and stir just enough to combine. Pour the egg/ice cream mixture over the bread. Shake the skillet gently to distribute the liquid evenly.

3. Cover with plastic wrap, put in a cool place, and allow the mixture to rest for about 30 minutes so that the bread cubes are saturated with the ice cream.

4. Preheat the oven to 350 degrees F.

5. Bake for 40 to 45 minutes until the cream mixture is set and it is slightly brown around the edges. Use pot holders or oven mitts to take the skillet out of the oven. Allow to cool for 5 to 10 minutes before inverting onto a serving dish. Serve immediately. No need for additional ice cream.

STRAWBERRY PIE

Makes 6 to 8 servings   Active Time: 40 minutes
Start to Finish: 4 hours

---

1 baked flaky pastry crust (see page 107)

6 cups (about 3 pints) fresh strawberries, washed, tops trimmed, and sliced in half or quarters

¾ cup sugar

3 tablespoons cornstarch

½ cup water

½ cup unsweetened strawberry preserves

1. In a saucepan over medium heat, mix sugar, cornstarch, and water. Stir in 1 cup of strawberry pieces. Cook, stirring until mixture begins to boil and thicken. Continue to cook and stir for about 5 minutes. Remove from the heat and allow to cool, about 20 minutes.

2. Spread the remaining strawberry pieces evenly in the pie crust. When the cooked mixture is cool, pour it over the larger pieces of fruit.

3. In a microwave-proof bowl, melt the strawberry preserves until just melted, about 20 seconds. Stir and drizzle the melted jam over the pie to distribute evenly.

4. Cover with plastic wrap and refrigerate for at least 3 hours and up to 1 day.

Tip: Dust the crust with sugar for an even sweeter pie!

IN CONGRE

unanimous Declaratio

When in the Course of human events, it ... to which the Law ...

We the P

insure domestic Tranquility for

and our Posterity, do ordain and

Article I

States of
of the thirteen united
eople of the United
for the common defence, promote the
establish this Constitution for the United

Menu 27

Now that it's officially summer, you're likely spending a lot more time outside, and doing a lot more cooking on the grill. This menu features two new recipes that will get you out in the backyard with your apron and tongs, and for dessert, a chance to use fresh peaches ripe from the harvest.

Grilled Chorizo-Stuffed Mushrooms

Cheesy Potato Casserole (page 147)

Grilled Chicken with Arugula and
Balsamic-Rosemary Vinaigrette

Peach Pie

GRILLED CHICKEN
with Arugula and Balsamic-Rosemary Vinaigrette

Makes 4 servings   Active Time: 25 minutes   Start to Finish: 2½ hours

8 bone-in, skin-on chicken thighs

1 lemon, ½ juiced and ½ sliced into wedges

2 tablespoons Dijon mustard

3 sprigs rosemary, leaves removed from 2

1 garlic glove, finely chopped

½ cup, plus 4 tablespoons olive oil

2 tablespoons balsamic vinegar

¼ teaspoon red pepper flakes

Coarsely ground pepper

Fresh sea salt

4 cups arugula, stemmed

While grilling, baste the chicken thighs with the remaining marinade and be sure to keep the grill covered, allowing the skin to cook to a crisp.

1. Combine the chicken thighs, lemon juice, Dijon mustard, 2 rosemary sprig leaves, garlic and the 4 tablespoons of olive oil in a large sealable plastic bag. Seal and firmly mix with your hands. Let rest at room temperature for 2 hours.

2. A half hour before grilling, prepare your gas or charcoal grill to medium-high heat.

3. Next, add the remaining sprig of rosemary and the ½ cup of olive oil into a small saucepan and set over medium-high heat. Bring to a simmer and then remove from heat. Discard the sprig of rosemary and pour the oil into a small bowl. Set aside.

4. When the coals are ready, at about 400 degrees F with the coals lightly covered with ash, remove the chicken from the marinade and season with coarsely ground pepper and sea salt. Then, place the chicken thighs skin side down on the grill, and let cook for about 9 minutes. Flip and cook for 4 to 5 more. When finished, they should feel springy if poked with a finger.

5. Remove the chicken thighs from grill and place on a large cutting board. Let rest for 5 to 10 minutes.

6. While waiting, mix the balsamic vinegar and red pepper flakes into the rosemary oil. Season with pepper and salt. Drizzle over arugula and plate evenly. Position chicken thighs on top of arugula salad and garnish with lemon wedges.

GRILLED CHORIZO-STUFFED MUSHROOMS

Makes 8 to 10 Servings   Active Time: 25 Minutes   Start To Finish: 50 Minutes

1 Spanish chorizo, casing removed

14 white mushrooms, stemmed

¼ cup, plus 2 tablespoons olive oil

1 medium white onion, finely chopped

4 cherry tomatoes, quartered

¼ cup chicken broth

1 small bunch parsley, finely chopped

Coarsely ground black pepper

Fresh sea salt

1. Prepare your gas or charcoal grill to medium heat. Leave a cast-iron skillet on the grill while heating so that it develops a faint, smoky flavor.

2. While waiting, add the chorizo into a food processor and puree into a thick paste. Remove and set aside.

3. When the grill is ready, at about 350 to 400 degrees F with the coals lightly covered with ash, brush the mushroom caps with the 2 tablespoons of olive oil. Next, place the mushroom tops on the grill and cook for about 2 minutes until the tops have browned. Remove from grill and place on a baking sheet.

4. Next, add the remaining ¼ cup of olive oil to the cast iron skillet, followed by the onion and cherry tomatoes. Cook until the onion is translucent, about 2 minutes, and then stir in the pureed chorizo. Continue to cook until the chorizo is lightly browned, about 3 minutes, and then add in the chicken broth and parsley. Cook for only a minute or so longer, and then remove from heat.

5. Using a spoon, add the chorizo mixture into the mushroom caps. Move the baking sheet to a cool side of the grill and cook for about 15 minutes until the chorizo has browned.

6. Remove from grill and serve hot.

For this pie you have to try serving it with bourbon whipped cream. You'll understand why this is so popular in the South, from whence the best peaches—and bourbon—hail. Simply beat heavy or whipping cream until soft peaks form. Add about ¼ cup sugar and continue beating until stiff peaks form. Gently beat in ¼ cup bourbon.

PEACH PIE

Makes 6 to 8 servings   Active Time: 1 hour
Start to Finish: 2 hours

---

1 flaky pastry crust recipe for a double crust (see page 107)

2 to 3 pounds peaches to yield 4 cups, peeled, cored, and sliced

1 teaspoon fresh squeezed lemon juice

¾ cup sugar

4 tablespoons flour

1 tablespoon butter

2 tablespoons light brown sugar

1 egg white

2 tablespoons sugar

1. Preheat the oven to 350 degrees F.

2. Bring a large pot of water to boil. Fill another large pot with cold water. When the water's boiling, submerge the peaches for a minute or two, then remove them with a slotted spoon and put them immediately into the cold water. This loosens the skin and makes them much easier to peel. Use enough peaches to yield 4 cups of peeled slices. In a large bowl, toss peaches with lemon juice, sugar, and flour, being sure to coat the pieces.

3. Put the skillet over medium heat and melt the butter in it. Add the brown sugar and cook, stirring constantly, until sugar is dissolved, 1 or 2 minutes. Carefully remove pan from heat.

4. Place 1 of the piecrusts over the sugar mixture. Fill with the peaches, and place the other crust over the peaches, crimping the edges together.

5. Brush the top crust with the egg white, and sprinkle the sugar over it. Cut 4 or 5 slits in the middle.

6. Put the skillet in the oven and bake for 60 to 70 minutes until golden brown and bubbly. Cover the outermost edge with aluminum foil in the last 10 minutes of baking to prevent it from burning.

7. Allow to cool before serving. Serve with bourbon whipped cream.

Menu 28

After the Fourth of July feast, here's a lighter menu with a seasonal focus on grilled seafood. It's also a great opportunity to visit your local farmer's market, as fresh fruit and vegetables take center stage, with the fruit featuring in a decadent dessert that screams summertime.

Grilled Lime Mahi-Mahi

Green Bean Almondine

Wild Rice Pilaf (page 71)

Banana-Strawberry Cream Pie

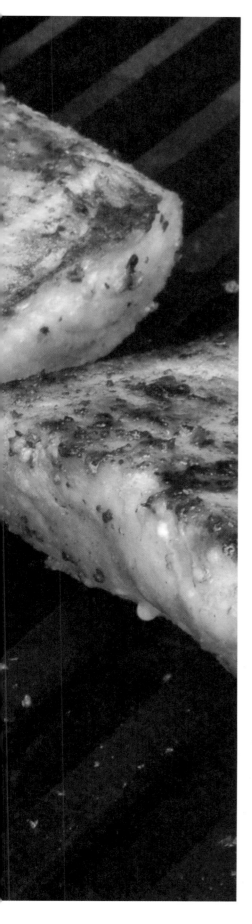

GRILLED LIME MAHI-MAHI

Makes 4 Servings.   Active Time: 45 Minutes
Start to Finish: 2 Hours and 30 Minutes

Mahi-Mahi Ingredients

½ cup olive oil

½ small lime, juiced

1 garlic clove, minced

1 teaspoon red pepper flakes

½ teaspoon cayenne pepper

4 mahi-mahi fillets

Coarsely ground black pepper

Fresh sea salt

Green Beans Ingredients

2 tablespoons olive oil

3 oz. prosciutto, ⅛ inch thick, sliced into cubes

2 to 3 pounds green beans, ends trimmed

2 garlic cloves, finely chopped

¼ cup pine nuts

¼ small lemon, juiced

Coarsely ground black pepper

Fresh sea salt

1. In a medium roasting pan, combine the olive oil, lime juice, garlic, red pepper flakes, and cayenne pepper and mix thoroughly. Place the mahi-mahi fillets into the marinade and let stand at room temperature for 1 to 2 hours, flipping once.

2. A half hour before cooking, place a cast-iron skillet on your gas or charcoal grill and prepare to medium heat. Leave the grill covered while heating, as it will add a faint smoky flavor to the skillet.

3. When the grill is ready, at about 400 degrees F with the coals lightly covered with ash, add the olive oil into the skillet. Wait until very hot, and then add the prosciutto and sear until browned. Next, stir in the pine nuts and toast, about 3 minutes. Stir in the garlic and green beans, then top with lemon juice. Season generously with coarsely ground black pepper and sea salt and cook until the green beans are charred and blistered, about 10 minutes.

4. While the green beans cook, remove the mahi-mahi fillets from the marinade and place directly over the heat source. Cover the grill and cook for about 4 to 5 minutes per side, until the fillets are flaky and moist when touched with a fork.

5. Remove the fillets and green beans from the grill and serve immediately.

GREEN BEANS ALMONDINE

Makes 6 to 8 servings   Active time: 10 minutes   Total time: 20 minutes

1 pound fresh green beans, trimmed

3 tablespoons butter

⅓ cups slivered almonds

1 teaspoon lemon juice

Salt and pepper to taste

1. Blanch the green beans in a large pot of boiling salted water until al dente (about 5 minutes), then shock them in an ice-water bath. Move out of the water and to the side to await the next step.

2. Next, heat a large skillet over medium heat and add the almonds. Stir constantly for about 30 seconds so they become lightly toasted. Mix in the butter and lemon juice to the almonds. When the butter is melted, add all of the beans and sauté for about two minutes, evenly coating the green beans with the mixture.

3. Season to taste with salt and pepper and serve.

BANANA-STRAWBERRY CREAM PIE

Makes 6 to 8 servings   Active Time: 60 Minutes   Start to Finish: Several hours or overnight

1 baked flaky pastry crust (see page 107)

½ cup sugar, divided

Pinch of salt

1 envelope unflavored gelatin (about 1 tablespoon)

3 eggs, separated

1¼ cups milk

1 teaspoon vanilla extract

¾ cup heavy cream

1 cup sliced strawberries, cut into dime-sized pieces, plus more for garnish

1 to 2 bananas, just ripe

Chocolate sauce to drizzle, if desired

1. In a small saucepan, stir together ¼ cup of the sugar, salt, and gelatin.

2. In a bowl, whisk together the egg yolk with the milk. Add the egg and milk mixture to the saucepan and stir to combine thoroughly. Over medium-low heat, cook, stirring constantly, as mixture warms and thickens. Do not bring to a boil. Cook until the mixture coats the back of a spoon. Remove from heat and stir in the vanilla. When slightly cooler, put the saucepan in the refrigerator to cool and further thicken the mixture, about 45 minutes.

3. In a large bowl, beat the egg whites with an electric mixer, working the rest of the sugar gradually into the whites as they're beaten until they stiffen and the sugar is dissolved.

4. Take the saucepan out of the refrigerator and whisk the cold custard until it's smooth. Fold it into the beaten egg whites. Stir in the strawberry pieces.

5. Slice the banana into ¼-inch slices and place in a single layer on top of the pie crust. Pour the strawberry cream filling over the banana slices and spread evenly. Cover with plastic wrap and refrigerate for several hours or up to 1 day before serving.

6. When ready to serve, remove plastic wrap and garnish with banana and strawberry slices. Drizzle with chocolate sauce if desired.

Menu 29

We're firing up the grill once again this week, and taking advantage of the warm weather. This menu features grilled pork chops, and a dessert and side tailor-made for late July. If you've got a vegetable garden, this is the beginning of the spinach harvest, and any Mainer will tell you this month signals the start of blueberry picking season.

Basic Grilled Double-Cut Rib Chops

Spinach Salad with Maple-Smoked Bacon

Cornbread

Blueberry Pie

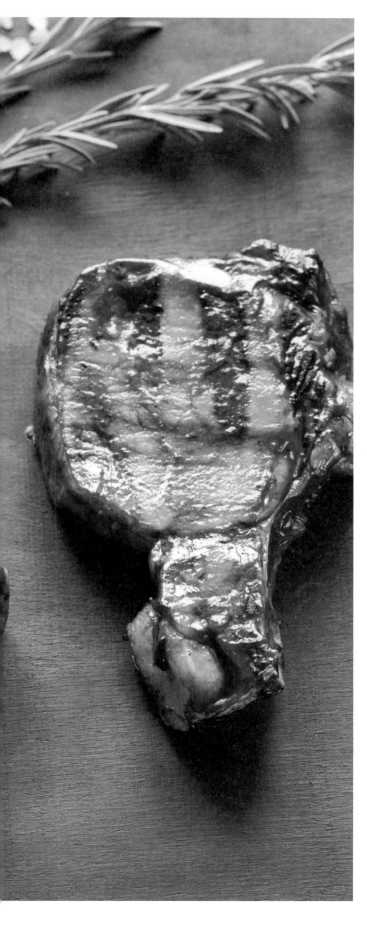

BASIC GRILLED
DOUBLE-CUT RIB CHOPS

Makes 4 to 6 Servings   Active Time: 25 Minutes
Start to Finish: 45 Minutes

---

4 to 6 double-cut rib chops (one chop per person)

Salt

Pepper

1. Preheat one side of your grill to 400 degrees F. If
    possible, create a two-zone cooking area: one zone
    will be your hot zone, concentrating your coals or heat
    source beneath one side of your grilling area, while
    the second zone will be arranged on the opposite side
    of the grill with little to no coals or flame beneath this
    surface area. Use the hot side to sear your chops, and
    the cool side to allow your chops to cook through the
    radiating heat. This will help ensure that your chops do
    not overcook and dry out.

2. Place the chops directly over the hot zone and sear
    both sides of the chops until evenly browned. Keep
    a watchful eye on the grill during this stage as fat
    drippings can create flare-ups that will char rather
    than sear the meat.

3. Once the chops are seared golden brown, move them over
    to the cooler zone and let them cook more thoroughly
    and slowly. If using a meat probe thermometer, look for
    temperatures in the center of your cut from 135 degrees
    F for medium rare and approximately 145 degrees F for a
    tender and flavorful medium.

*If you demand more flavor from your pork, try
adding different hardwoods to your fire (or into a
wet chip chamber if cooking over a gas grill.) Apple
and cherry woods offers a mild but lovely fruit
flavor. In fact, many fine chefs prefer apple wood
for smoking pork, beef, chicken or even fish.*

SPINACH SALAD
with Maple-Smoked Bacon

Makes 6 Servings   Active Time: 35 Minutes   Start to Finish: 45 Minutes

---

1 pound spinach, stemmed

1 medium red onion, sliced into ¼-inch rings

¼ cup dried cranberries

8 thick slices of bacon, trimmed of excess fat

2 tablespoons balsamic vinegar

1 teaspoon Dijon mustard

1 teaspoon red pepper flakes (optional)

½ cup olive oil

Coarsely ground black pepper

Fresh sea salt

1. One hour before grilling, soak the maple woodchips in water.

2. Next, place a large cast-iron skillet on your gas or charcoal grill and prepare to medium heat. Leave the grill covered while heating, as it will add a faint smoky flavor to the skillet.

3. While waiting, rinse the stemmed spinach and dry thoroughly. Place the spinach in a medium bowl and mix in the red onion and dried cranberries. Transfer to the refrigerator and set aside.

4. When the grill is ready, at about 400 degrees F with the coals lightly covered with ash, throw the woodchips over the coals and cover the grill. When the grill is smoking, add the bacon to the cast-iron skillet, close the grill's lid, and cook until crispy, about 4 minutes. Transfer to a plate covered with paper towels and then break into ½-inch pieces. Set aside.

5. In a small bowl, whisk together the balsamic vinegar, Dijon mustard, and red pepper flakes, and then gradually incorporate the olive oil. Season with coarsely ground black pepper and fresh sea salt, and then mix with the spinach salad and bacon bits. Serve chilled.

Variation: Those who like the heat might want to toss in a couple pepperoncini peppers!

Cornbread

Makes 6 to 8 servings   Active Time: 20 Minutes   Start to Finish: 1 Hour

---

2 cups finely ground yellow cornmeal

1 cup flour

¼ cup sugar

2 teaspoons baking powder

1 teaspoon baking soda

1 teaspoon salt

5 tablespoons unsalted butter, divided

1½ cups milk

2 eggs

1. Preheat the oven to 400 degrees F.

2. In a large bowl, combine cornmeal, flour, sugar, baking powder, baking soda, and salt. Put ½ cup milk in a measuring cup. Add 2 tablespoons butter, cut into pieces. Put in the microwave and heat on high for 1 minute so that butter is melted into the milk. Pour this over the dry ingredients and begin stirring. Gradually add the additional cup of milk and stir, then add the eggs and continue stirring until thoroughly combined.

3. Heat a cast-iron skillet over medium heat and melt the 3 remaining tablespoons of butter in it. Add the batter and shake the pan gently to evenly distribute.

4. Transfer the skillet to the oven and cook for 25 to 30 minutes, until light golden brown and a toothpick inserted in the middle comes out clean.

5. Using pot holders or oven mitts, remove the skillet from the oven and let the bread cool for 10 to 15 minutes before slicing and serving. Top with honey, if desired.

BLUEBERRY PIE

Makes 6 to 8 servings   Active Time: 60 Minutes
Start to Finish: 2 hours

1 flaky pastry crust recipe for a double crust
(see page 107)

4 cups fresh or frozen blueberries

1 tablespoon freshly squeezed lemon juice

1 cup sugar

3 tablespoons flour

1 tablespoon butter

2 tablespoons brown sugar

1 egg white

2 tablespoons sugar

1. Preheat the oven to 350 degrees F.

2. If using frozen blueberries, it's not necessary
    to thaw them completely. In a large bowl, toss
    blueberries with lemon juice, sugar, and flour,
    being sure to coat the pieces.

3. Put the skillet over medium heat and melt the
    butter in it. Add the brown sugar and cook,
    stirring constantly, until sugar is dissolved, 1 or 2
    minutes. Carefully remove pan from heat.

4. Place 1 of the piecrusts over the sugar mixture.
    Fill with blueberries, and place the other crust
    over the blueberries, crimping the edges together.

5. Brush the top crust with the egg white, and
    sprinkle the sugar over it. Cut 4 or 5 slits in the
    middle.

6. Put the skillet in the oven and bake for 50 to 60
    minutes until golden brown and bubbly. Cover the
    outermost edge with aluminum foil in the last 10
    minutes of baking to prevent it from burning.

7. Allow to cool before serving.

Menu 30

This meal brings a spicy twist to the traditional steak and potatoes, with the smoky flavor of chipotle (a dried and smoked jalapeno) enhancing the flavor of the rib eye. It also features another visit to the local farmer's market, where wholesome beans, vine-ripened tomatoes, and fresh berries compliment the heartier beef and starch components of the menu.

Chipotle Rib Eye

White Beans and Diced Tomatoes

Classic Baked Potato (page 191)

Berry Delicious Popsicles

CHIPOTLE RIB EYE

Makes 2 to 3 servings   Active Time: 20 minutes
Start to Finish: 1 hour and 30 minutes

Steak Ingredients

2 bone-in rib eyes, about 1¼ to 1½ inches thick

1 tablespoon olive oil

Rub Ingredients

2 dry chipotle peppers, seeded and finely minced

1 tablespoon dried oregano

1 tablespoon dried cilantro

1 tablespoon coarsely ground black pepper

2 teaspoons ground cumin

1 teaspoon onion powder

½ teaspoon dry mustard

Fresh sea salt

1. Combine the rub ingredients and mix thoroughly.

2. Rub a very thin layer of olive oil to both sides of the steaks
    and then generously apply the dry rub, firmly pressing it all
    around the steak. Let rest at room temperature for at least
    1 hour.

3. A half hour before cooking, prepare your gas or charcoal
    grill to medium-high heat.

4. When the grill is ready, at about 400 to 450 degrees F with
    the coals lightly covered with ash, place the steaks on the
    grill and cook for about 6 to 7 minutes until blood begins
    to rise from the tops. When the steaks are charred, flip and
    cook for 4 to 5 more minutes for medium-rare and 5 to 6
    more minutes for medium. The steaks should feel slightly
    firm if poked in the center.

5. Remove the steaks from the grill and transfer to a large
    cutting board. Let stand for 5 to 10 minutes, allowing the
    steaks to properly store their juices and flavor. Serve warm.

WHITE BEANS AND DICED TOMATOES

Makes 6 servings
Active Time: 15 minutes
Start to Finish: 15 minutes

---

2 15-oz. cans cannellini beans, washed

1 pint cherry tomatoes, halved

½ cup basil, coarsely chopped

¼ cup Italian-leaf parsley

3 tablespoons extra-virgin olive oil

½ medium lemon, juiced

2 garlic cloves, minced

1 tablespoon balsamic vinegar

¼ cup freshly grated Parmesan cheese

Coarsely ground black pepper

Fresh sea salt

1. In a large bowl, mix together the cannellini beans, tomatoes, basil and parsley. Transfer to the refrigerator and remove just before mixing with the dressing.

2. In a small cup, whisk together the olive oil, lemon juice, garlic and balsamic vinegar. Set aside.

3. Remove the cannellini beans and tomatoes from the refrigerator, and then toss with the vinaigrette. Top with ¼ cup of freshly grated Parmesan cheese, and then season with coarsely ground black pepper and fresh sea salt.

BERRY DELICIOUS POPSICLE

Yield: 10 popsicles   Active time: 15 minutes
Total time: 5 hours

Tools Required

Popsicle mold

Popsicle sticks

Blender

Ingredients

3 cups of your favorite berries (I recommend blueberries and pitted cherries)

¼ cup lemon juice

¼ cup raw honey

1. Wash your berries and place them in your blender, along with the lemon juice and honey. Puree until smooth, about 30 seconds.

2. Pour into a popsicle mold and insert popsicle stick.

3. Freeze until popsicles hold firm (three to five hours).

4. Briefly submerge the mold into lukewarm water. When the popsicles begin to separate from the mold, remove immediately. Pop the popsicles out of the mold, and enjoy!

Variations:

• Variation possibilities are endless. Enhance the flavor by adding any variety of "toss-ins," like fresh grated ginger, organic dark cocoa powder, pure vanilla or almond extract, unsweetened coconut flakes, or even sea salt!

• Try adding in kiwi slices, pineapple, or other tropical fruit combinations for an entirely different flavor experience.

Menu 31

The dog days of August can certainly bring the heat! This menu is light and refreshing, featuring a combination of summer flavors straight from the herb garden. And if you or a friend have your own chicken coop, here's a great way to make use of those farm-fresh eggs—even if they're farm fresh from the local supermarket.

Tomato-Basil Tart

Bacon-and-Eggs Spinach Salad

Strawberry and Mint Salad

Peach Galette

TOMATO-BASIL TART

Makes 4 to 6 servings
Active Time: ½ hour
Start to Finish: 1½ hour

---

1 flaky pastry crust recipe for a single crust (see page 107)

1 ½ pounds tomatoes, sliced about ¼-inch thick, seeds removed

1 tablespoon kosher salt

2 tablespoons olive oil, plus more for drizzling

1 Vidalia onion, thinly sliced

Salt and freshly ground black pepper

1 cup (8 oz.) fresh chèvre (goat cheese)

8-10 basil leaves, cut into threads

1. Preheat the oven to 350 degrees F.

2. Put the tomato slices on a plate lined with paper towels, and sprinkle with the salt. Let the salt sit on the tomatoes for about 15 minutes, and turn the slices over.

3. In the cast iron skillet, heat the olive oil over medium heat and add the onions. Cook, stirring, until the onions are lightly browned, about 3 minutes. Season with salt and pepper. Transfer them to a bowl but keep the oil in the skillet.

4. On a lightly floured surface, roll out the crust so that it is just larger than the bottom of the pan and lay the pastry crust in the pan.

5. Spread the onions over bottom of the crust and dot with the goat cheese. Arrange the tomato slices so that they cover the bottom. Drizzle lightly with olive oil.

6. Put the skillet in the oven and bake at 350 degrees F for 20 minutes then increase the heat to 400 degrees F and bake an additional 10 minutes until top of tart is toasty. Sprinkle with sliced basil leaves.

BACON-AND-EGGS SPINACH SALAD

Makes 6 servings   Active Time: 15 minutes   Start to Finish: 40 minutes

1 pound spinach

3 large eggs

8 thick slices of bacon, trimmed of excess fat

2 tablespoons white wine vinegar

2 tablespoons red wine vinegar

1 teaspoon Dijon mustard

2 tablespoons olive oil

1 medium red onion, sliced

Coarsely ground black pepper

Fresh sea salt

1. Next, place a large cast-iron skillet on your gas or charcoal grill and prepare to medium heat. Leave the grill covered while heating, as it will add a faint smoky flavor to the skillet.

2. While waiting, rinse the spinach and dry thoroughly. Place the spinach in a medium bowl and store it in the refrigerator.

3. Fill a medium saucepan with water and place over medium-heat. Bring to a boil and then add the eggs and remove from heat. Cover the saucepan and let the eggs rest in the hot water for about 10 to 14 minutes. Remove from water and let cool in the refrigerator.

4. When the grill is ready, at about 400 degrees F with the coals lightly covered with ash, throw the woodchips over the coals and cover the grill. When the grill is smoking, add the bacon into the cast-iron skillet, close the grill's lid, and cook until crispy, about 4 minutes. Transfer to a plate covered with paper towels and set aside.

5. In a small bowl, whisk together the white wine vinegar, red wine vinegar, Dijon mustard, and olive oil and then set aside.

6. Remove the eggs from the refrigerator and then peel off their shells. Slice the eggs in half and add over the spinach salad. Drizzle the vinaigrette onto the spinach and then top with the bacon bits and sliced onion. Season the eggs with the coarsely ground black pepper and fresh sea salt and then serve the salad immediately.

STRAWBERRY AND MINT SALAD

Makes 4 servings   Active Time: 15 minutes   Start to Finish: 15 minutes

4 cups fresh
strawberries

1 lime

Honey, to taste

¼ cup fresh mint,
torn

1. Wash and slice the strawberries into quarters. Toss into a large bowl.

2. Drizzle with the lime juice and sprinkle the mint over the strawberries.

3. Drizzle with honey, to taste. Garnish with an additional sprig of mint, if desired.

4. Serve, and enjoy!

Variations:

• Add orange slices for a citrus-y twist, and drizzle even more lime juice, to taste.

• Substitute fresh two fresh basil leaves (thinly sliced) for the mint, and drizzle the finished project with lemon juice rather than lime juice, for an entirely different flavor combination that's just as tasty.

PEACH GALETTE

Makes 6 to 8 servings   Active Time: ¾ hour
Start to Finish: 1½ hour

1 flaky pastry crust recipe for a single crust
(see page 107)

3 cups fresh peaches, peeled, stones removed,
and sliced

½ cup sugar

Juice of ½ lemon (seeds removed)

3 tablespoons cornstarch

Pinch of salt

2 tablespoons peach jam

1 teaspoon Amaretto liqueur (optional)

1 egg, beaten

1 tablespoon granulated sugar

1. Preheat the oven to 400 degrees F.

2. The crust in the skillet should be slightly larger
    than the bottom of the pan so that it can be
    folded over along the edges.

3. In a large bowl, mix the fruit with the sugar,
    lemon juice, cornstarch, and pinch of salt. Stir
    well to be sure to coat all the fruit.

4. If using the liqueur, mix it in with the jam in
    a small bowl before smearing the jam onto the
    center of the crust.

5. Place the fruit in a mound in the center of the
    pie crust. Fold the edges of the crust over to form
    an edge of about 1 inch of crust. Brush the crust
    with the beaten egg and sprinkle it with sugar.

6. Put the skillet in the oven and bake until the
    filling is bubbly, which is necessary for it to
    thicken sufficiently, about 35 to 40 minutes.

7. Allow to cool before serving.

Menu 32

We cannot tell a lie: This menu features some truly American recipes. Southern barbeque is the featured item, with sides of coleslaw and spiced corn that could have been right at home on the tables of the earliest settlers.

Smoked Pulled Barbecue Chicken Sandwiches

Coleslaw (page 336)

Spiced Corn (page 47)

Peach Cobbler

SMOKED PULLED BARBECUE
CHICKEN SANDWICHES

Makes 4 to 6 servings   Active Time: 40 minutes   Start to Finish: 10 hours

Tools

2 to 3 cups hickory or oak woodchips

Cast-iron skillet

Chicken Ingredients

1 teaspoon chili powder

¼ teaspoon cayenne pepper

2 teaspoons Tabasco

½ teaspoon chipotle chile powder

2 to 3 pounds skinless, boneless chicken breasts

6 hamburger buns

Sauce Ingredients

2 tablespoons clarified butter

4 garlic cloves, finely chopped

½ cup white onion, minced

½ medium shallot, finely chopped

¾ cup tomatoes, crushed

1 cup apple cider vinegar

2 tablespoons honey

Coarsely ground black pepper

Fresh sea salt

1. Combine the rub ingredients for the chicken in a large bowl and then add the chicken breasts. Rub the spices over the chicken and then place the bowl in the refrigerator. Let marinate for 2 to 12 hours, the longer the better.

2. One hour before grilling, add the woodchips into a bowl of water and let soak. At the same time, prepare your gas or charcoal grill to medium heat. Leave the skillet on the grill while heating so that it develops a faint, smoky flavor.

3. When the grill is ready, at about 350 to 400 degrees F with the coals lightly covered with ash, scatter half of the woodchips over the coals and then place the chicken breasts on the grill. Cover the grill, aligning the air vent away from the woodchips so that their smoke rolls around the chicken breasts before escaping. Cook for about 7 to 8 minutes on each side and then remove from grill. Transfer the chicken to a large cutting board, let rest for 5 minutes, and then shred the chicken with 2 forks. Set aside.

4. Scatter the remaining woodchips over the coals and add the clarified butter into the skillet. When hot, add the garlic, onion, and shallot and sauté until the garlic is golden and the onion and shallot are translucent. Add the remaining ingredients and simmer or about 15 minutes, or until the barbecue sauce has thickened. Mix in the chicken and reduce heat. Cook for 5 more minutes and then remove from heat.

5. Let the chicken rest for 5 minutes, allowing the chicken to properly absorb the sauce, and then serve on warm buns. Drizzle more sauce on the meat before adding the top bun, if desired.

To get the perfect "pulled" and "shredded" texture to the chicken and still achieve the smoked flavor, you must simply grill the chicken at first and then quickly braise it in a cast-iron skillet on the grill at medium heat.

PEACH COBBLER

Makes 8 to 10 servings   Active Time: 15 minutes   Total time: 1 hour

---

About 4 cups peach slices, peeled and pitted

1 cup sugar, divided

½ cup water

8 tablespoons butter, melted

1½ cups self-rising flour

1½ cups milk

Ground cinnamon to taste

1. Preheat your oven to 350 degrees F.

2. Once peaches are pitted, sliced, and skinned, combine them with a ½ cup of sugar and the water in a saucepan and mix well. After the mixture begins to boil, allow it to simmer for about 10 minutes, then remove it from heat.

3. Prepare the baking dish by pouring in the melted butter.

4. Gently spoon the fruit into the dish. Slowly pour in the syrup remaining in the saucepan.

5. In a medium bowl, combine the remaining sugar, flour, and milk and mix until there are no more clumps. Then, pour this over the fruit but do not stir to combine. Sprinkle the top with cinnamon, then bake for 30 to 45 minutes.

6. Allow to cool slightly before serving with your choice of whipped cream or vanilla ice cream.

Menu 33

We normally associate stews with the cold winter, but when the stew features fresh seafood and is cooked over the grill, it becomes a lighter meal perfect for the warm summer months. The lighter nature of the seafood stew is complimented here with a crisp house salad and herb focaccia, plus a dessert made from ripe blackberries and peaches, two quintessential late-summer fruit harvests.

Grilled Seafood Stew

Garden Salad (page 65)

Italian Herb Focaccia

Blackberry-Peach Pie

GRILLED SEAFOOD STEW

Makes 4 to 6 servings   Active Time: 45 minutes   Start to Finish: 1 hour

¼ cup olive oil

1 large shallot, finely chopped

4 garlic cloves, minced

¼ small green pepper, chopped

½ teaspoon dried oregano

½ teaspoon red pepper flakes

3 cups plum tomatoes, stemmed & crushed

2 tablespoons flat-leaf parsley, leaves removed

2 thyme sprigs

1 bay leaf

½ small lemon, juiced

2 cups clam juice

1 cup dry white wine

24 littleneck clams, scrubbed

18 mussels, scrubbed

14 large shrimp, peeled & deveined

4 oz of cleaned squid; cut into ½ inch wide rings, tentacles removed

10 2-by-1 inch pieces of striped bass

Coarsely ground black pepper

Fresh sea salt

1. Place a large Dutch oven on your gas or charcoal grill and prepare to medium-high heat. Leave the grill covered while heating, as it will add a faint smoky flavor to the skillet.

2. When the grill is ready, about 450 to 500 degrees F and the coals are lightly covered with ash, heat the olive oil in the Dutch oven. Next, when the oil is hot, add in the shallot and minced garlic and cook for about 2 minutes, until the shallot is translucent and the garlic is golden, not brown. Add in the green pepper, oregano, pepper flakes and cook until soft, about 5 minutes.

3. Add the tomatoes, parsley, thyme, bay leaf, lemon juice and clam juice and dry white wine and boil until thickened, about 15 minutes. Stir in the clams, mussels, and shrimp and cook until the shells open and the shrimp is firm. Add the pieces of calamari and striped bass and cook for another 3 minutes until the striped bass is opaque through the middle.

4. Remove the Dutch oven from the heat and season with coarsely ground black pepper and salt. Serve in warmed bowls.

Serve in a large bowls and, if you would like, garnish with finely chopped, fresh flat-leaf parsley leaves. Place a bowl to the side for empty shells.

ITALIAN HERB FOCACCIA

Makes 4 to 6 servings   Active Time: 30 Minutes   Start to Finish: 60 Minutes

1 teaspoon active dry yeast

1 cup water (110 to 115 degrees F)

2 to 2½ cups flour

1 teaspoon salt

½ teaspoon dried oregano

½ teaspoon dried thyme

¼ teaspoon dried basil

1 clove garlic, minced

3 tablespoons olive oil, plus more for drizzling over bread before baking

Sea salt (coarse grained) and freshly ground black pepper

Grated Parmesan for topping

1. Proof the yeast by mixing it with the warm water. Let sit for 10 minutes until foamy.

2. In a bowl, combine the flour, salt, oregano, thyme and basil, and stir into yeast mix. Stir to combine well. Stir in the garlic. Transfer to a lightly floured surface and knead the dough until it loses its stickiness, adding more flour as needed, about 10 minutes.

3. Coat the bottom and sides of a large mixing bowl (ceramic is best) with olive oil. Place the ball of dough in the bowl, cover loosely with plastic wrap, put it in a naturally warm, draft-free location, and let it rise until doubled in size, about 45 minutes to 1 hour.

4. Preheat the oven to 450 degrees F.

5. Put a tablespoon of olive oil in the skillet, and press the dough into it. Drizzle some olive oil over it and sprinkle with salt and pepper, then with Parmesan cheese. Cover loosely with plastic wrap and let rise for about 20 minutes.

6. Put in the middle of the oven and bake for 25 to 30 minutes until golden and hot. Remove from oven and let rest for 5 minutes before removing from skillet to cool further.

BLACKBERRY-PEACH PIE

Makes 6 to 8 servings   Active Time: 30 Minutes
Start to Finish: 60 Minutes

---

1 flaky pastry crust recipe for a single crust (see page 107)

4 cups fresh peaches, peeled, pitted, and cut into pieces

¾ cup sugar

3 tablespoons flour

½ teaspoon grated lemon peel

1 tablespoon fresh squeezed lemon juice

¼ teaspoon ground ginger

2 cups fresh blackberries

1 egg white

2 tablespoons sugar

1. Preheat the oven to 375 degrees F.

2. In a large bowl, toss peaches with sugar, flour, lemon peel, lemon juice, and ginger. Gently stir in blackberries.

3. Put the crust in a cast-iron skillet. The crust should be larger than the bottom of the pan so it can be folded over along the edges.

4. Place fruit mix in the middle of the crust. Fold the edges of the crust over to form an edge of about 1 inch of crust.

5. Brush the crust with the egg white, and sprinkle it with sugar.

6. Put the skillet in the oven and bake for about 35-40 minutes, until the filling is bubbly and has thickened sufficiently.

7. Allow to cool before serving, and top with fresh whipped cream.

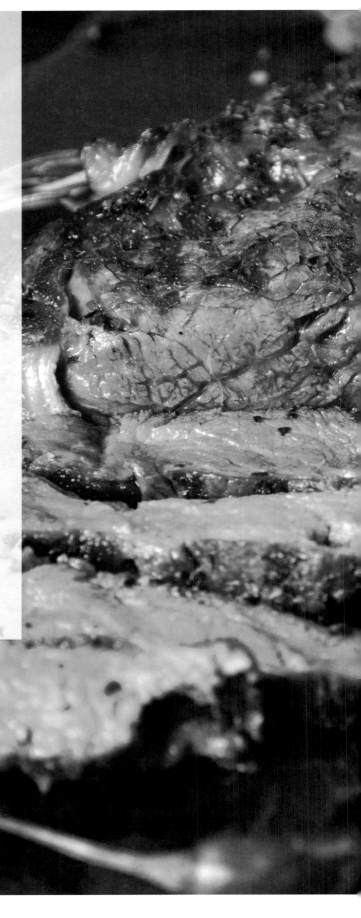

Menu 34

August is when our gardens really come to life, and if you've planted summer squash, peppers, and zucchini in your garden, now is just about the time you'll be ready to harvest. This menu makes the most of the sunny weather and your green thumb by grilling these late summer vegetables, as well as tri-tip steaks. Ripe peaches feature in a delicious summery cake for dessert. One secret is putting a fresh homemade twist on a cake mix without anyone being the wiser. Such is the case with this summery twist on upside-down cake.

Marinated Tri-Tip Steaks

Grilled Balsamic Peppers

Grilled Yellow Squash and Zucchini

Peachy Keen Cake

MARINATED TRI-TIP STEAKS

Makes 3 servings   Active Time: 45 minutes   Start to Finish: 14 hours

Steak Ingredients

1 tri-tip roast, about 1½ inches thick and 2 to 2½ pounds

Marinade Ingredients

2 cups red wine

2 tablespoons red wine vinegar

2 garlic cloves, crushed

2 sprigs of rosemary, leaves removed and minced

2 sprigs of thyme, leaves removed and minced

½ small white onion, finely chopped

1 teaspoon fresh lemon juice

½ teaspoon dried oregano

Coarsely ground black pepper

Fresh sea salt

1. The day before grilling, combine the ingredients for marinade in a large sealable plastic bag and let rest at room temperature. After 20 minutes, add the tri-tip roast to the bag so that it is completely submerged; more wine may be necessary. Seal and place in refrigerator and let marinate overnight.

2. One hour before grilling, remove the tri-tip bag from the refrigerator and let stand at room temperature.

3. Prepare your gas or charcoal grill, designating 2 sections: one for direct medium-high heat and the other for indirect heat.

4. When the grill is ready, at about 400 to 450 degrees F with the coals lightly covered with ash, remove the roast from the marinade and grill over direct heat for about 5 minutes per side. Next, move the roast to the indirect heat and cover the grill. Cook for another 20 to 30 minutes, flipping every 5 minutes.

5. Remove the steaks from the grill and transfer to a large cutting board. Let stand for 10 minutes, allowing the steaks to properly store their juices and flavor, and then slice across the grain into thin slices. Serve warm.

Tip: It is important to note that this dish requires marinating overnight so that it softens and becomes more tender on the grill.

GRILLED BALSAMIC PEPPERS

Makes 4 to 5 servings
Active Time: 15 minutes
Start to Finish: 30 minutes

2 red bell peppers, stemmed, seeded and chopped into quarters

2 yellow bell peppers, stemmed, seeded and chopped into quarters

2 green bell peppers, stemmed, seeded and chopped into quarters

4 tablespoons olive oil

2 tablespoons balsamic vinegar

8 basil leaves

Coarsely ground black pepper

Fresh sea salt

1. Combine all the ingredients into a large bowl and mix thoroughly.

2. Place a cast-iron skillet on your gas or charcoal grill and prepare to medium heat. Leave the grill covered while heating, as it will add a faint smoky flavor to the skillet.

3. When the grill is ready, about 400 to 500 degrees F, place the balsamic peppers into the skillet and cook until tender and lightly charred, about 7 to 9 minutes.

4. Remove from grill and serve hot.

GRILLED YELLOW SQUASH AND ZUCCHINI

Makes 8 to 10 servings
Active Time: 15 minutes
Start to Finish: 35 minutes

4 medium zucchini, sliced into circles

2 medium yellow squash, sliced into circles

¼ cup olive oil

Coarsely ground black pepper

Fresh sea salt

1. Prepare your gas or charcoal grill to medium-high heat.

2. While waiting, toss the vegetables, olive oil, black pepper, and salt in a small bowl and set aside.

3. When the grill is ready, about 400 to 500 degrees F, add the vegetables onto the grill and cook, flipping once, until tender — about 10 to 15 minutes.

4. Remove from grill and serve warm.

PEACHY KEEN CAKE

Makes 8 servings   Active Time: 20 minutes
Start to Finish: 1 hour

---

8 tablespoons (1 stick) butter

2 peaches, thinly sliced, or 1 can sliced peaches with no sugar added, drained

1 box (15.25 oz.) yellow cake mix

1 cup water

½ cup vegetable oil

6 oz. unsweetened apple sauce

4 eggs

¼ teaspoon almond extract

Vanilla or butter pecan ice cream for serving

1. Preheat the oven to 350 degrees F.

2. In the skillet, melt the butter over medium heat. When it's melted, add the fruit. Allow the fruit to simmer in the butter over low to medium heat until the butter is bubbling but not browning.

3. In a large bowl, combine the cake mix, water, oil, applesauce, eggs, and almond extract. Stir to combine.

4. When the butter in the skillet is bubbling, turn off the heat, arrange the peaches in a somewhat even layer, and pour the batter over the fruit.

5. Bake 35 to 40 minutes, until browned on the top and sides and a toothpick inserted in the middle comes out clean.

6. Allow to cool for about 10 minutes. The skillet will still be hot. Put a large serving plate on the counter and, working quickly and deliberately, flip the skillet so the cake is inverted onto the plate. Serve with vanilla or butter pecan ice cream.

Tip: If flipping the cake gets a little messy, that can be covered up by adding a scoop of ice cream to each serving.

Labor Day

Labor Day traditionally signals the end of the summer, and the weekend provides one last chance for a family picnic before the chill of autumn sets in. We've got a more formal meal option (steak kebabs with salsa verde) and a casual one (sloppy joes) with common sides: Chilled Tomatoes and Garlic; Macaroni Salad; and Potato Salad. The upcoming change of seasons is reflected in the dessert choices, with Strawberry Rhubarb Crisp for those holding on to summer, and Apple Pie for those welcoming the fall.

Marinated Steak Kebabs with Salsa Verde

Chilled Tomatoes and Garlic

Sloppy Joes

Macaroni Salad

Potato Salad (page 206)

Strawberry Rhubarb Crisp

Apple Pie

MARINATED STEAK KEBABS
with Salsa Verde

Makes 3 to 4 servings   Active time: 45 minutes
Start to Finish: 4 hours

Kebab Ingredients

2 to 3 pounds top sirloin

1 cup olive oil

¼ cup basil leaves

1 sprig rosemary, leaves removed

1 garlic clove, minced

1 bag skewers

Salsa Verde Ingredients

1 cup Italian parsley leaves

½ cup cilantro

¼ very small shallot

1 anchovy filet

1 tablespoon capers

2 garlic cloves

1 teaspoon red wine vinegar

½ cup olive oil

1. Cut the top sirloin into 1½- to 2-inch cubes. Combine the olive oil, basil leaves, rosemary, and garlic in a large sealable bag, then add the cuts of meat. Seal tight and let rest at room temperature for 2 to 3 hours.

2. A half hour before cooking, prepare your gas or charcoal grill to medium-high heat.

3. When the sirloin cuts have finished marinating, remove from bag and take 3 to 4 pieces of meat and pierce with the skewers. At the same time, drizzle the olive oil over the tomatoes in a bowl and sprinkle with thyme. Season with black pepper. Set aside.

4. In a small food processor, add the parsley, cilantro, shallot, anchovy, capers, garlic cloves and red wine vinegar. Pulse into a thick paste. Remove from processor and place into a small bowl. Whisk in the olive oil and set aside.

5. When the grill is ready, at about 400 degrees F with the coals lightly covered with ash, place the kebabs on the grill. Grill the kebabs for about 8 to 9 minutes for medium-rare, 10 minutes for medium. Rotate the kebabs about every 2 minutes so each side is cooked evenly.

6. Remove kebabs from grill and transfer to a large cutting board. Let rest for five minutes and then serve warm with Salsa Verde.

MACARONI SALAD

Makes 4 servings   Active time: 25 minutes   Total time: 1 hour 30 minutes

1 cup mayonnaise

2 tablespoons vinegar

1 tablespoon mustard

1 teaspoon sugar

⅓ teaspoon pepper

½ lb. macaroni, cooked and drained

1 cup sliced celery

1 cup green pepper, finely chopped

½ cup red pepper, finely chopped

½ cup green onion, finely chopped

1. For the dressing, combine mayonnaise, vinegar, mustard, sugar, salt, and pepper in a small bowl and set aside.

2. Prepare the macaroni and, in a large bowl, mix in the celery, peppers, and onion.

3. Add the dressing and stir to coat the macaroni and vegetables evenly.

4. Cover and chill for about an hour before serving.

Chilled Tomatoes
with Garlic

Makes 4 to 6 servings   Active Time: 10 minutes   Start to Finish: 15 minutes

10 whole tomatoes of your choice

4 large garlic cloves, chopped

¼ cup olive oil

4 chives, finely chopped

Coarsely ground black pepper

Fresh sea salt

1. Stem the tomatoes, cut them into quarters, and put them in a medium bowl.

2. Add the garlic, olive oil and chives, and then season with coarsely ground black pepper and sea salt. Serve chilled.

SLOPPY JOES

Makes 6 to 8 burgers   Active time: 15 minutes   Total time: 1 hour 10 minutes

1½ lb. extra lean ground beef

½ medium onion, diced

2 cloves garlic, minced

1 green pepper, diced

2 cups water

¾ cups ketchup

1 dash Worcestershire sauce

2 tablespoons brown sugar

1 teaspoon Dijon mustard

1½ teaspoon salt, or to taste

½ teaspoon ground black pepper

Cayenne pepper to taste (optional)

1. Place ground beef and onion into a large skillet to brown over medium heat before stirring in the garlic and bell pepper. Once the vegetables are softened, add 1 cup of water and stir, simmering for about 5 minutes to mix all the flavors.

2. Mix in the ketchup, Worcestershire sauce, brown sugar, Dijon mustard, salt, and black pepper. Add 1 more cup of water. Once simmering, reduce the heat down to low for 40 minutes. Stir occasionally until the liquid has mostly evaporated and the mixture is the consistency of your liking.

3. Season with salt, pepper, and cayenne pepper to taste, and scoop out onto buns to serve.

STRAWBERRY RHUBARB CRISP

Makes 4 servings   Active Time: 30 Minutes
Start to Finish: 60 Minutes

1½ cups rhubarb, cut into ½-inch pieces

1½ cups strawberries, sliced

2 tablespoons sugar

2 teaspoons flour

¾ cup oats (quick cooking but not instant)

4 tablespoons butter, chilled, cut into pieces

¼ cup dark brown sugar

⅓ cup flour

1. Preheat the oven to 450 degrees F.

2. In a bowl, combine the rhubarb pieces, strawberry slices, sugar, and flour, and toss to coat the fruit. Transfer to a baking dish.

3. In another bowl, work the butter in with the sugar using a fork. Add the oats and flour and continue to work with the fork to create a crumbly mix.Sprinkle it over the fruit in the dish.

4. Put the dish in the oven and bake for about 50 minutes until the topping is golden and the fruit is bubbly. Serve warm with whipped cream or ice cream.

In the early 1900s American rhubarb farmers successfully lobbied for their vegetable to be officially designated as a fruit so that they could get lower tax rates and less stringent interstate shipping laws.

APPLE PIE

Makes 6 to 8 servings   Active Time: 60 Minutes
Start to Finish: 2 hours

---

1 flaky pastry crust recipe for a double crust (see page 107)

6 Granny Smith apples, peeled, cored, and sliced

1 teaspoon ground cinnamon

¾ cup sugar

1 teaspoon fresh squeezed lemon juice

1 tablespoon butter

1 tablespoon light brown sugar

1 egg white

1. Preheat the oven to 350 degrees F.

2. In a large bowl, toss apples with cinnamon, sugar, and lemon juice.

3. Put the skillet over medium heat and melt the butter in it. Add the brown sugar and cook, stirring constantly, until sugar is dissolved, 1 or 2 minutes. Carefully remove pan from heat.

4. Place 1 of the piecrusts over the sugar mixture. Fill with the apple/spice mix, and place the other crust over the apples, crimping the edges together.

5. Brush the top crust with the egg white. Cut 4 or 5 slits in the middle.

6. Put the skillet in the oven and bake for about 60 minutes until golden brown and bubbly. Cover the outermost edge with aluminum foil in the last 10 minutes of baking to prevent it from burning.

7. Allow to cool before serving. Serve with whipped cream or ice cream.

You can flavor whipped cream with liqueur for an especially yummy topping. Beat heavy or whipping cream until soft peaks form. Add about ¼ cup sugar and continue beating until stiff peaks form. Gently beat in ¼ cup liqueur, such as apple brandy or Cointreau.

317

5 Ways to Celebrate Labor Day:

A BBQ, of course!

Shopping for American-made gifts and American-grown food

Volunteer with veterans or bring cookies to your local police or fire station

With family

At a sporting event

Menu 35

Here's a meal that's inspired by the Tex-Mex cuisine of the American southwest. Mexican food has become increasingly popular in the United States, with traditional Mexican recipes being updated with American ingredients. In fact, salsa now tops ketchup as the top-selling condiment in the country. But no need to go out and buy your condiments — you can make your own homemade corn salsa recipe (page 165) to go with this menu. (Add Spiced Corn from page 47 too!)

Chicken Quesadillas with Guacamole

Corn Salsa (page 165)

Spiced Corn (page 47)

Cilantro-Lime Rice (page 168)

Pineapple-Coconut Popsicles

CHICKEN QUESADILLAS
with Guacamole

Makes 4 servings   Active Time: 45 minutes   Start to Finish: 1½ hours

Quesadilla Ingredients

3 tablespoons olive oil

1 red onion, sliced thin

1 clove garlic, minced

3 cups cooked chicken, diced

4 (8-inch) corn or flour tortillas

2 cups shredded sharp cheddar cheese

½ cup pitted black olives, sliced thin

½ cup salsa

1 avocado, peeled, pit removed, and sliced thin

Guacamole Ingredients

2 large Mexican Haas avocados, halved and pitted

½ small lime, juiced

¼ small white onion, finely chopped

¼ to ½ cup cilantro, chopped

1 jalapeno, stemmed, seeded and finely chopped

Coarsely ground black pepper

Fresh sea salt

1. Heat a 12-inch skillet over medium-high heat and add 2 tablespoons of olive oil, tilting to coat the pan as it heats. Add the onion and garlic and cook, stirring, until onion is translucent, about 3 minutes. Add cooked chicken and stir to combine and warm the chicken. Transfer to a bowl, cover with foil, and keep warm.

2. While the chicken rests, add your guacamole ingredients to a medium bowl and break apart with a fork. Combine the ingredients coarsely, leaving chunks if you like a chunky guacamole. Set aside.

3. Wipe skillet clean with a paper towel, return to heat, and add a tablespoon of oil, coating the pan. Add two tortillas, folded in half. Fill each half with the chicken mixture, and add some cheese, olives, salsa, and avocado. Fold the top down on each tortilla and press, cooking the bottom. Flip the tortillas and continue to cook for about 5 minutes.

4. Keep cooked quesadillas warm in the oven while you cook through the batch. Serve warm with guacamole and additional salsa on the side.

Variations

- Substitute sliced leftover steak for the chicken.
- Substitute sliced jalapenos for the olives, or include both.
- Drizzle with Sriracha before serving.
- Serve with lime slices to squeeze over the quesadillas, especially if spicy.

PINEAPPLE-COCONUT POPSICLES

Makes about 10 popsicles,
depending on the size of your mold
Active Time: 10 minutes
Start to Finish: 3 to 4 hours

13.5-oz can whole (or full-fat) organic
coconut milk

1 cup fresh pineapple, sliced into chunks

¼ cup raw honey

1. Place the ingredients in a blender. Purée
   until smooth, about
   30 seconds.

2. Pour into a popsicle mold and insert
   popsicle stick.

3. Freeze until popsicles hold firm (three to
   five hours).

4. Briefly submerge the mold into lukewarm water.
   When the popsicles begin to separate from the
   mold, remove immediately. Pop the popsicles out
   of the mold, and enjoy!

Menu 36

September always reminds us of the end of summer, not because of weather, but because it's back-to-school time. Moms and dads are busy again shuttling the kids to school and to practice, and life seems to move at a fever pitch. This menu hopes to give the adults a bit of a break with some more simple recipes, while a dessert of s'mores looks to comfort the kid in all of us.

Spicy Shrimp

Spinach and Shallots

Mango-Avocado Salad

Skillet S'mores

SPICY SHRIMP

Makes 4 to 6 servings   Active time: 15 minutes
Total time: 35 minutes

---

1 tablespoon celery salt

¼ teaspoon cayenne pepper

¼ teaspoon paprika

¼ teaspoon ground allspice

1 teaspoon coarsely ground black pepper

½ teaspoon kosher salt

30 large shrimp, peeled and deveined

2 tablespoons olive oil

1. Combine all the spices into a small bowl and mix well.

2. Place the peeled and deveined shrimp to a large bowl and toss with olive oil. Add the spices into the bowl and coat evenly. Set aside while preparing the grill.

3. Preheat your gas or charcoal grill to medium-high heat.

4. When the grill is ready, at about 450 to 500 degrees F with the coals lightly covered with ash, add the shrimp to the grill and grill over direct heat. Cook until the shrimp are slightly firm and opaque throughout. Remove from grill and let cool for 5 minutes. Serve warm.

MANGO-AVOCADO SALAD

2 medium mangoes, cubed

2 large avocados, halved, pitted and cubed

¼ small red onion, coarsely chopped

2 cups chopped tomatoes

1 cup basil leaves, thinly sliced

½ small lemon or lime, juiced

1 tablespoon olive oil

2 teaspoons coarsely ground black pepper

1 teaspoon fresh sea salt

1. Combine the mango, avocado, red onion, tomatoes, and basil and mix well.

2. Add the lemon or lime juice and olive oil and mix lightly.

3. Season with pepper and salt before serving.

Spinach and Shallots

3 tablespoons olive oil

4 large shallots, sliced thin

2 pounds fresh spinach, tough stems removed, rinsed, and thoroughly dried

1 tablespoon balsamic vinegar

Salt and pepper

1. Heat skillet over medium-high heat. Add olive oil and shallots and cook, stirring, until shallots are translucent, about 2 minutes.

2. Add the spinach and cook, stirring, until all the leaves are covered in the oil/onion mix, another 2 or 3 minutes. The spinach will start to reduce quickly. Reduce the heat and keep stirring so none of it burns. If desired, you can turn the heat to low and cover the skillet so the leaves steam-cook.

3. When the spinach leaves are wilted and still bright green, splash them with the balsamic vinegar, shaking the pan to distribute. Season with salt and pepper and serve.

Variation:
If you prefer less onion flavor, use two shallots instead of four.

This dish works best with more mature spinach. Reserve baby spinach greens for salads and use the larger leaves for this dish.

SKILLET S'MORES

Makes 6 to 8 servings   Active Time: 20 minutes   Start to Finish: 30 minutes

1 (16.5-oz.) bag semisweet chocolate chips

16 marshmallows, cut in half

Graham crackers

1. Preheat the oven to 450 degrees F.

2. Put the chocolate chips in the skillet and top with the cut marshmallows, clean side facing up.

3. Bake in the oven until marshmallows brown on top, about 5 minutes.

4. Serve with graham crackers for scooping and a side of ghost stories.

If you didn't get your fill of s'mores over the summer, don't think you can't have them without a campfire.

Menu 37

In some of the more northern climates, the onset of fall means it's sadly time to winterize the grill and move much of the cooking indoors again. Stovetop cooking is on the menu, with three skillet recipes to welcome the autumn months, plus a simple shortbread cookie dessert to sweeten the move inside.

Spareribs

Garlic Rosemary Rolls (page 156)

Skillet Eggplant Parm (page 180)

Shortbread Cookie Bars

SPARERIBS

Makes 2 to 4 servings   Active Time: 2 hours
Start to Finish: 2 hours

2 pounds pork spareribs

Salt and pepper for seasoning

Juice from ½ lemon

1 to 2 cups barbeque sauce

1. Preheat the oven to 350 degrees F.

2. Wash and dry the ribs, cutting into sections that
   will fit in the skillet. Season both sides with salt
   and pepper.

3. Put the ribs in the skillet, sprinkle with fresh-
   squeezed lemon juice, and put the skillet in
   the oven. Bake for about 90 minutes, turning
   halfway through cooking time.

4. For the second half of the cooking time, brush
   with barbeque sauce, if desired, and turn again
   for the last 15 minutes, putting barbeque sauce
   on the other side of the ribs. Serve immediately.

SHORTBREAD COOKIE BARS

Makes 6 to 8   Active time: 25 minutes
Start to Finish: 60 minutes

1 cup flour

¼ teaspoon salt

¼ cup sugar

8 tablespoons (1 stick) unsalted butter, chilled

½ teaspoon vanilla extract

1. Preheat the oven to 300 degrees F. Heat the skillet in the oven while making the dough.

2. In a large bowl, combine the flour, salt, and sugar, whisking to combine.

3. Cut the butter into slices and add to the flour mixture. The best way to work it into the flour is with your hands. As it starts to come together, add the vanilla extract. Work with it until it resembles coarse meal.

4. Gather the dough into a ball. On a lightly floured surface, roll it out into a circle that's just smaller than the surface of the cast iron skillet—about 8 inches in diameter. Slice the round into 8 wedges.

5. Remove the skillet from the oven and place the wedges in it to recreate the circle of dough. Bake for about 45 minutes or until the shortbread is a pale golden color. Remove from the oven and allow to cool for about 10 minutes before transferring the cookies to a plate.

Fall

Fall is harvest season, when we enjoy the fruits of our summer labors. Holidays like Thanksgiving and Rosh Hashanah bring us together at the dining table, where we spend time reflecting with friends and family, and prepare for the cold.

As the leaves change and the temperature drops, it's time to bring what's left of the herb garden inside. It's also time to plant winter vegetables, including cabbage, brussels sprouts, garlic, greens and peas. With winter approaching, you may want to stock up on some basic kitchen ingredients such as flour and sugar, and put a few sticks of butter in the freezer. No one wants to run to the store in bad weather, especially for a cup of sugar. It's also time to check your kitchen's smoke detector again.

Be sure to winterize your grill before the weather turns sour. Clean and scrub the grates, clean and empty the drip pan, and use an oven cleaner to remove any grease from the interior of the grill body. Disconnect and store the propane tank, and cover your grill, particularly if it will live outside for the winter.

The autumnal menus provided here reflect the shorter days and cooler temperatures. These are heartier meals, rich with proteins and dense fall vegetables that will and bolster you for the long winter months.

Menu 38

September heralds the first harvest of heartier fall vegetables such as beets, carrots, potatoes, radishes, cabbage, and brussels sprouts. This menu includes some of these fall garden favorites paired with a traditional beef brisket and a classic chocolate cake for dessert. It's a great opportunity to use the yield of your gardening labors.

Blackened Texas Brisket

Coleslaw

Glazed Carrots

Chocolate Cake

BLACKENED TEXAS BRISKET
with Coleslaw

Makes 3 to 4 servings   Active Time: 8 to 9 hours   Start to Finish: 10 to 11 hours

Tools

6 to 8 cups hickory or oak woodchips

1 large, aluminum foil pan

1 smoker box (if using gas grill)

Rub Ingredients

¼ cup of paprika

3 tablespoons coarsely ground black pepper

1 tablespoon ground chipotle chile

1 tablespoon chili powder

2 teaspoons cayenne pepper

1 teaspoon ground cumin

1 teaspoon dried oregano

Fresh sea salt

Steak Ingredients

1 center-cut beef brisket, 5 to 6 pounds and about ½ inches thick

2 tablespoons olive oil

Coleslaw Ingredients

¼ cup apple cider vinegar

¼ cup raw honey

1 garlic clove, minced

1 teaspoon celery salt

1 teaspoon coarsely ground black pepper

1 teaspoon fresh sea salt

½ teaspoon dry mustard

½ head purple cabbage

½ head green cabbage

2 carrots, peeled and finely chopped

1. Combine the rub ingredients in a small bowl and whisk thoroughly. Rub the brisket with the olive oil and then generously apply the rub ingredients, firmly kneading it into the meat. Wrap the brisket in plastic wrap and let rest at room temperature from 2 to 10 hours (the longer the better).

2. While waiting, soak the woodchips in water for 1 to 2 hours.

3. A half hour before cooking, prepare your gas or charcoal grill to low heat: about 250 degrees F. You want to designate two separate heat sections on the grill: one for direct-heat and the other for indirect-heat. To do this, simply arrange the coals towards one side of the grill.

4. When the grill is ready (the coals should be lightly covered with ash), drain 1 cup of the woodchips and spread over the coals or pour in the smoker box. Place the grate on the grill and then lay the brisket, fatty-side up, in the large aluminum pan. Position the pan over the cool section of the grill and then cover with the lid, aligning the air vent away from the woodchips so that their smoke rolls around the brisket before escaping. Cook for 5½ to 6 hours, rekindling the fire with coals and fresh wood chips every hour or so. When the internal temperature reads 190 to 200 degrees F, and the meat is very tender when pierced with a fork, remove from the grill.

5. Transfer to a large cutting board and let stand for 20 to 30 minutes without touching.

6. While waiting, put a saucepan over medium-low heat and add all of the ingredients for the coleslaw besides for the cabbage and carrots. Bring to a boil and simmer for 5 minutes. Add the cabbage and carrots to a medium-sized bowl. Remove the dressing from heat and slowly stir into the cabbage and carrots. Refrigerate for 30 minutes.

7. Slice the brisket diagonally into ¼-inch strips and serve with coleslaw.

GLAZED CARROTS

Makes 4 servings   Active Time: 20 minutes   Start to Finish: 40 minutes

1½ pounds carrots

¾ cup water

4 tablespoons butter

2 tablespoons sugar

Salt

Chopped fresh parsley

1. Peel and trim the carrots. Cut them in half and cut the halves in half length-wise.

2. Put the carrots in the skillet with the water, butter, and sugar. Bring to boil over medium-high heat.

3. When boiling, reduce the heat to low and simmer for another 10 minutes, stirring the carrots occasionally.

4. When the carrots are tender and there is a buttery sauce, sprinkle with salt. Garnish with chopped parsley and serve.

CHOCOLATE CAKE

Makes 4 servings   Active Time: 20 minutes
Start to Finish: 1 hour

---

6 tablespoons butter, cut in pieces

1 cup sugar

2 eggs

½ teaspoon vanilla extract

1 cup flour

1 teaspoon baking powder

2 tablespoons unsweetened cocoa powder

½ cup milk

1. Preheat the oven to 350 degrees F.

2. In a large bowl, cream the butter and sugar together until light. Add the eggs one at a time, combining thoroughly after each addition. Stir in the vanilla extract.

3. In a small bowl, combine the flour, baking powder, and cocoa powder, and mix the dry ingredients together. Alternately add the flour mix and the milk to the butter-sugar mix until thoroughly combined.

4. Grease the skillet with some butter and add the cake batter.

5. Put in the oven and bake for about 30 to 35 minutes, until the top is golden and the cake springs to the touch and a toothpick inserted in the middle comes out clean. Cool and cut into wedges.

Tip: For a doubly impressive cake, double this recipe and top with frosting, jam and fresh fruit!

Variations: There are so many ways to top this simple chocolate cake, including whipped cream, frosting, fresh berries, berries and cream, chocolate syrup, ice cream (almost any flavor), or marshmallow fluff.

Menu 39

It's that time of year again, when Americans across the country turn their attention to the gridiron. Nowhere is more focused on football than the American South, where Friday means high school games under the lights, and Saturday means college tailgating and a lifetime passion. Start your meal with Skillet Wings, perfect for any tailgate.

Skillet Wings

Kale and Sausage Soup

Cornbread (page 280)

Skillet Tarte Tatin

SKILLET WINGS

Makes 3 to 6 servings   Active Time: 30 minutes   Start to Finish: 1 hour

---

6 whole chicken wings

1 tablespoon butter

1 tablespoon vegetable oil

Salt and pepper

¼ teaspoon cayenne pepper

7 oz. Frank's Red Hot sauce

Blue cheese dressing

Celery and carrot sticks

1. Preheat the oven to 500 degrees F.

2. With a sharp knife, cut the wings at the joint so that you have three sections: the single-boned section, the double-boned section, and the tip. Discard the tips.

3. When the oven is almost to 500 degrees F, put the skillet over medium-high heat and add the butter and oil. When this gets hot, add the wing sections and stir. Season with salt and pepper, sprinkle with cayenne, stir again, then coat the wings with a portion of the hot sauce (use only enough to coat the wings, saving more for later).

4. Put the skillet in the oven and cook the wings for a couple of minutes. Remove the skillet from the oven (wearing oven mitts!), flip over each wing section, and coat with more hot sauce. Put the skillet back in the oven and cook for another 2 minutes. Repeat this procedure for about 20 minutes, basting with the hot sauce in the skillet, until the wings are fully cooked and crispy all over.

5. Serve with blue cheese dressing and a side of celery and carrot sticks.

KALE AND SAUSAGE SOUP

Makes 6 servings   Active Time: 45 minutes   Start to Finish: 1 hour

2 tablespoons olive oil

1 medium yellow onion, finely chopped

1 garlic clove, finely chopped

¾ pound homemade pork or chicken sausage, cut into ½-inch pieces

¼ teaspoon red pepper flakes

3 cups homemade Chicken Stock (page 37)

2 cups water

1 pound fresh kale, stemmed and chopped

Coarsely ground black pepper

Fresh sea salt

1. Place a large Dutch oven on your gas or charcoal grill and prepare to medium heat. Leave the grill covered while heating, as it will add a faint smoky flavor.

2. When the grill is ready, at about 400 degrees F with the coals are lightly covered with ash, add the olive oil to the Dutch oven, followed by the onion, garlic, and sausage pieces. Cook until the onion is brown and the sausage has browned, about 7 minutes. Remove the sausage from the pan and set aside.

3. Next, stir in the pepper flakes, chicken stock, and water and bring to a boil. Cook, uncovered, for about 20 minutes. Add in the kale and boil for about 5 more minutes until tender. Stir in the sausage and cook for about 2 more minutes.

4. Remove the Dutch oven from the grill and season with coarsely ground black pepper and fresh sea salt. Serve hot.

SKILLET TARTE TATIN

Makes 6 to 8 servings   Active Time: 1 hour   Start to Finish: 1½ hours (plus 1 hour for refrigeration)

---

1 cup flour

½ teaspoon salt

1 tablespoon sugar

6 tablespoons unsalted butter, cut into small pieces

3 tablespoons ice water

1 cup (2 sticks) unsalted butter, cut into small pieces

1½ cups sugar

8 to 10 apples, peeled, cored, and halved (see sidebar)

The best apples for this dessert are ones that are semi-tart and crisp. These include Mutsu, Honeycrisp, Jonagold, and Golden Delicious.

1. To make the pastry, whisk together the flour, salt, and sugar in a large bowl. Using your fingers, work the butter into the flour mixture until you have coarse clumps. Sprinkle the ice water over the mixture and continue to work it with your hands until it just holds together. Shape it into a ball, wrap it in plastic wrap, and refrigerate it for at least one hour but even overnight.

2. Place the pieces of butter evenly over the bottom of the skillet, then sprinkle the sugar evenly over everything. Next, start placing the apple halves in a circular pattern, starting on the outside of the pan and working in. The halves should support each other and all face the same direction. Place either one or two halves in the center when finished working around the outside. As the cake bakes, the slices will slide down a bit.

3. Place the skillet on the stove and turn the heat to medium-high. Cook the apples in the pan, uncovered, until the sugar and butter start to caramelize, about 35 minutes. While they're cooking, spoon some of the melted juices over the apples (but don't overdo it).

4. Preheat the oven to 400 degrees F, and position a rack in the center.

5. Take the chilled dough out of the refrigerator and, working on a lightly floured surface, roll it out into a circle just big enough to cover the skillet (about 12 to 14 inches). Gently drape the pastry over the apples, tucking the pastry in around the sides.

6. Put the skillet in the oven and bake for about 25 minutes, until the pastry is golden brown.

7. Remove the skillet from the oven and allow to cool for about 5 minutes. Find a plate that is an inch or two larger than the top of the skillet and place it over the top. You will be inverting the tart onto the plate. Be sure to use oven mitts or secure pot holders, as the skillet will be hot.

8. Holding the plate tightly against the top of the skillet, turn the skillet over so the plate is now on the bottom. If some of the apples are stuck to the bottom, gently remove them and place them on the tart.

9. Allow to cool a few more minutes, or set aside until ready to serve (it's better if it's served warm).

10. Serve with fresh whipped cream, crème fraiche, or vanilla ice cream.

Menu 40

America's relationship with France began well before the American revolution, when much of today's country was comprised of French territories. Our friendship with the French has only grown, and much of our culinary tradition is greatly influenced by the French cooking heritage. This menu certainly reflects that influence, with two decidedly Gallic recipes, and a tempting French inspired dessert.

Boeuf Bourguignon

French Onion Soup

Roasted Red Potatoes

Pear Clafouti

I have a great use for the leftover red wine; I drink it. If you don't want to drink it, here's what to do: Boil it down in a saucepan until it's reduced by half, then freeze it in ice cube trays. When you're making a dish in the future that calls for red wine, just pull out a few cubes.

BOEUF BOURGUIGNON

Makes 6 to 8 servings   Active Time: 25 minutes
Minimum cook time: 4 hours in a medium slow cooker

---

2 pounds stewing beef, fat trimmed, and cut into 1-inch cubes

2 tablespoons olive oil

1 large carrot, chopped

3 garlic cloves, minced

1 head of broccoli, chopped into bite-sized pieces

2 cups dry red wine

½ cup Beef Stock (page 37) or purchased stock

1 tablespoon tomato paste

3 tablespoons chopped fresh parsley

1 teaspoon herbes de Provence or dried thyme

1 bay leaf

1½ tablespoons cornstarch

Salt and freshly ground black pepper to taste

1. Preheat the oven broiler, and line a broiler pan with heavy-duty aluminum foil. Broil beef for 3 minutes per side, or until browned. Transfer beef to the slow cooker, and pour in any juices that have collected in the pan.

2. Heat oil in a medium skillet over medium heat. Add carrot, garlic, and broccoli. Cook, stirring frequently, for 4 to 5 minutes, or until vegetables are soft. Scrape mixture into the slow cooker.

3. Add wine, stock, tomato paste, parsley, herbes de Provence, and bay leaf to the slow cooker, and stir well. Cook on Low for 8 to 10 hours or on High for 4 to 5 hours, or until beef is tender.

4. If cooking on Low, raise the heat to High. Mix cornstarch and 2 tablespoons cold water in a small cup, and stir cornstarch mixture into the slow cooker. Cook for an additional 15 to 20 minutes, or until juices are bubbling and slightly thickened. Remove and discard bay leaf, season to taste with salt and pepper, and serve hot.

Note: The dish can be prepared up to 2 days in advance and refrigerated, tightly covered. Reheat it, covered, in a 350 degrees F oven for 20 to 25 minutes, or until hot.

Variation:

Substitute boneless lamb shoulder for the beef, and add 2 tablespoons chopped fresh rosemary or 2 teaspoons dried to the recipe.

CLASSIC FRENCH ONION SOUP

Makes 6 to 8 servings   Active Time: 20 minutes   Minimum cooking time: 8½ hours in a medium slow cooker

---

4 tablespoons (½ stick) unsalted butter, cut into small pieces

¼ cup olive oil

3 pounds sweet onions, such as Vidalia or Bermuda, thinly sliced

1 tablespoon granulated sugar

Salt and freshly ground black pepper to taste

5 cups Beef Stock (page 37) or purchased stock

¾ cup dry red wine

3 tablespoons chopped fresh parsley

1 bay leaf

1 tablespoon fresh thyme or ½ teaspoon dried

6 slices gluten-free French or Italian bread, cut ½-inch thick

⅓ cup freshly grated Parmesan cheese

1 tablespoon cornstarch

1½ cups grated Gruyère or Swiss cheese

1. Set the slow cooker on High, and add butter and olive oil. Add onions once butter melts, and add sugar, salt, and pepper. Toss well to coat onions. Cook for 1 hour, remove the cover, and stir onions. Cook for an additional 3 to 4 hours, or until onions are golden brown.

2. Add beef, stock, wine, parsley, bay leaf, and thyme to the slow cooker, and stir well. Cook on Low for 4 to 6 hours or on High for 2 to 3 hours, or until onions are very soft.

3. While soup cooks, preheat the oven to 450 degrees F and cover a baking sheet with aluminum foil. Sprinkle bread with Parmesan cheese, and bake slices for 5 to 8 minutes, or until browned. Remove, and set aside.

4. Preheat the oven broiler. If cooking on Low, raise the heat to High. Mix cornstarch and 2 tablespoons cold water in a small cup. Stir mixture into the slow cooker, and cook for an additional 15 to 20 minutes, or until the liquid is bubbling and has slightly thickened. Remove and discard bay leaf, and season to taste with salt and pepper.

5. To serve, ladle hot soup into oven-proof soup bowls and top each with toast slice. Divide Gruyère on top of toast and broil 6 inches from heating element for 1 to 2 minutes, or until cheese melts and browns. Serve immediately.

Note: The soup can be prepared up to 3 days in advance and refrigerated, tightly covered. Reheat it, covered, over low heat, stirring occasionally.

If you don't have ovenproof soup bowls, you can still enjoy the gooey toast topping. Arrange the toast slices on a baking sheet lined with aluminum foil, and top with the cheese. Broil until the cheese melts, and then transfer the toasts to soup bowls with a wide spatula.

12 to 14 small red potatoes, scrubbed clean

2 to 3 tablespoons olive oil

Freshly ground pepper

Coarse sea salt

Chopped fresh parsley

Rosemary, for garnish

1. Preheat the oven to 375 degrees F.

2. In a bowl, drizzle oil over the potatoes. Grind some fresh pepper on the potatoes. Put them in the skillet to form a single layer. Sprinkle the potatoes with sea salt.

3. Bake in the oven for 25 to 40 minutes, turning halfway through the cooking time, until potatoes are cooked through. Serve hot with rosemary or chopped parsley as garnish.

PEAR CLAFOUTI

Makes 4 to 6 servings   Active Time: 20 minutes
Start to Finish: 45 minutes

8 tablespoons melted butter

½ cup sugar

⅔ cup flour

½ teaspoon salt

1 teaspoon almond extract

3 eggs

1 cup milk

4 tablespoons unsalted butter

4 pears

½ cup + 2 teaspoons sugar

1. Preheat the oven to 400 degrees F.

2. In a large bowl, mix together 6 tablespoons of the
    butter, sugar, flour, salt, almond extract, eggs, and
    milk until all ingredients are blended and smooth.
    Set aside.

3. Put 2 tablespoons of butter in the cast-iron skillet
    and put it in the oven to heat up.

4. In another skillet on the stove, working over
    medium-high heat, add the additional butter until
    melted. Add the fruit and sugar to the butter and
    cook, stirring, until the pears are just soft and
    glazed, about 3 minutes.

5. Remove the skillet from the oven and pour in half
    the batter. Spoon the cooked pears over the batter,
    and then add the remaining batter. Sprinkle with the
    sugar.

6. Bake in the oven for 25 to 30 minutes until the
    clafouti is golden brown and set in the center. Serve
    warm with whipped cream or confectioner's sugar if
    desired, or just by itself.

*Although clafouti is most delicious served
warm, it is plenty tasty served at room temperature or even chilled.*

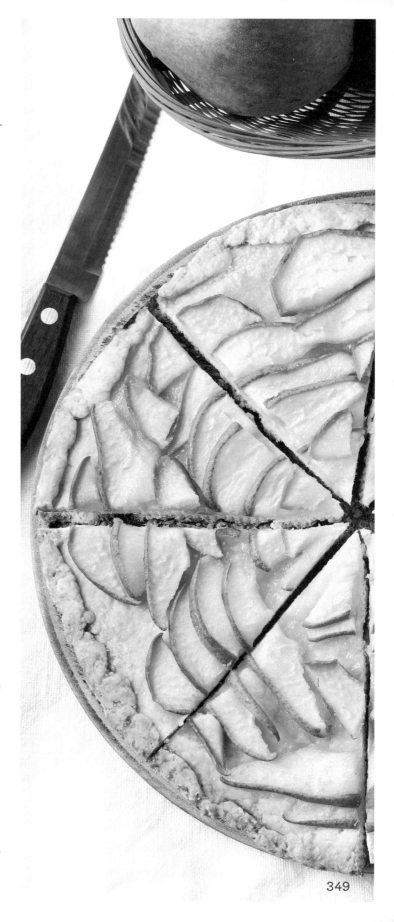

Menu 41

This menu would be right at home in your local pub, featuring steak frites paired with a hearty mushroom side. But the star of the season is pumpkin, the main attraction of many an upcoming dessert. Our meal closes with a pumpkin banana bread sure to make any jack-o-lantern smile.

Steak Frites

Marvelous Mushrooms

Pumpkin Banana Bread

STEAK FRITES

Makes 2 Servings   Active Time: 30 Minutes   Start to Finish: 2 Hours

Steak Ingredients

2 small steaks (best is sirloin, rib eye, or shell), about 1 inch thick

3 tablespoons unsalted butter

Salt and pepper to taste

Fresh parsley for garnish

Frites Ingredients

1 pound Yukon gold potatoes, peeled, washed, and cut into thin strips

3 cups peanut oil (Peanut oil is the best oil to fry in, but vegetable oil is a suitable substitute.)

Salt and pepper to taste

1. Preheat the oven to 200 degrees F.

2. Prepare everything ahead of time so you can cook the steaks immediately after the fries. If you wait too long, the fries will get soft. Line a baking sheet with paper towels (for the fries when they're cooked). Put the steaks on a plate in the refrigerator (keep them cold until ready for to go in the pan). Make sure your potato strips are clean and dry.

3. Put the oil in the skillet and add the potatoes. Bring the oil to a boil over medium-high heat (careful of splattering). As the oil gets hotter, the potatoes will get limp and just start to brown (about 15 minutes). At this point, start turning them with tongs to get all sides crispy and browned. Cook another 5 minutes or so.

4. Transfer the fries to the baking sheet and sprinkle with salt. Put in the oven to stay warm, covering with additional paper towels so they stay crisp.

5. Drain the fat from the skillet into a heat proof glass container (like a measuring cup). Put the skillet back on the burner and add the butter. Take the steaks out of the fridge. When the butter is hot but not smoking, put the steaks in the skillet. Sear them over the high heat for a minute per side, then reduce the heat to medium. Sprinkle with salt and pepper and turn them every few minutes. They're cooked in about 8 minutes (so that they're somewhat rare and juicy inside).

6. Transfer to plates, and pile the French fries next to them. Garnish with parsley. Voila!

351

MARVELOUS MUSHROOMS

Makes 4 servings   Active Time: 20 minutes   Start to Finish: 30 minutes

6 tablespoons butter, cut into pieces

1 pound mushrooms, cut into slices

1 teaspoon Vermouth

Salt and pepper to taste

1. Heat the skillet over medium-high heat. Add the butter. When melted, add the mushrooms. Cook, stirring, until the mushrooms begin to soften, about 5 minutes. Reduce the heat to low and let the mushrooms simmer, stirring occasionally, until they cook down, about 15 to 20 minutes.

2. Add the Vermouth and stir, then season with salt and pepper. Allow to simmer until the mushrooms practically melt in your mouth. Serve hot.

There are many kinds of mushrooms available, and you can mix and match them as you desire. But my favorite to use with this dish is the basic white mushroom.

PUMPKIN BANANA BREAD

Makes 1 loaf   Active Time: ½ hour   Start to Finish: 2 hours

8 tablespoons (1 stick) butter, softened

⅔ cup light brown sugar

2 tablespoons honey

2 large eggs

1 cup pumpkin purée (unsweetened)

1 cup mashed very ripe bananas (about 2 or 3)

2 tablespoons water

1 teaspoon vanilla extract

1½ cups flour (white or whole wheat)

¼ teaspoon baking powder

1 teaspoon baking soda

¾ teaspoon salt

½ teaspoon ground cinnamon

½ teaspoon ground nutmeg

½ cup chopped walnuts (optional)

1. Preheat the oven to 350 degrees F. Put the skillet in the oven while it preheats.

2. In a large bowl, beat together the butter, sugar, honey, eggs, pumpkin, banana, water, and vanilla. In a separate bowl, whisk together the flour, baking powder, baking soda, salt, cinnamon, and nutmeg. Add the dry ingredients to the bowl of wet ingredients. Stir until thoroughly combined. Fold in the chopped walnuts.

3. Using pot holders or oven mitts, carefully remove the skillet from the oven. Pour in the batter and return the pan to the oven. Bake for about 60 minutes, until the bread sounds hollow when tapped on the top and a toothpick or knife inserted in the middle comes out clean.

4. Let rest for about 20 minutes. Gently invert onto a plate. Allow to cool before cutting into wedges and serving.

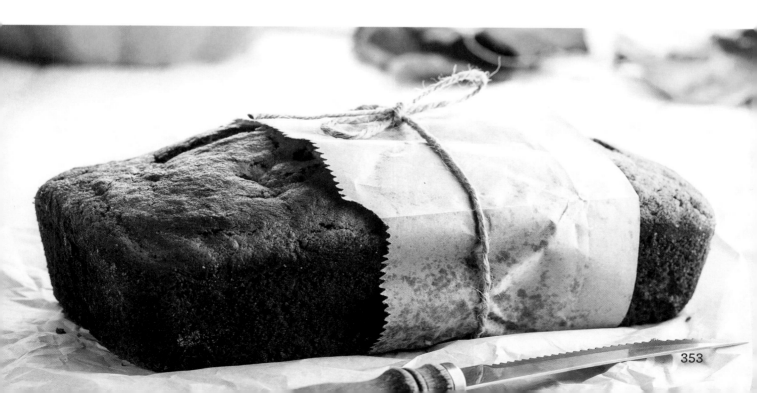

Menu 42

Indian summer has likely passed, and as the days get colder and the nights get longer, here's a menu that's sure to keep off the chill after raking the leaves. A hearty shepherd's pie is both filling and warms the bones, while dessert combines two fall flavors in a rustic homemade pie.

Shepherd's Pie

Peas and Onions

Dinner Rolls (page 179)

Pumpkin-Walnut Pie

SHEPHERD'S PIE

Makes 4 to 6 servings   Active Time: 45 minutes   Start to Finish: 1½ hours

---

6 russet potatoes, peeled and cubed

½ teaspoon salt

½ cup (8 tablespoons) butter, cut into individual tablespoons

½ to ¾ cup milk, or ½ cup milk and ¼ cup plain yogurt

Salt and pepper to taste

1 tablespoon olive oil

½ yellow onion, chopped fine

1 pound ground beef

1 (15-oz.) can of petit pois (peas), drained, or 2 cups high-quality frozen peas

½ of a 15-oz. can of corn kernels, drained (if desired)

Salt and pepper to taste

1. Preheat the oven to 350 degrees F.

2. After peeling and cubing the potatoes, give them a final rinse to get all the dirt off. Put the potato pieces in a large saucepan or pot and cover with cold water. Add the salt. Bring the water to a boil, reduce to a simmer, and cook the potatoes until soft, about 20 minutes. When they can be easily pierced with a sharp knife, they're cooked.

3. Drain the potato pieces and put them in a large bowl. Add 6 tablespoons of the butter and ½ cup of the milk and use a potato masher to make the mashed potatoes. Add additional milk or yogurt to get a creamy but not soupy consistency. Season with salt and pepper and set aside.

4. In the cast-iron skillet over medium heat, put the tablespoon of olive oil and cook the onion, stirring to just soften, about 2 minutes. Add the ground beef and break apart to cook, stirring while the meat browns. When there is just a little pinkness to the meat, drain the fat from it. Stir in the peas and, if desired, the corn kernels. Season with salt and pepper.

5. Spread the mashed potatoes over the meat and vegetables into a baking dish, distributing the potatoes evenly and smoothing the top. Cut the remaining 2 tablespoons of butter into slivers and dot the potatoes with them.

6. Cover with foil and bake for 30 minutes. Remove the foil and cook another 10 minutes until the potatoes are just browned.

7. Allow to cool about 5 minutes before serving.

How this recipe came to be called a "pie" is curious, since it doesn't really have a crust. Instead, it has a top layer of mashed potatoes, which blankets the beef mixture underneath and helps keep it juicy while it bakes. In that sense, it works like a pie. Semantics aside, it's one of the best comfort foods you can make.

PEAS AND ONIONS

Makes 4 servings   Active Time: 5 minutes   Start to Finish: 20 minutes

3 tablespoons butter

½ onion, chopped

1 pound shelled peas, fresh or frozen

½ cup vegetable or chicken broth

Coarsely ground black pepper

Salt

1. Heat 2 tablespoons of butter in a sauté pan over medium-high heat. Sauté the chopped onions.

2. Add the peas and broth and bring to a boil, stirring frequently.

3. When the stock has reduced by about half, turn off the heat and add 1 tablespoon butter and salt and pepper to taste.

PUMPKIN-WALNUT PIE

Makes 6 to 8 servings   Active Time: 30 Minutes
Start to Finish: 75 Minutes

---

1 flaky pastry crust recipe for a single crust (see page 107)

1 (15-oz.) can pumpkin puree (not pumpkin pie mix)

1 (14-oz.) can sweetened condensed milk (not evaporated)

2 eggs

2 tablespoons 100% natural maple syrup

½ teaspoon ground cinnamon

¼ teaspoon ground ginger

¼ teaspoon ground nutmeg

¼ cup packed brown sugar

¼ cup finely chopped walnuts

2 tablespoons flour

2 tablespoons butter, chilled and cut into pieces

1. Preheat the oven to 425 degrees F.

2. In a large bowl, combine the pumpkin puree, sweetened condensed milk, eggs, maple syrup, and spices. Whisk or stir until thoroughly combined. Pour into unbaked pie crust. Put the cast iron skillet in the oven and bake for 10 minutes.

3. While pie is baking, in a small bowl, combine the brown sugar, walnuts, and flour. Work in the butter with your fingers until the mixture is crumbly.

4. Reduce the oven temperature to 350 degrees F. Carefully take the pie out of the oven and top with the brown sugar/walnut mixture, distributing evenly. Use foil to cover the edges of the crust to prevent them from burning.

5. Return skillet to the oven and bake 30 to 35 minutes or until a knife inserted about an inch from the edge comes out clean. Allow to cool completely, and then refrigerate until ready to serve.

6. Serve with fresh whipped cream or vanilla ice cream.

Menu 43

The American Northwest has a long-standing history of salmon fishing, dating back to local Native American tribes who decorated their totem poles with images of the revered catch. This menu celebrates America's love of salmon with a recipe for salmon cakes, and a side featuring salmon's best embellishment, sour cream and dill.

Salmon Cakes

Glazed Carrots (page 337)

Sour Cream and Dill Scones

Nutty Apple-Cranberry Pie

SALMON CAKES

Makes 6 to 8 cakes   Active Time: 60 minutes
Start to Finish: 90 minutes

---

2 (14.75-oz.) cans of salmon (preferably Red Salmon over Pink Salmon)

2 large eggs, lightly beaten

4 tablespoons bread crumbs

¼ cup onion, minced

1 teaspoon Frank's Red Hot sauce

1 teaspoon dried parsley flakes

Salt and freshly ground pepper to taste

2 tablespoons oil (preferably peanut, but olive is fine)

Lemon wedges

1. Drain the liquid from the cans of salmon, and empty the fish into a bowl, flaking it apart with a fork. Add the eggs, bread crumbs, minced onion, hot sauce, and parsley flakes and stir, combining well. Season with salt and pepper.

2. Heat the skillet over medium-high heat. Add 1 tablespoon of the oil. Add 3 or 4 individual heaping spoons full of fish mix to the skillet, pressing down on the tops of each to form a patty (cake). Brown the cakes on each side for about 5 minutes. Try to turn the cakes over just once. If you're worried about them being cooked through, put a lid on the skillet for a minute or so after they've browned on each side.

3. Transfer the cakes to a plate and cover with foil to keep them warm while you cook the next batch. Serve on a platter with lemon wedges.

Tip: You may choose to use canned salmon for this recipe. The quality isn't as high as using freshly steamed salmon, but it's quite good. With the healthy add-ins, and the fact that the end product is a cake that will be topped with a dressing like tartar or cocktail sauce, the canned salmon is great for ease of use and taste.

Variations:

-Salmon cakes can be served many ways:

-Eat them as you would hamburgers, on a bun with lettuce, tomato, red onion, and instead of ketchup or mustard, tartar or cocktail sauce.

-Serve a cake on top of a green salad with a lemon-dill dressing on the side.

-Make mini cakes and serve as finger foods with toothpicks and dipping sauces.

SOUR CREAM AND DILL SCONES

Makes 4 to 6 servings   Active Time: 30 minutes
Start to Finish: 50 minutes

2 cups flour

1 teaspoon baking powder

½ teaspoon salt

1 teaspoon freshly ground black pepper

4 tablespoons butter, chilled, cut into pieces

¾ cup sour cream

1 tablespoon finely chopped fresh dill

1 egg beaten with a little milk

1. Preheat the oven to 400 degrees F. Position a rack in the middle of the oven.

2. In a large bowl, whisk together the flour, baking powder, salt, and pepper. Add the butter pieces and mix with an electric mixer until just blended, or mix with a fork so that the dough is somewhat crumbly.

3. Stir in the sour cream and dill, being careful not to overmix.

4. With flour on your hands, transfer the dough to a lightly floured surface. Form the dough into a circle about ½-inch thick. With a long knife, cut the dough into 6 to 8 wedges.

5. Butter the cast iron skillet, and put the scone wedges in a circle in it, leaving some space between the pieces.

6. Brush with the beaten egg. Bake for 20 to 25 minutes, or until golden.

NUTTY APPLE-CRANBERRY PIE

Serves 6 to 8   Active Time: 60 Minutes   Start to Finish: 2 hours

1 cup chopped walnuts

4 pounds Granny Smith apples

1 cup fresh cranberries

1 teaspoon ground cinnamon

¼ teaspoon ground ginger

1 cup sugar

1 teaspoon lemon juice

8 tablespoons (1 stick) butter

1 cup light brown sugar

1 (14.1-oz.) package
refrigerated piecrusts

1 egg white

2 tablespoons sugar

1. Preheat the oven to 450 degrees F.

2. Spread the walnut pieces out on a cookie sheet and bake until toasted, about 5 to 8 minutes, removing the cookie sheet mid-way to shake and turn the nuts. Keep an eye on them so they don't burn. Remove the cookie sheet from the oven and allow the nuts to cool. Reduce the oven temperature to 350 degrees F.

3. Peel and core the apples, and cut into ½-inch-thick wedges. In a large bowl, combine the apples with cranberries, cinnamon, ginger, sugar, and lemon juice. Stir in the walnut pieces.

4. Put the skillet over medium heat and melt the butter in it. Add the brown sugar and cook, stirring constantly, until sugar is dissolved, one or two minutes. Remove pan from heat.

5. Roll out 1 of the piecrusts and gently place it over the sugar mixture. Fill with the apple/cranberry mix, and place the other crust over the apples, crimping the edges together.

6. Brush the top crust with the egg white, and sprinkle the sugar over it. Cut 4 or 5 slits in the middle.

7. Put the skillet in the oven and bake for 60 to 70 minutes until golden brown and bubbly. Cover the outermost edge with aluminum foil in the last 10 minutes of baking to prevent it from burning.

8. Allow to cool before serving.

Menu 44

Many a "leaf-peeper" has spent a weekend viewing the dazzling fall foliage in New England, when the colors of the trees explode like fireworks. October is high season for leaf-peeping in Maine, New Hampshire, and Vermont, and this menu celebrates the region with a handful of recipes that evoke New England in the fall.

Pot Roast

New England Spider Cake

Bone Marrow Mashed Potatoes
(page 224)

Slow Cooker Pumpkin Custard

POT ROAST

Makes 4 to 6 servings   Active Time: 15 minutes   Start to Finish: 4½ hours

---

1 (2- to 2½-pound) boneless chuck roast or rump roast

3 tablespoons olive oil

1 large sweet onion, such as Vidalia or Bermuda, diced

3 garlic cloves, minced

2 cups Beef Stock (page 37) or purchased stock

2 potatoes, cut into halves or wedges

2 carrots, cut into 1-inch lengths, and halved if thick

3 tablespoons chopped fresh rosemary or 1 tablespoon dried

2 tablespoons chopped fresh parsley

1 tablespoon chopped fresh thyme or ½ teaspoon dried

1½ tablespoons cornstarch

Salt and freshly ground black pepper to taste

1. Preheat the oven broiler, and line a broiler pan with heavy-duty aluminum foil. Broil beef for 3 to 4 minutes per side, or until browned. Transfer beef to the slow cooker, and pour in any juices that have collected in the pan.

2. Heat oil in a medium skillet over medium-high heat. Add onion and garlic, and cook, stirring frequently, for 3 minutes, or until onion is translucent. Scrape mixture into the slow cooker.

3. Add stock, potatoes, carrots, and rosemary to the slow cooker, and stir well. Cook on Low for 8 to 10 hours or on High for 4 to 5 hours, or until beef is very tender. Remove as much grease as possible from the slow cooker with a soup ladle.

4. If cooking on Low, raise the heat to High. Mix cornstarch with 2 tablespoons cold water in a small cup, and stir cornstarch mixture into the slow cooker. Cook on High for 15 to 20 minutes, or until juices are bubbling and slightly thickened. Season to taste with salt and pepper, and serve hot.

5. Remove beef from the slow cooker, and slice it against the grain into thin slices. Serve immediately.

Note: The dish can be prepared up to 2 days in advance and refrigerated, tightly covered. Reheat it, covered, in a 350°F oven for 20 to 25 minutes, or until hot.

While roasted meats need time to "rest" during which the juices are reabsorbed into the fibers of the meat, that is not necessary for braised dishes. The juices from the meat are integrated into the sauce which then moistens the meat.

NEW ENGLAND SPIDER CAKE

Serves 4 to 6   Active Time: 30 minutes   Start to Finish: 40 minutes

1¼ cups yellow corn meal

½ cup sugar

1 teaspoon baking soda

1 teaspoon salt

2 cups buttermilk

2 large eggs

2 tablespoons unsalted butter

1. Preheat the oven to 400 degrees F and position a rack in the middle.

2. In a large bowl, combine the corn meal, sugar, baking soda, and salt. In a separate bowl, beat the eggs with the buttermilk until thoroughly combined. Gradually add it to the cornmeal mixture.

3. Heat the cast iron skillet over high heat and add the butter. When melted and swirled around to cover the whole bottom, pour in the batter.

4. Transfer the skillet to the oven and bake about 20 minutes, until the cake is golden brown and springy to the touch. Melt some additional butter on the surface when you take it out of the oven, and serve with jam, fresh berries, or maple syrup.

Early settlers in New England used a version of today's cast-iron skillet that had legs on it so it could sit in the fire. While Spider Cake is essentially a type of cornbread, made and cooked this way the outside becomes crisp and the inside forms a custardy layer.

SLOW COOKER PUMPKIN CUSTARD

Makes 6 to 8 servings   Active Time: 20 minutes
Start to Finish: 3½ to 7½ hours

6 egg yolks

1¼ cup coconut milk

1 teaspoon pumpkin pie spice mix

½ cup coconut crystals

½ teaspoon vanilla extract

⅛ teaspoon salt

⅓ cup pumpkin puree

1. Put an oven-safe casserole dish in the slow cooker. Add water around the dish so that it reaches about halfway up the side of the dish.

2. In a large bowl using a whisk, beat the egg yolks until thoroughly combined and a lighter, lemony color. Add the coconut milk, spice mix, crystals, vanilla, and salt until well combined. Fold in the pumpkin puree. Pour the mixture into the dish inside the slow cooker.

3. Cover and cook on Low for 5 to 6 hours or on High for 2 to 4 hours. The custard should be thick but not too firm. Turn the cooker off and let the dish cool slightly in the water. Then remove it and refrigerate for 1 hour or longer before serving.

Halloween

Nowadays, Halloween is about getting the best candy and bobbing for apples, among other traditions. Witches, ghosts, and the latest action figures and princesses roam the streets of spooky decorations. As fall begins with the changing leaves and a successful harvest, celebrate with some delicious snacks and sweets from the holiday's staple: the pumpkin!

Pumpkin Seeds

Pumpkin Cake

Pumpkin Pie

PUMPKIN CAKE

Makes 6 to 8 servings   Active Time: 15 minutes
Start to Finish: 1 hour 45 minutes

---

2 cups fresh, cooked or canned pumpkin

½ cup oil

¾ teaspoon (more, if you like) cinnamon

1 egg

2 cups sugar

½ teaspoon (more of this too, if you like) pumpkin spice

¾ teaspoon salt

2 teaspoon soda

½ cup chopped nuts (optional, but pecans are great!)

2½ cups all-purpose flour

½ cup raisins (optional, but use only a ¼ cup if you are using fresh pumpkin or it will be too moist.)

1. Mix all ingredients together, beating until smooth.

2. Fill greased and floured bundt pan, bread pan, or 1 pound coffee can (half full).

3. Bake 1 hour and 30 minutes in a 350 degrees F oven. Watch the cooking time because it will be slightly different depending on the baking container you use.

PUMPKIN SEEDS

Seeds of one pumpkin

Salt, to taste

Variations:

• There is no rocket science required here. You can make as many different flavors of pumpkin seeds as you can imagine. Replace the salt from the recipe above with the suggested seasoning. Here are some we suggest that you try:

• Cheesy Pumpkin Seeds: Sprinkle with cheesy popcorn seasoning.

• Tex-Mex Style: Sprinkle powdered taco seasoning onto the seeds. This is better mixed in a bowl first. Add more red pepper powder for a really hot seed!

• Cajun Style: Mix seeds in a bowl with a packet of Cajun seasonings mix. If you like it really spicy, add extra hot sauce.

• Garlic Salt: Yum!

1. Extract seeds from pumpkin.

2. Separate and discard pulp.

3. Thoroughly wash seeds in warm water.

4. Spread seeds out onto a cookie sheet.

5. Sprinkle generously with salt.

6. Put into oven and bake at 350 degrees F for approximately 20 minutes.

7. Check every five minutes and stir, adding more salt or to taste.

8. Check seeds to see if they are done by taking a sample out. Allow seeds to cool before tasting them. If the insides are dry, they are done.

9. Allow to cool and serve. Leftover seeds can be kept fresh in an airtight container or frozen for extended periods.

PUMPKIN PIE

Makes to 8 servings   Active Time: ½ hour
Start to Finish: 1 hour

---

1 flaky pastry crust recipe for a single crust
(see page 107)

1 (15-oz.) can pumpkin puree

1 (12-oz.) can evaporated milk

2 eggs, lightly beaten

½ cup sugar

½ teaspoon salt

1 teaspoon cinnamon

¼ teaspoon ground ginger

¼ teaspoon ground nutmeg

1 tablespoon butter

1 tablespoon light brown sugar

1. Preheat the oven to 400 degrees F.

2. In a large bowl, combine the pumpkin puree,
    evaporated milk, eggs, sugar, salt, cinnamon,
    ginger, and nutmeg. Stir to combine
    thoroughly.

3. Put the skillet over medium heat and melt the
    butter in it. Add the brown sugar and cook,
    stirring constantly, until sugar is dissolved, 1
    or 2 minutes. Carefully remove pan from heat.

4. Place the piecrust over the sugar mixture. Fill
    with the pumpkin mix.

5. Put the skillet in the oven and bake for 15
    minutes, then reduce the heat to 325 degrees F
    and bake an additional 30 to 45 minutes until
    the filling is firm and a toothpick inserted in
    the middle comes out clean. Don't overcook.

6. Allow to cool before serving. Serve with fresh
    whipped cream laced with a splash of apple
    liquor like Calvados or Applejack.

The Pumpkin

By John Greenleaf Whittier

Oh, greenly and fair in the lands of the sun,
The vines of the gourd and the rich melon run,
And the rock and the tree and the cottage enfold,
With broad leaves all greenness and blossoms all gold,
Like that which o'er Nineveh's prophet once grew,
While he waited to know that his warning was true,
And longed for the storm-cloud, and listened in vain
For the rush of the whirlwind and red fire-rain.

On the banks of the Xenil the dark Spanish maiden
Comes up with the fruit of the tangled vine laden;
And the Creole of Cuba laughs out to behold
Through orange-leaves shining the broad spheres of gold;
Yet with dearer delight from his home in the North,
On the fields of his harvest the Yankee looks forth,
Where crook-necks are coiling and yellow fruit shines,
And the sun of September melts down on his vines.

Ah! on Thanksgiving day, when from East and from West,
From North and from South comes the pilgrim and guest;
When the gray-haired New Englander sees round his board
The old broken links of affection restored;
When the care-wearied man seeks his mother once more,
And the worn matron smiles where the girl smiled before;
What moistens the lip and what brightens the eye,
What calls back the past, like the rich Pumpkin pie?

Oh, fruit loved of boyhood! the old days recalling,
When wood-grapes were purpling and brown nuts were falling!
When wild, ugly faces we carved in its skin,
Glaring out through the dark with a candle within!
When we laughed round the corn-heap, with hearts all in tune,
Our chair a broad pumpkin,—our lantern the moon,
Telling tales of the fairy who traveled like steam
In a pumpkin-shell coach, with two rats for her team!

Then thanks for thy present! none sweeter or better
E'er smoked from an oven or circled a platter!
Fairer hands never wrought at a pastry more fine,
Brighter eyes never watched o'er its baking, than thine!

And the prayer, which my mouth is too full to express,
Swells my heart that thy shadow may never be less,
That the days of thy lot may be lengthened below,
And the fame of thy worth like a pumpkin-vine grow,
And thy life be as sweet, and its last sunset sky
Golden-tinted and fair as thy own Pumpkin pie!

Menu 45

The days seem shorter and shorter, and the nights are getting colder fast. Italian food is always a good way to battle the cold, and veal parmigiana is a stick-to-your ribs favorite. There's also a slow cooker recipe on the menu, to limit your time in the kitchen and let you savor the remaining daylight.

Italian Salad (page 93)

Veal Parmigiana

Slow Cooker Risotto

Almond Pine Nut Macaroons

VEAL PARMIGIANA

Makes 4 Servings   Active Time: 30 Minutes
Start to Finish: 1 Hour

½ cup flour

Salt and pepper

½ cup breadcrumbs (Italian seasoned)

¼ cup grated Parmesan cheese

1 egg

½ cup milk

4 veal cutlets

3 tablespoons olive oil

2 cloves garlic, peeled and cut in half

4 oz. mozzarella, shredded

24 oz. jar marinara sauce (or 2 cups home-made)

1. Preheat the oven to 450 degrees F.

2. In a shallow bowl, season the flour with salt and pepper.

3. In another shallow bowl, mix the breadcrumbs and Parmesan cheese.

4. In a third shallow bowl, whisk the egg with the milk until combined.

5. Line a plate with wax paper. Dip the cutlets in flour, then egg/milk, then breadcrumb mix, coating both sides. Place the breaded cutlets on the wax paper until ready to cook.

6. Heat the cast iron skillet over medium-high heat and add the olive oil. When it's hot, add the olive oil and the garlic pieces. Brown the cutlets in the oil, cooking for 2 to 3 minutes per side. Remove the wax paper, and put the cutlets on the plate.

7. Lower the heat to medium and add the marinara sauce, stirring until sauce bubbles. Reduce heat to low and simmer for about 10 minutes.

8. Put the cutlets in the skillet and sprinkle with additional Parmesan. Divide the shredded mozzarella between the cutlets, put it on top of each, and put the skillet in the oven. Cook until cheese melts and begins to brown, about 5 minutes. Serve immediately.

SLOW COOKER RISOTTO

Makes 4 servings   Active Time: 15 minutes   Total Time: 2 hours 15 minutes

3 tablespoons unsalted butter

1 medium white onion, chopped

1 cup Arborio rice

3 cups low-sodium chicken broth

½ cup Parmesan cheese

2 tablespoons fresh parsley, minced

Salt to taste

1. Heat butter in a medium saucepan over medium-high heat. Add onion and cook, stirring frequently, for 3 minutes or until onion is translucent. Add rice and stir to coat grains. Raise the heat to high and add about ¼ to ½ cup broth. Stir for about two minutes, or until it is almost evaporated. Scrape mixture into the slow cooker.

2. Add the remaining broth to the slow cooker and stir well. Cook on High for 2 hours or until rice is soft and liquid is absorbed. Stir in cheese and parsley, season with salt, and serve hot.

Once you've made this Italian rice known for its porridge-like consistency in the slow cooker—without all the stirring of traditionally made risotto—you'll never do the stovetop version again!

ALMOND PINE NUT MACAROONS

Makes 3 dozen   Active Time: 15 minutes   Start to Finish: 40 minutes

---

8 oz. can almond paste

1¼ cups granulated sugar

2 large egg whites, room temperature

¾ cup pine nuts

1. Preheat the oven to 325 degrees F, and line two baking sheets with parchment paper or silicon baking mats.

2. Break almond paste into small pieces and place it in a mixing bowl along with sugar. Beat a medium speed with an electric mixer until combined. Increase the speed to high, add egg whites, and beat until mixture is light and fluffy. This can also be done in a food processor fitted with the steel blade.

3. Drop heaping tablespoons of dough onto the prepared baking sheets. Pat pine nuts into tops of cookies.

4. Bake cookies for 18 to 20 minutes or until lightly browned. Place baking sheets on wire racks, and cool completely.

Tip: When buying almond paste, be sure it's almond paste and not marzipan, which is already sweetened.

Variation: Substitute chopped blanched almonds or chopped walnuts for the pine nuts.

379

Menu 46

Chinese food is popular across the country, and this meal plan gives you the opportunity to try making Chinese at home. The menu includes a homemade version of the classic General Tso's Chicken, and a Pineapple Upside-Down Cake. Pineapple is traditionally used in Chinese cooking, as it portends the arrival of wealth and good fortune.

General Tso's Chicken

White Rice

Steamed Broccoli

Pineapple Upside-Down Cake

GENERAL TSO'S CHICKEN

Makes 4 servings   Active Time: 1½ hours
Start to Finish: 2 hours

1 large egg

1½ teaspoons toasted sesame oil

¼ cup + 1 tablespoon low-sodium soy sauce

¼ cup + 2 tablespoons cornstarch

1 pound skinless, boneless chicken thighs, cut into bite-sized pieces

1 tablespoon vegetable oil, plus more for frying

2 tablespoons fresh ginger, chopped fine

3 cloves garlic, minced

1 cup chicken broth

2 teaspoons Sriracha

3 tablespoons sugar

3 scallions, sliced thin

1. Carefully crack the egg over a medium-sized bowl, separating the white and yolk so the white goes into the bowl. Put the yolk in a cup and refrigerate for another use. Add the sesame oil, 1 tablespoon of soy sauce, and the cornstarch. Whisk to combine. Add the chicken pieces and marinate at room temperature for about 30 minutes.

2. In a small skillet or saucepan, heat the tablespoon of oil over medium-high heat. Add the ginger and garlic and stir for about a minute. Add in the broth, Sriracha, sugar, remaining soy sauce, and tablespoon of cornstarch, whisking to combine the ingredients. Continue to whisk will cooking the sauce until it gets thick and glossy. Reduce the heat to low and cover to keep it warm.

3. Heat the cast-iron skillet over medium-high heat and add about ½ inch of oil. When hot, add the chicken one piece at a time so it doesn't splatter too much. Turn the pieces with a slotted spoon so that they brown on all sides. Cook until crispy, about 5 minutes. As the pieces are cooked, transfer them to a plate lined with paper towels to drain.

4. When all the pieces are cooked, stir them with the scallions into the sauce. Serve hot.

WHITE RICE

For 4 servings, plan about 1 cup of rice.

To add an easy burst of flavor...

• Mix in dried cranberries and chopped pecans at the end.

• Finely chopped herbs such as parsley, scallions, basil, or cilantro provide great taste and color.

• Replace half the water you boil the rice in with coconut milk or carrot juice for an infused flavor.

STEAMED BROCCOLI

For 4 servings, plan about a pound to a pound and a half of broccoli.

To add an easy burst of flavor, mix in...

• Minced garlic, lemon juice, and Parmesan

• A light drizzle of olive oil with sundried tomatoes and black olives

• Dried cranberries with chopped walnuts and orange zest into the finished steamed broccoli

If General Tso's Chicken is one of your family favorites when you're out, there's no reason you can't make it at home. Serve with white rice and steamed broccoli. To coordinate the three parts, make the rice ahead of time and reheat on the stove over a low flame. The broccoli can be partially steamed ahead of time and then finished with additional steaming of about 10 minutes.

PINEAPPLE UPSIDE-DOWN CAKE

Makes 8 to 10 servings   Active Time: 1 hour   Start to Finish: 2 hours

Topping
Ingredients

4 tablespoons butter

1 (18-oz.) can pineapple rings, plus juice

½ cup dark brown sugar

Maraschino cherries (optional)

Cake
Ingredients

4 tablespoons butter, chilled

1 cup light brown sugar

2 eggs

1 cup buttermilk

1 teaspoon vanilla extract

1½ cups flour

1½ teaspoons baking powder

½ teaspoon salt

1. Preheat the oven to 350 degrees F.

2. Heat the skillet over medium-high heat. Add the butter, and stir in the juice from the jar of pineapples and the brown sugar. Stir continuously while the sugar melts, and continue stirring until the liquid boils and starts to thicken. Cook until the sauce turns a thick, dark, caramel consistency.

3. Remove from heat and place the pineapple rings in the liquid, working from the outside in. Place a cherry in each ring if adding cherries. Put the skillet in the oven while preparing the batter.

4. To make the cake, beat the cold butter and light brown sugar with an electric mixer until light and creamy. Beat in the eggs one at a time, making sure the first is thoroughly mixed in before adding the next.

5. In a small bowl, whisk together the flour, baking powder, and salt. Alternate adding the dry and liquid ingredients to the butter/sugar mix until all are combined but not overly smooth.

6. Remove the skillet from the oven and pour the batter over the pineapple rings. Replace in the oven and bake for 45 minutes until cake is golden and a knife inserted in the middle comes out clean.

7. Take the skillet out of the oven and let it rest for about 10 minutes.

8. Find a plate that is an inch or two larger than the top of the skillet and place it over the top. You will be inverting the cake onto the plate. Be sure to use oven mitts or secure pot holders, as the skillet will be hot. Holding the plate tightly against the top of the skillet, turn the skillet over so the plate is now on the bottom. If some of the pineapple is stuck to the bottom, gently remove it and place it on the cake.

9. Allow to cool a few more minutes, or set aside until ready to serve (it's better if it's served warm).

In 1925, Dole sponsored a pineapple recipe contest, promising to publish winning recipes in a book. It received over 50,000 recipes, and over 2,000 of them were for pineapple upside-down cake. It's been a classic of American cooking ever since.

Menu 47

The end of November coincides with the end of the pecan harvest, which starts in September and runs through the end of this month. This menu features a Southern-themed meal of creamy chicken stew and biscuits, topped off with a chocolate caramel pecan pie to celebrate this traditionally southern crop.

Creamy Chicken Stew with Wild Mushrooms

Biscuits (page 139)

Sweet Couscous with Nuts and Dried Fruit

Chocolate Caramel Pecan Pie

CREAMY CHICKEN STEW
with Wild Mushrooms

Makes 4 to 6 servings   Active Time: 15 minutes   Start to Finish: 2½ hours

---

1½ pounds boneless, skinless chicken (breast, thighs, or a combination)

¾ pound fresh shiitake mushrooms

2 tablespoons unsalted butter

2 tablespoons vegetable oil

1 onion, chopped

3 garlic cloves, minced

1 cup Chicken Stock (page 37) or purchased stock

½ cup dry white wine

2 tablespoons chopped fresh parsley

1 tablespoon fresh thyme or ½ teaspoon dried

1 tablespoon cornstarch

½ cup heavy cream

Salt and freshly ground black pepper to taste

1. Rinse chicken and pat dry with paper towels. Trim fat, and cut chicken into 1-inch cubes. Wipe mushrooms with a damp paper towel, discard stems, and cut in half if large.

2. Heat butter and oil in a medium skillet over medium-high heat. Add onion and garlic, and cook, stirring frequently, for 2 minutes. Add mushrooms, and cook, stirring frequently, for 3 to 4 minutes, or until mushrooms begin to soften. Scrape mixture into the slow cooker.

3. Add chicken, stock, wine, parsley, and thyme to the slow cooker, and stir well. Cook on Low for 4 to 6 hours or on High for 2 to 3 hours, or until chicken is cooked through and no longer pink and vegetables are tender.

4. If cooking on Low, raise the heat to High. Stir cornstarch into cream, and stir cream mixture into the slow cooker. Cook for an additional 15 to 20 minutes, or until juices are bubbling and slightly thickened. Season to taste with salt and pepper, and serve hot.

Note: The dish can be prepared up to 2 days in advance and refrigerated, tightly covered. Reheat it, covered, over low heat until hot, stirring occasionally.

Variation:
Substitute boneless pork loin for the chicken.
Brown the pork in a skillet.

SWEET COUSCOUS

with Nuts and Dried Fruit

Makes 4 to 6 servings
Active Time: 2 minutes
Total Time: 20 minutes

2⅓ cups water

¼ cup sugar

1 cup total dried fruit of your choice (cranberries, apricots, raisins, apple, cherries, etc.)

2½ cups (about 1 lb.) couscous

½ cup coarsely chopped toasted slivered almonds

¼ cup extra-virgin olive oil, if desired

1. Combine water, sugar, and your choices of dried fruit in a medium saucepan and bring the mixture to a boil over medium-high heat while stirring constantly. Remove the pan from the heat before stirring in the couscous, then cover the pan with a tight lid and wait for the couscous to absorb all the water (about 5 to 10 minutes).

2. Using a fork, fluff up the mixture and break up any lumps. Add in the slivered almonds. Allow the dish to sit and cool for about 10 minutes before serving. For a moister texture, olive oil can be mixed in as well before serving.

CHOCOLATE CARAMEL PECAN PIE

Makes 6 to 8 servings   Active Time: 20 minutes
Start to Finish: 1¾ hours

1½ cups granulated sugar

1 cup heavy cream

4 tablespoons (½ stick) unsalted butter, cut into small pieces

¼ cup bourbon

2 large eggs

1 cup pecan halves, toasted at 350 degrees F for 5 minutes

4 oz. bittersweet chocolate, melted

1 (9-inch) pie shell

1. Combine sugar and ½ cup water in a small saucepan and place over medium-high heat. Cook, without stirring, until liquid is golden brown and caramelized. Turn off the heat and add cream slowly, stirring with a long-handled spoon; it will bubble up at first. Once cream has been added, cook the caramel over low heat for 2 minutes. Strain the mixture into a mixing bowl and allow it to cool for 10 minutes.

2. Preheat the oven to 400 degrees F.

3. Beat butter, bourbon, and eggs into caramel and whisk until smooth. Stir in pecans. Spread melted chocolate in bottom of pie shell and pour pecan filling over it. Bake for 15 minutes, then turn the over down to 350 degrees F and bake another 15 minutes. Allow pie to cool on a wire rack until room temperature.

Variations:

• Use rum or brandy instead of bourbon.

• Use walnuts instead of pecans.

Caramelizing sugar is not difficult, but one pitfall is allowing the sugar to actually reach dark brown before removing the pan from the heat. The liquid and pot are very hot by the time the sugar starts to color, so take the pan off the heat when the syrup is a medium brown; it will

Thanksgiving

Thanksgiving is the crown jewel of American holidays, when family and food collide in a celebration of gratitude. This holiday meal has all the Thanksgiving classics, including the turkey, the stuffing, and the green bean casserole. There's also a recipe for homemade cranberry sauce. The debate still rages in many a home over which is more favored, the homemade sauce, or the out-of-the-can loaf-style cranberry sauce, but with this menu, you've got the option to decide for yourself.

389

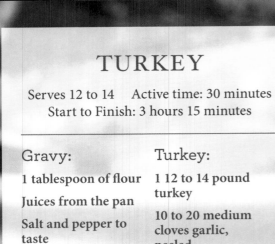

TURKEY

Serves 12 to 14   Active time: 30 minutes
Start to Finish: 3 hours 15 minutes

Gravy:

1 tablespoon of flour

Juices from the pan

Salt and pepper to taste

Turkey:

1 12 to 14 pound turkey

10 to 20 medium cloves garlic, peeled

1½ lemons

Butter

Salt and pepper

Poultry seasoning

1. Preheat oven to 375 degrees F.

2. Remove the neck, giblets, and liver from the cavity of the turkey. Rinse the turkey with cold water and pat it dry with paper towels. Place the turkey breast side up in a roasting pan.

3. Put the peeled garlic cloves in the cavity of the turkey. Cut the lemon in half, remove any seeds, and squirt the juice of one lemon over the turkey. Cut the squeezed lemon half into pieces and put them into the cavity with the garlic cloves.

4. Stick some slivers of butter under the skin of the breast and sprinkle the turkey with salt and pepper and then lightly dust it with the poultry seasoning. Be sure to put the salt, pepper, and poultry seasoning into the cavity too.

5. Next, create a foil "tent" over the bird, which will keep it moist. Fashion the tent by cutting two large pieces of foil and folding them together along the longest side to create a crimped edge. Position the tent over the turkey and secure the edges around the roasting pan.

6. Roast at 375 degrees F for 45 minutes before reducing the heat. Cook for another 90 minutes at 350 degrees F, then remove the foil tent and continue to cook for another 30 minutes. Turn the heat up to 400 degrees F for the last 15 minutes. Check for doneness by "shaking" the legs and piercing the lower breast to see the color of the juice. If it needs more time, reduce the oven temperature to 350 degrees F and check it every 10 to 15 min.

7. Remove the turkey to a warmed platter, cover with a towel, and let sit for a half hour before carving.

8. Make a delicious gravy by putting the roasting pan over a burner on the oven, turning the burner to low, and using a fork to mix the juices with the cooked bits that are stuck to the pan.

9. Sprinkle 1 tablespoon of flour over the juices, using the fork to mash and blend the flour into the juices. Don't let the mixture come to a boil, just keep it warm, stirring the flour with the fork to break up any clumps. Add more flour if it's too runny, but avoid adding too much at once. When it's nice and smooth, season with salt and pepper, and pour into a gravy boat or small heat proof pitcher.

10. If the giblets, liver, and neck interest you: Take the neck out of the paper and rinse all parts under cold water. Place on a paper towel to absorb extra water. Cut the giblets and liver into nickel-sized pieces and put them around the turkey on the roasting pan. Put the neck into the cavity. When you reduce the oven temp to 350, take the neck out of the cavity and put it in the pan with the other pieces. When the turkey is cooked, the juices have flowed into the pan, and you've removed the bird to a platter to make the gravy, remove the neck. As you're mashing the flour into the gravy, mashed the cooked liver pieces, too, so they combine with the gravy. The gravy will be much tastier with these additions.

SLOW COOKER STUFFING

Serves 8 to 10   Active Time: 10 minutes   Start to Finish: 4 to 8 hours

---

3 large apples, peeled and cored

1 large onion, diced

1 cup diced celery

6 cups bread crumbs or 10 cups dried bread cubes

1 teaspoon fresh thyme, chopped

1 teaspoon salt

½ teaspoon pepper

3 eggs

6 cups chicken stock or broth

1 cup butter, cut into pieces

¼ cup fresh parsley, chopped

Salt and pepper to taste

1. Add the apples, onion, and celery, to a large skillet and cook, stirring, until onions are translucent, about 5 minutes. Add the onion mix to a bowl.

2. Stir the bread crumbs or cubed bread into the bowl with the onion mix. Add thyme, salt, and pepper, stirring to combine. Put seasoned bread into the slow cooker.

3. In the bowl in which the bread mixture was prepared, whisk the eggs together lightly and add the chicken stock. Whisk briefly to combine. Pour over bread mixture. Dot with butter.

4. Cover and cook on Low for 6 to 8 hours or on High for 4 to 5 hours. Transfer to a bowl to serve, garnishing with the chopped parsley.

TURKEY LEGS

Makes 3 to 4 servings   Active Time: 45 minutes   Start to Finish: 60 minutes

---

2 tablespoons butter

3 or 4 turkey drumsticks

Salt and pepper to taste

½ cup white wine

1 teaspoon thyme

Those turkey legs served at theme parks are always juicy and meaty. This is the closest you'll come to replicating that taste.

1. Preheat the oven to 375 degrees F.

2. Wash and dry the drumsticks, and cut away any excess skin. Season with salt and pepper all over.

3. Heat the skillet over medium-high heat and add the butter. When hot, add the turkey legs and start to brown them. Allow to cook on each side to brown and sear the skin, about 4 minutes a side.

4. Add the wine and thyme to the pan and tilt it to distribute the liquid and herbs. Cook over the heat for another 2 or 3 minutes. Season with additional salt and pepper.

5. Put the skillet in the oven and bake for about 40 minutes. Flip the legs about halfway through the cooking time. The meat should pull away from the bone. Check that it's cooked through by piercing the thickest part to see if the juices run clear. Serve hot.

SWEET POTATO CASSEROLE

Serves 6 to 8   Active time: 20 minutes   Total time: 1 hour

2½ pounds sweet potatoes, peeled and cut into 1 inch cubes

¾ cup packed brown sugar

¼ cup butter, softened

1½ teaspoon salt

½ teaspoon vanilla extract

½ cup finely chopped pecans, divided

Cooking spray

2 cups miniature marshmallows

1. Place your sweet potatoes in a large pot and fill with water until just submerged. Bring the pot to a boil before reducing the heat, allowing the potatoes to simmer for about 15 minutes or until they are very tender. Drain and allow to cool.

2. Preheat the oven to 375 degrees F and prepare a large casserole dish with nonstick cooking spray.

3. Return the potatoes to the large pot and add the sugar, butter, salt, and vanilla extract. Mash the sweet potatoes with a potato masher, then stir in ¼ cup pecans.

4. Add the potato mixture to the casserole dish and spread out evenly. Sprinkle out the remaining pecans and top evenly with miniature marshmallows, then bake for 25 minutes until golden and melty.

CRANBERRY SAUCE

Makes 2½ cups   Active Time: 15 minutes   Start to Finish: 15 minutes (plus 6 hours for refrigeration)

4 cups raw cranberries

⅓ **cup honey**

½ **cup orange juice**

½ **small lemon, juiced**

1. Combine the cranberries, honey, orange juice, and lemon juice in a medium saucepan over medium heat.

2. Simmer for about 15 minutes, until the sauce thickens and the berries have broken apart.

3. Transfer to a bowl and refrigerate overnight.

Reducing the amount of sugar and adding Grade B (dark) maple syrup creates a pumpkin pie whose flavor is richer and more nuanced than a regular pumpkin pie. Top with a maple-pecan topping for an over-the-top taste!

MAPLE PUMPKIN PIE

Makes 6 to 8 servings   Active Time: ½ hour   Start to Finish: 2 hours

1 flaky pastry crust recipe for a single crust (see page 107)

1 (15-oz.) can pumpkin puree

1 (12-oz.) can evaporated milk

2 eggs, lightly beaten

¼ cup sugar

¼ cup 100% natural Grade B (dark) maple syrup

½ teaspoon salt

1 teaspoon cinnamon

¼ teaspoon ground ginger

¼ teaspoon ground nutmeg

1 tablespoon butter

1 tablespoon light brown sugar

4 tablespoons butter, melted

4 tablespoons 100% natural Grade B (dark) maple syrup

1. Preheat the oven to 400 degrees F.

2. In a large bowl, combine the pumpkin puree, evaporated milk, eggs, sugar, maple syrup, salt, cinnamon, ginger, and nutmeg. Stir to combine thoroughly.

3. Put the skillet over medium heat and melt the butter in it. Add the brown sugar and cook, stirring constantly, until sugar is dissolved, 1 or 2 minutes. Carefully remove pan from heat.

4. Place the piecrust over the sugar mixture. Fill with the pumpkin mix.

5. Put the skillet in the oven and bake for 15 minutes, then reduce the heat to 325 degrees F and bake an additional 30 to 45 minutes until the filling is firm and a toothpick inserted in the middle comes out clean. Don't overcook.

6. Make the maple topping by putting the butter and maple syrup in a bowl and stirring to thoroughly combine. Spoon the mixture and carefully spread over the top of the pie. Preheat the broiler to high. Place an oven rack on the top shelf. Broil the pie until the topping is just toasted, keeping an eye on it to be sure it doesn't burn, about 5 minutes. Cool slightly before serving.

PECAN PIE

Makes 8 to 10 servings
Active Time: ½ hour
Start to Finish: 1½ hours

1 flaky pastry crust recipe for a single crust (see page 107)

3 eggs

1 cup dark corn syrup

½ cup sugar

¼ cup butter, melted

1 teaspoon vanilla extract

1 cup pecan halves or broken pieces

1. Preheat the oven to 350 degrees F.

2. In a large bowl, whisk the eggs until thoroughly combined. Add the corn syrup, sugar, melted butter, and vanilla. Whisk until combined, and then stir in the pecan pieces.

3. Pour the filling into the pie crust, shaking the skillet gently to distribute evenly.

4. Put the skillet in the oven and bake for about 60 minutes or until a knife inserted toward the middle comes out clean. If the edge of the crust starts to overly brown, remove the skillet from the oven and put tin foil over the exposed crust until the filling is set.

5. Allow to cool to room temperature before serving.

Thanksgiving:
Where would we be without pie?

Menu 48

This menu is a hearty winter warmer, featuring a classic Beef Stroganoff and scalloped potatoes. And if those two creamy dishes aren't enough to satisfy the largest of appetites, we'll end with a rich, dense German chocolate cake that's sure to leave all at the table feeling full and happy.

Shrimp Cocktail with Homemade Cocktail Sauce (page 43)

Beef Stroganoff

Scalloped Potatoes

German Chocolate Cake with Coconut Pecan Frosting

BEEF STROGANOFF

Makes 4 to 6 Servings   Active Time: 40 Minutes
Start to Finish: 90 Minutes

1 pound ground beef

1 small onion, minced

2 cloves garlic, pressed

½ cup finely chopped mushroom caps

1½ cups beef broth

¼ cup dry sherry

1 tablespoon Worcestershire sauce

¼ cup flour

½ cup sour cream

Salt and pepper to taste

Egg noodles

1. In a bowl, combine the ground beef with the minced onion, pressed garlic, and mushroom pieces, mixing well. Form into small meatballs.

2. Heat the skillet over medium-high heat. Add the meatballs gently so they fit in the skillet (or work in batches). Fry them in the skillet turning so that all sides get browned, about 3 minutes a side. Transfer the meatballs to a plate and cover with foil to keep warm.

3. In the skillet, add the beef broth, sherry, and Worcestershire sauce. Bring to a boil, scraping the browned bits of meatball off the bottom of the pan. Put the flour in a bowl and add some of the hot sauce, using a whisk to form a paste. Add a bit more sauce to the bowl, and when the hot sauce is incorporated with the flour, stir all of it into the skillet and mix. Continue to cook until the sauce thickens somewhat.

4. Reduce the heat and add the sour cream. Add the meatballs back to the skillet. When everything is hot, serve over egg noodles. Season with salt and pepper.

This dish must be served over egg noodles. Nothing else will do. Chop some fresh parsley to use as a garnish if desired, and have some bread available to lap up the extra sauce.

SCALLOPED POTATOES

Makes 4 to 6 servings
Active Time: ½ hour
Start to Finish: 4 hours

---

6 medium Idaho potatoes, thinly sliced

1 white onion, thinly sliced

1 cup low-fat shredded cheddar cheese

½ cup fresh parsley, minced

10 domestic mushrooms, cleaned and thinly sliced

½ cup low-fat milk

½ cup butter, melted

½ teaspoon paprika

Salt to taste

1. Spray the inside of the slow cooker liberally with nonstick cooking spray. In the slow cooker, alternate layers of potatoes, onions, cheese, parsley, and mushrooms until all are used up.

2. In a small bowl, combine the milk, butter, paprika, and salt. Pour this mixture over the ingredients in the slow cooker.

3. Cover and cook on Low for 7 to 9 or on High for 3 to 4 hours until potatoes are cooked through and bubbly. Serve hot.

Once you have the potatoes peeled and sliced, it's just a matter of stacking them in the slow cooker, adding the other ingredients, and returning to a masterpiece.

GERMAN CHOCOLATE CAKE

Makes 8 servings   Active Time: 20 Minutes   Start to Finish: 1 hour

8 tablespoons (1 stick) butter

1 (15.25-oz.) box of devil's food cake mix

⅓ cup chocolate Ovaltine

1 cup unsweetened coconut flakes

1 cup water

½ cup vegetable oil

6 oz. unsweetened applesauce

4 eggs

1. Preheat the oven to 350 degrees F.

2. In the cast iron skillet, melt the butter over low to medium heat.

3. In a large bowl, combine the cake mix, Ovaltine, coconut flakes, water, oil, applesauce, and eggs. Stir to combine.

4. Pour the batter over the butter. Bake 25 to 30 minutes until browned on the top and sides and a toothpick inserted in the middle comes out clean.

5. Allow to cool for about 10 minutes. The skillet will still be hot. Put a large serving plate on the counter and, working quickly and deliberately, flip the skillet so the cake is inverted onto the plate. Allow to cool an additional 15 to 20 minutes before frosting with Coconut Pecan Frosting (see below). Top with whole pecans.

COCONUT PECAN FROSTING

½ cup evaporated milk

½ cup sugar

1 egg yolk

4 tablespoons (¼ cup) butter, cut into slices

½ teaspoon vanilla extract

½ cup sweetened flaked coconut

1 cup pecans (½ cup chopped in the frosting + ½ cup whole for garnish)

1. Makes enough to top one layer — so double this recipe if you're frosting fiends.

2. In a large saucepan, combine the evaporated milk, sugar, egg yolk, butter, and vanilla. Cook over medium heat, stirring frequently, until thickened, about 10 to 12 minutes.

3. Add the coconut and pecans, stirring to combine.

4. Allow to cool, stirring occasionally. Spread over the top of the cooled skillet cake and refrigerate until ready to serve.

Menu 49

December is one of the coldest months, and if it hasn't happened already, the first snowstorm of the season can't be far away. It's a perfect time to warm up with a bowl of chili. Broccoli is the perfect side, and Peppermint Patty Brownies will remind you of the cold, crisp chill outside.

Chili Con Carne

Steamed Broccoli (page 382)

Italian Salad (page 93)

Peppermint Patty Brownies

CHILI CON CARNE

Makes 4 to 6 servings   Active time: 20 minutes
Minimum cook time: 3 hours in a medium slow cooker

1½ pounds stewing beef, fat trimmed, and cut into ½-inch cubes

2 tablespoons vegetable oil

1 large onion, diced

4 garlic cloves, minced

1 jalapeno or serrano chile, seeds and ribs removed, and finely chopped

½ green bell pepper, seeds and ribs removed, and finely chopped

3 tablespoons chili powder

1 tablespoon smoked Spanish paprika

1 tablespoon ground cumin

1 teaspoon dried oregano

1 (8-ounce) can tomato sauce

2 (14.5-ounce) cans diced tomatoes, drained

1 chipotle chile in adobo sauce, finely chopped

2 teaspoons adobo sauce

1 (15-ounce) can red kidney beans, drained and rinsed

1 cup corn kernels

Salt and freshly ground black pepper to taste

For serving: sour cream, chopped onion, grated Monterey Jack cheese

Note: The dish can be prepared up to 2 days in advance and refrigerated, tightly covered. Reheat it, covered, over low heat until hot, stirring occasionally.

1. Preheat the oven broiler, and line a broiler pan with heavy-duty aluminum foil. Broil beef for 3 minutes per side, or until browned. Transfer beef to the slow cooker, and pour in any juices that have collected in the pan.

2. Heat oil in a medium skillet over medium-high heat. Add onion, garlic, chile, and green bell pepper. Cook, stirring frequently, for 3 minutes, or until onion is translucent. Reduce the heat to low, and stir in chili powder, paprika, cumin, and oregano. Cook for 1 minute, stirring constantly. Scrape mixture into the slow cooker.

3. Add tomato sauce, tomatoes, chipotle chile, and adobo sauce to the slow cooker, and stir well. Cook on Low for 4 to 6 hours or on High for 2 to 3 hours. Add beans and corn, and cook for an additional 2 hours on Low or 1 hour on High, or until beef is very tender. Season to taste with salt and pepper, and serve hot.

4. When serving, pass sour cream, onion, and cheese separately.

Tip: You can go as dark as you like with the chocolate, but 70% is likely best.

PEPPERMINT PATTY BROWNIES

Makes 6 to 8 servings   Active Time: 40 minutes
Start to Finish: 1½ hours

---

8 tablespoons (1 stick) unsalted butter + 1 tablespoon

8 oz. dark chocolate chips

1 cup sugar

3 eggs at room temperature

½ teaspoon peppermint extract

½ cup + 2 tablespoons all-purpose flour

2 tablespoons unsweetened cocoa powder

¼ teaspoon salt

1½ cups York Peppermint Patty pieces

1. Preheat the oven to 350 degrees F.

2. In a microwave-safe bowl, melt the butter and chocolate pieces together, cooking in 15-second increments and stirring after each increment. The butter and chocolate should be just melted together and smooth.

3. In a large bowl, whisk the sugar in with the eggs. Add the peppermint and stir to combine. Working in batches, start mixing the melted chocolate into the sugar/egg mixture, stirring vigorously to combine after each addition. In a small bowl, mix the flour, cocoa powder, and salt. Gently fold the dry ingredients into the chocolate mix. Next, fold in the Peppermint Patty pieces.

4. Over medium heat, melt 1 tablespoon butter in the cast iron skillet. When melted, pour in the batter. Bake for about 30 minutes or until a toothpick inserted in the center comes out with a few moist crumbs. It may need a couple more minutes, but be careful not to overbake this or you'll lose the great gooiness. When it's ready, remove from the oven and allow to cool about 10 minutes. Serve in wedges with mint chocolate chip ice cream.

Hanukkah

This is the time of year when Jewish households will be gathering to celebrate Hanukkah, an eight-day holiday of light that commemorates the rededication of the ancient temple in Jerusalem and the miracle of the temple's lamp oil lasting eight days. On each night, a new candle is lit on the nine-branched menorah, with one candle (the shamash) used to light the others. Among the traditional recipes included are those that use oil—celebrating the miracle—and, of course, beef brisket and noodle kugel.

Beef Brisket

Noodle Kugel

Matzoh Potato Pancakes

Applesauce

Chocolate Cake (page 338)

Challah Bread

Donuts

BEEF BRISKET

Makes 6 to 8 servings   Active Time: 30 minutes
Start to Finish: 9 hours

8-pound brisket, with a layer of fat on it or with marbling of fat

1 teaspoon vegetable oil

Salt and pepper

1. Preheat the oven to 250 degrees F.

2. Heat a large cast-iron skillet over medium-high heat. When it's hot, add the vegetable oil, then put the brisket in fat side down so it starts to cook. Sear the meat on both sides, about 3 minutes a side, and season with salt and pepper.

3. Put the skillet in the oven with the brisket facing fat side up. Cook for 8 hours, checking on it every few hours to be sure it isn't drying out, but this is unlikely.

4. Cook until the meat is very tender, falling apart with a fork.

NOODLE KUGEL

Makes 6 to 8 servings   Active time: 5 minutes
Start to Finish: 1 hour

½ pound kosher egg noodles

½ stick butter, melted

1 pound cottage cheese

2 cups sour cream

6 eggs

1 teaspoon ground cinnamon

½ cup raisins

1. Preheat your oven to 375 degrees F and prepare a large casserole dish with nonstick cooking spray.

2. Prepare the noodles according to package instructions and strain.

3. In a large bowl, mix together all ingredients for even distribution. Bake the casserole for 30 to 45 minutes until the top is golden brown. Allow to cool slightly before serving.

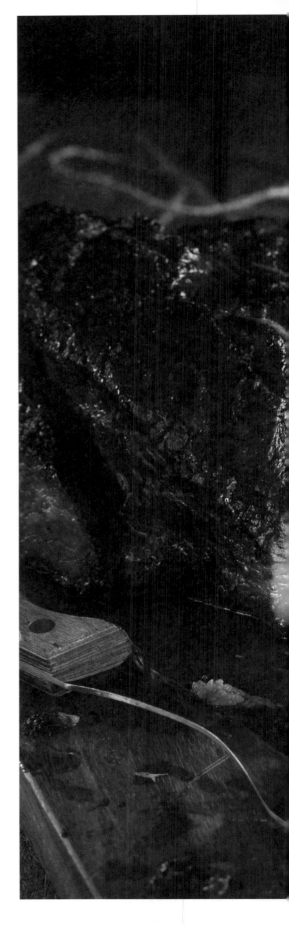

Some serious BBQ competitions feature brisket, and different chefs have different "secret ingredients" to transform this cut. Some use barbeque rubs with everything from cayenne to cumin to special peppers. Some start the heat high and then lower it. If you want a flavored brisket, explore putting a rub together. You'll need to add it as you would the salt and pepper in this recipe. But I prefer to serve the basic brisket with different barbeque sauces on the side.

MATZOH POTATO PANCAKES

6 large russet potatoes, washed and peeled

1 large onion

3 eggs, beaten

¼ to ½ cup matzoh meal

Salt and freshly ground pepper

1 cup canola or vegetable oil

1. Using a hand grater or a food processor with a shredding attachment, grate the potatoes onto a large baking dish, and then transfer to a colander in the sink.

2. Grate the onion or use a knife to process into a very fine dice. Put the grated onion into a bowl.

3. Squeeze as much liquid out of the potatoes as possible. Take half of the grated potatoes, mix them with the onions, and process the mixture in a food processor or blender to create a rough puree. Don't overblend or chop, as the mix will get too starchy.

4. Put the puree in a separate colander so that it can drain. Let both colanders drain for another 20 to 30 minutes. Push down on both to release more liquid and squeeze them again before continuing with the recipe.

5. Combine the two batches into a large bowl, and add the eggs and matzoh meal. Stir to thoroughly combine. Season with salt and pepper.

6. Heat the skillet over medium-high heat and add the oil. Be careful making the pancakes, as the oil can splatter. Take spoonfuls of the potato mix and place them in the oil. Cook for about 3 minutes a side. The pancakes should be golden brown on the outside, and cooked through on the inside. You may need to adjust the temperature of the oil to get the right cooking temperature, especially if you have more than three in the skillet at one time.

7. When cooked, transfer with a slotted spoon to a plate lined with paper towels. Keep warm until ready to eat. Season with additional salt and pepper.

Variations:
- Serve with chunky unsweetened applesauce and a small dollop of sour cream.
- Serve as you would French fries—with salt and vinegar, with ketchup, with gravy, or with salsa.
- For a nontraditional taco, top potato pancakes with chili and cheese.

Applesauce

Makes 15 pints
Active Time: 15 minutes
Start to Finish: 35 minutes

---

4 pounds apples

½ cup apple cider or water

Optional:

1 tablespoon cinnamon

1 teaspoon grated nutmeg

½ teaspoon cloves

Pinch of sugar

1. After removing the cores, cut apples into quarters, and then place in large pot and add apple cider or water.

2. Put the lid on the pot and let simmer for 15 to 20 minutes until it has broken down.

3. Remove apple skins with tongs, and use a potato masher to further break down fruit. Add additional spices to taste if desired.

CHALLAH BREAD

Makes 2 loaves
Active Time: 30 Minutes
Start to Finish: 4 Hours

2½ cups warm water

1 tablespoon active dry yeast

½ cup honey

4 tablespoons vegetable oil

3 eggs

1 tablespoon salt

8 cups unbleached all-purpose flour

1 tablespoon poppy seeds (optional)

1. Dissolve honey in warm water and add yeast within a large bowl.
    Let stand for about 10 minutes, until foamy, before adding the oil,
    2 eggs, and salt. Add the flour one cup at a time to the mixture,
    mixing well after each addition and gradually transitioning to
    kneading with your hands as the dough thickens.

2. Knead the dough until it is smooth, elastic, and no longer sticky,
    adding flour as needed. Allow the dough to then rest, covered
    in a damp cloth, until the dough had doubled in bulk (about 1½
    hours).

3. Turn out the dough onto a floured board or counter, knead
    slightly to decrease the risen volume, and divide the dough in
    half. Knead each half for about five minutes before dividing each
    into thirds. Roll each portion out into a long snake about 1½
    inches in diameter.

4. Prepare two baking trays with nonstick spray.

5. Take three dough snakes and pinch one of each of their ends
    together before braiding, and pinch the other ends to hold the
    braid in place. Place one per baking pan, and once again cover
    with a damp towel to let them rise for about one hour.

6. Preheat your oven to 375 degrees F.

7. Beat the remaining egg and give each loaf a generous brushing.
    Sprinkle with poppy seeds if desired, then bake for about
    40 minutes until the bread has a golden exterior and has a
    nice hollow sound. Allow an hour to cool on a baking rack
    before slicing.

DONUTS

Makes 18 donuts   Active Time: 15 minutes   Total Time: 15 minutes

2 tablespoons white vinegar

⅜ cup milk

2 tablespoons shortening

½ cup white sugar

1 egg

½ teaspoon vanilla extract

2 cups sifted all-purpose flour

½ teaspoon baking soda

¼ teaspoon salt

1 quart oil for deep frying

½ cup confectioners' sugar for dusting

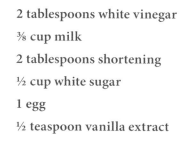

1. Stir the vinegar into the milk, and let stand for a few minutes until the mixture thickens.

2. In a separate large bowl, cream together the shortening and sugar. Ensure there are no lumps and that the mixture is smooth.

3. In a smaller bowl, prepare the dry ingredients together.

4. To combine, alternate adding small batches of the dry ingredients and the milk/vinegar mixture into the creamed sugar until all is well blended.

5. Roll the dough out on a floured surface to about ⅓-inch thick. Cut the donuts using a donut cutter or two different sized cookie cutters. Set the cut dough aside and gather the scraps, reroll, and cut as necessary until all dough is used. You may also save the inner cut circles of the donut rings to fry for donut holes!

6. In a deep skillet or deep fryer, heat the oil to 375 degrees F. Gently place in the donuts to avoid splashing. The donuts should immediately float and grow puffy. Flip them over once golden brown to fry the other side as well. Place fried donuts onto a cookie sheet covered with paper towels to absorb extra oil and let cool. Dust with confectioners' sugar and serve.

7. Donuts are best eaten the same day, but can be stored in an airtight container for 2 to 3 days.

Variations:

• Use cinnamon sugar as a dusting for an extra burst of sweet flavor!

• For a simple glaze, combine 1½ cups confectioners' sugar, ½ teaspoon of salt, and ½ teaspoon of vanilla extract with a ¼ cup cold water. Blend until no lumps remain. You can either carefully drizzle the glaze atop the donuts or completely dip the pastry in for a complete coating.

• For a chocolate glaze, combine 1½ cup confectioners' sugar, 4 tablespoons cocoa powder, and 1 teaspoon vanilla extract with a ¼ cup of cold water. Blend until no lumps remain. While the glaze is still wet, you can add in additional fun, such as sprinkles!

I have a little dreidel
I made it out of clay
And when it's dry and ready
Oh dreidel, I shall play

Oh, dreidel, dreidel, dreidel
I made you out of clay
And when you're dry and ready
Oh Dreidel we shall play

Oh, dreidel, dreidel, dreidel
I made you out of wood
And when you are all ready
I'll play you when I could

Oh, dreidel, dreidel, dreidel
I made you out of glass
And when you are all ready
I'll play you on the grass

Oh, dreidel, dreidel, dreidel
I made you out of gold
And when you are all ready
I'll play you in the cold

I have a little dreidel,
I made it out of clay,
When it's dry and ready,
then dreidel I shall play,

Oh, dreidel, dreidel, dreidel,
I made it out of clay,
Oh, dreidel, dreidel, dreidel,
then dreidel I shall play.

417

Menu 50

Roasted Chicken is another of those classic dishes, and nothing quite fills the house like the aroma of a seasoned chicken roasting in the oven. The slow roasting of the chicken also warms the kitchen, making it the center of activity on a cold winter day. Toasted barley with mushrooms and a spicy upside-down cake add to the warmth.

Roasted Chicken

Roasted Root Vegetables

Toasted Barley with Mushrooms

Apple and Gingerbread Upside-Down Cake

ROASTED CHICKEN

Makes 4 to 6 servings   Active Time: 15 minutes   Start to Finish: 1 hour 15 minutes

1 4 to 6 pound
chicken

10 to 20 medium
cloves garlic, peeled

1 lemon

salt and pepper

poultry seasoning
(thyme, sage,
marjoram, rosemary,
black pepper, and
nutmeg)

1. Preheat oven to 375 degrees F.

2. Remove the neck, giblets, and liver from the cavity of the chicken. Rinse the chicken with cold water and pat it dry with paper towels. Place the chicken breast side up in a roasting pan.

3. Put the peeled garlic cloves in the cavity of the chicken. Cut the lemon in half, remove any seeds, and squirt the juice of one half lemon over the chicken. Cut the squeezed lemon half into pieces and put them into the cavity with the garlic cloves.

4. Sprinkle the chicken with salt and pepper and then lightly dust it with the poultry seasoning. Be sure to put the salt, pepper, and poultry seasoning into the cavity too.

5. Place the roasting dish in the oven and cook for 30 minutes. Lower the heat to 350 degrees F and cook for another hour. Pull the pan out of the oven and test the bird for doneness. The legs should shake easily and when you pierce the lower part of the breast, near the thigh, the juices should run clear. If there is resistance in the leg and/or the juices are pink, put the chicken back in the oven. Check it every 10 to 15 min until the juices run clear. The skin will be brown and crisky. Resist the urge to take it out too soon!

6. Remove the chicken to a warmed platter and let it sit for about 10 min before carving.

7. Make a delicious gravy by putting the roasting pan over a burner on the oven, turning the burner to low, and using a fork to mix the juices with the cooked bits that are stuck to the pan.

8. Sprinkle 1 Tbsp of flour over the juices, using the fork to mash and blend the flour into the juices. Don't let the mixture come to a boil, just keep it warm, stirring the flour with the fork to break up any clumps. Add more flour if it's too runny, but avoid adding too much at once. When it's nice and smooth, season with salt and pepper, and pour into a gravy boat or small heat proof pitcher.

9. If the giblets, liver, and neck interest you: Take the neck out of the paper and rinse all parts under cold water. Place on a paper towel to absorb extra water. Cut the giblets and liver into nickel sized pieces and put them around the chicken on the roasting pan. Put the neck into the cavity. When you reduce the oven temp to 350, take the neck out of the cavity and pit it in the pan with the other pieces. When the chicken is cooked, the juices have flowed into the pan, and you've removed the bird to a platter to make the gravy, remove the neck. As you're mashing the flour into the gravy, mashed the cooked liver pieces, too, so they combine with the gravy. The gravy will be much tastier with these additions.

ROASTED ROOT VEGETABLES

Makes 4 To 6 Servings   Active Time: 20 Minutes   Start To Finish: 60 Minutes

---

2 small parsnips, trimmed and scrubbed clean

1 turnip, trimmed and scrubbed clean

4 small beets, trimmed and scrubbed clean

4 medium carrots, trimmed, scrubbed clean

½ onion, cut into slices

1 small bulb fennel, trimmed and cut into slivers

¼ cup olive oil

Salt and pepper to taste

2 teaspoons dried rosemary, crumbled

1. Preheat the oven to 400 degrees F.

2. Cut the cleaned vegetables in half or quarters to form bite-sized pieces.

3. In a large bowl, combine all cut vegetables and pour the olive oil over them. Season with salt and pepper and toss to coat.

4. Put the vegetables in the skillet and sprinkle the rosemary over everything.

5. Put the skillet in the oven and bake for about 40 minutes, turning the vegetables over after the first 20 minutes. Serve warm.

TOASTED BARLEY

with Mushrooms

Makes 4 to 6 servings
Active Time: 20 minutes
Start to Finish: 3 hours

1 cup pearl barley

3 tablespoons unsalted butter

1 tablespoon olive oil

1 shallot, minced

½ pound domestic mushrooms, cleaned, caps removed, and sliced

¼ pound Portobello mushrooms, cleaned and cut into 1-inch pieces

2 cups vegetable broth

2 teaspoon fresh thyme

1 bay leaf

Salt to taste

1. Place a medium skillet over medium-high heat. Add barley and cook, stirring frequently, for 3 to 5 minutes, or until barley is lightly toasted. Transfer barley to the slow cooker.

2. Add butter and oil to the skillet. When butter melts, add shallot and mushrooms. Cook, stirring frequently, for 3 to 5 minutes, or until mushrooms begin to soften. Scrape mixture into the slow cooker.

3. Add broth, thyme, and bay leaf to the slow cooker, and stir well. Cover and cook on Low for 4 to 6 hours or on High for 2 to 3 hours, or until barley is soft. Season with salt and serve hot.

Toasting grains is an additional step for many recipes, but the results are worth the effort. Toasting cooks the starch on the exterior of the grain so the dish doesn't become gummy. Although barley is best toasted dry, any species of rice can be toasted in butter or oil. With rice, the grains just need to become opaque; they don't need to brown.

APPLE AND GINGERBREAD UPSIDE-DOWN CAKE

Makes 8 servings
Active Time: 20 minutes
Start to Finish: 1½ hours

2 Red Delicious apples

¾ cup (1½ sticks) unsalted butter, softened, divided

1¼ cups firmly packed light brown sugar, divided

¾ cup brown rice flour

½ cup potato starch

¼ cup tapioca flour

1½ teaspoons baking soda

1 teaspoon ground cinnamon

1 teaspoon ground ginger

¾ teaspoon xanthan gum

¼ teaspoon ground cloves

1/4 teaspoon salt

1 cup molasses

1 cup boiling water

1 large egg, lightly beaten

Vanilla ice cream (optional)

1. Preheat the oven to 350 degrees F. Slice apples vertically into thin slices through the core. Melt ¼ cup (1/2 stick) butter in a 10-inch cast iron or other ovenproof skillet over medium heat. Reduce heat to low, and sprinkle ¾ cup brown sugar evenly over butter; then cook, without stirring, for 3 minutes. Not all the sugar will dissolve. Remove the skillet from the heat and arrange apple slices close together on top of brown sugar.

2. Whisk together brown rice flower, potato starch, tapioca flour, baking soda, cinnamon, ginger, xanthum gum, cloves, and salt in a mixing bowl.

3. Reduce mixer speed to low, and add flour mixture in 3 batches, alternating with molasses mixture, beginning and ending with flour mixture. Beat until just combined. Gently spoon batter over apples, and spread evenly.

4. Bake cake for 40-45 minutes, or until golden brown and a cake tester inserted in the center comes out clean. Run a thin knife around the edge of the skillet. Wearing oven mitts, immediately invert a serving plate over the skillet and, holding the skillet and plate together firmly, invert them. Carefully lift off the skillet. If necessary, replace any fruit that might have stuck to the bottom of the skillet. Cool at least 15 minutes or to room temperature before serving, and offer vanilla ice cream.

Variation: Use pears instead of apples.

Menu 51

The featured ingredient on this menu is lamb. While most people associate lamb with Easter, this spicy meal is perfect for heating up a dreary December day. The creamy polenta adds a hearty component to the meal, while savory molasses cookies will get friends and the family in the holiday spirit.

Spanish Lamb Shanks

Fontina Polenta

Chickpea and Carrot Salad

Molasses Cookies

SPANISH LAMB SHANKS

Makes 4 to 6 servings   Active Time: 20 minutes
Start to Finish: 4½ hours

---

4 to 6 (12- to 14-ounce) lamb shanks

3 tablespoons olive oil

1 large sweet onion, diced

1 teaspoon granulated sugar

Salt and freshly ground black pepper to taste

3 garlic cloves, minced

1 tablespoon smoked Spanish paprika

½ cup dried porcini mushrooms

2 cups Beef Stock (page 37) or purchased stock

2 juice oranges, washed

1½ cups dry red wine

3 tablespoons tomato paste

3 tablespoons chopped fresh rosemary or 1 tablespoon dried

2 tablespoons chopped fresh parsley

2 bay leaves

1½ tablespoons cornstarch

1. Preheat the oven broiler, and line a broiler pan with heavy-duty aluminum foil. Broil lamb shanks for 3 minutes per side, or until browned. Transfer lamb to the slow cooker, and pour in any juices that have collected in the pan.

2. Heat oil in a skillet over medium heat. Add onion, sugar, salt, and pepper, and toss to coat onions. Cover the pan, and cook for 10 minutes, stirring occasionally. Uncover the pan, and cook over medium-high heat, stirring frequently, for 10 to 15 minutes, or until the onions are browned. Reduce the heat to low, stir in garlic and paprika, and cook for 1 minute, stirring constantly. Scrape mixture into the slow cooker.

3. While onions cook, combine mushrooms and stock in a small saucepan. Bring to a boil over high heat, remove the pan from the heat, and allow mushrooms to soak for 10 minutes. Remove mushrooms from the stock with a slotted spoon, and chop. Strain stock through a sieve lined with a paper coffee filter or paper towel. Add mushrooms and stock to the slow cooker, and stir well.

4. Grate zest from oranges, and squeeze juice from oranges. Add zest and orange juice, wine, tomato paste, rosemary, parsley, and bay leaves to the slow cooker, and stir well. Cook shanks on Low for 8 to 10 hours or on High for 4 to 5 hours, or until lamb is very tender.

5. If cooking on Low, raise the heat to High. Mix cornstarch with 2 tablespoons cold water in a small cup, and add cornstarch mixture to the slow cooker. Cook for an additional 15 to 20 minutes, or until the juices are bubbling and slightly thickened. Remove and discard bay leaves, season to taste with salt and pepper, and serve hot.

Note: The dish can be prepared up to 2 days in advance and refrigerated, tightly covered. Reheat it, covered, in a 350 degrees F oven for 20 to 25 minutes, or until hot.

FONTINA POLENTA

Makes 4 to 6 servings   Active Time: 10 minutes   Minimum cook time: 3 hours in a medium slow cooker

---

5 cups Chicken Stock (page 37) or purchased stock

1 cup half-and-half

1 cup polenta or yellow cornmeal

1 tablespoon fresh thyme or 1/2 teaspoon dried

3 tablespoons unsalted butter, cut into small pieces

1 cup grated Fontina cheese

Salt and freshly ground black pepper to taste

Vegetable oil spray

1. Grease the inside of the slow cooker liberally with vegetable oil spray.

2. Combine stock, half-and-half, polenta, and thyme in the slow cooker. Whisk well, and cook on High for 1 1/2 hours, or until mixture begins to boil.

3. Whisk well again, and cook on High for an additional 1 1/2 hours or on Low for 3 hours, or until polenta is very thick.

4. Stir in butter and cheese, and season to taste with salt and pepper. Serve immediately as a side dish or topped with sauce. The polenta can remain on Warm for up to 4 hours.

5. **Note**: The dish can be prepared up to 2 days in advance and refrigerated, tightly covered. Reheat it, covered, in a 350°F oven for 20 to 25 minutes, or until hot.

Variations

-Substitute jalapeño Jack for the Fontina, and add 1 (4-ounce) can diced mild green chiles to the slow cooker.

-Add 2 tablespoons chopped fresh herbs, such as sage, rosemary, or thyme at the onset of the cooking time.

-Add 1/2 cup dried porcini mushrooms, broken into small pieces and rinsed, to the slow cooker, and stir in 1 tablespoon truffle oil at the end of the cooking time.

-Add 1 (14.5-ounce) can diced tomatoes, undrained, 1 tablespoon tomato paste, and 2 tablespoons chopped fresh basil or oregano to the slow cooker, and reduce the amount of stock to 3 cups.

-Substitute sharp cheddar for the Fontina, and add 1/4 pound bacon, cooked until crisp and crumbled, to the slow cooker when whisking halfway through the cooking time.

-Add 1 cup fresh corn kernels or frozen corn, thawed, to the slow cooker when whisking the polenta halfway through the cooking time.

-Serve polenta instead of an English muffin as the base for eggs Benedict, or make it American and serve it at breakfast in place of grits.

-An alternative way to serve polenta is to pack the hot polenta into a well-oiled loaf pan and chill it well. Once chilled you can cut it into 3/4-inch slices and either grill them or saute them in butter or olive oil. You can also spread the polenta in a shallow baking dish to a thickness of 3/4 inch, and then chill the mixture, cut it into long narrow rectangles, and pan-fry them.

CHICKPEA AND CARROT SALAD

Makes 4 servings.   Active Time: 15 minutes
Total Time: 20 minutes

---

2 (15 oz.) cans of chickpeas, rinsed and drained, or 3 cups cooked chickpeas

2 cups grated carrots (about 5 to 6 medium carrots)

⅔ cups chopped celery

½ cup thinly sliced green onions

½ cup chopped dill

½ cup toasted pumpkin seeds

⅓ cup extra virgin olive oil

2 to 3 tablespoons sherry vinegar

1 medium to large clove garlic, pressed or minced

¼ tsp salt

Freshly ground black pepper

1. Combine chickpeas, carrots, celery, onions, dill, and toasted pumpkin seeds in a medium bowl and set aside.

2. To make the dressing, combine the olive oil, 2 tablespoons vinegar, garlic, and salt. Whisk together until well blended and pour over the salad mixture. Stir well to combine everything.

3. Add any additional vinegar, salt, or pepper to taste. Allow the salad to chill in the refrigerator for about 30 minutes before serving.

Variations

- Mix together other herbs with the dill, such as chopped cilantro and/or parsley.

- For extra flavor, try adding in your favorite olives or crumbled cheese.

MOLASSES COOKIES

Makes About 12 Cookies,
Depending On The Size
Active Time: 15 Minutes
Start To Finish: 25 Minutes

¾ cup (1½ sticks) unsalted butter

1 cup packed brown sugar

1 egg

⅓ cup molasses

2 cups flour

2 teaspoons baking soda

1 teaspoon cinnamon

1 teaspoon ginger

½ teaspoon cloves

¼ teaspoon salt

¼ cup white sugar, set aside in a bowl for rolling

1. Preheat the oven to 375 degrees F and line a baking sheet with parchment paper.

2. In a large bowl, cream together the butter, sugar, egg, and molasses.

3. In a medium bowl, mix all the remaining ingredients, except the white sugar for rolling.

4. Add the dry ingredients to the molasses mixture and stir to combine.

5. Chill the dough for 1 hour.

6. Shape the chilled dough into rounded tablespoonfuls, roll in the white sugar, and place on the parchment-lined baking sheet, at least 1 inch apart.

7. Bake the cookies for 10 minutes, until just set.

8. Remove from the oven and let cool on a wire cooling rack.

Christmas

It's the most wonderful time of the year, and a season rich with traditions. This holiday menu is steeped in those traditions, including a Yorkshire Pudding that would make Bob Crachit's grandmother proud. It's a time to gather your loved ones around the table, pass the potatoes, empty the stockings, and spread some yuletide cheer.

Prime Rib

Yorkshire Pudding

Slow Cooker Christmas Ham

Mashed Potatoes (page 87)

Green Bean Casserole (page 132)

Creamed Spinach

Christmas Sugar Cookies with Royal Icing

Chocolate Walnut Fudge

PRIME RIB

Makes 6 To 8 Servings   Active Time: 1 Hour
Start To Finish: 5 Hours

1 6-rib rib roast with ribs removed

5 medium garlic cloves, crushed into a fine paste

4 tablespoons coarsely ground black pepper

3 tablespoons fresh sea salt, coarse if possible

6 bunches fresh rosemary

6 bunches fresh thyme

1. Remove the rib roast from the refrigerator 30 minutes before cooking and let stand at room temperature. Preheat the oven to 450 degrees F.

2. Generously apply the garlic paste onto the meat side and both ends of the prime rib, followed by the fresh sea salt and coarsely ground pepper.

3. Chop 1 bunch of rosemary and 1 bunch of thyme and place in a small bowl. Mix with more salt and pepper. Press the herb mixture against the side of the meat so it sticks.

4. Place a roasting rack in the center of a roasting pan. Take the remaining rosemary and thyme bunches and set on the rack so that they form a bed, alternating the rosemary and thyme.

5. Place the roast meat side down onto the herb-covered rack.

6. Place the roast in the oven and cook for 20 minutes; then lower temperature to 325 degrees F. Cook the roast for about 3 to 4 more hours until internal temperature reaches 130 degrees F.

7. Remove the roast from the oven, transfer to a large carving board, and let stand for about 15 minutes before carving.

Tip: Save your drippings for Yorkshire Pudding!

YORKSHIRE PUDDING

Makes 6 to 8 servings   Active Time: 15 minutes   Start to Finish: 1 hour 45 minutes

1½ cups flour

¾ teaspoon salt

¾ cup milk, room temperature

3 large eggs, room temperature

¾ cup water, room temperature

½ cup beef drippings

1. Preheat the oven to 400 degrees F or decrease the temperature when you take your roast beef out of the oven.

2. In a large bowl, mix the flour and salt together with a whisk. Make a well in the center of the flour, add the milk and whisk until blended. Next beat the eggs into the batter until thoroughly combined. Add the water, stir this in thoroughly, and set aside for about an hour.

3. When your roast comes out of the oven, pour off ½ cup of drippings and put them in the cast iron skillet. Put the skillet in the oven and let the drippings get very hot so that they sizzle. Stir the batter while you're waiting so it's blended. Remove the skillet from the oven, pour the batter in, and return it immediately.

4. Bake for about 30 minutes or until the sides have risen and are gently browned.

5. Bring to the table where the roast beef awaits, and serve with extra juices on the side.

CREAMED SPINACH

Makes 4 Servings   Active Time: 15 Minutes   Start To Finish: 20 Minutes

1 tablespoon unsalted butter

1 small shallot, diced

2 garlic cloves, minced

2 pounds baby spinach, stems trimmed

1/3 cup heavy cream

Coarsely ground black pepper

Fresh sea salt

1. Place the butter in a large cast-iron skillet on the stove over medium heat. When hot, add the diced shallot and garlic, and cook 3 to 4 minutes, until the garlic is golden and the shallot is translucent.

2. Add the spinach to the skillet in batches and cook until the spinach is warmed through. Pour in the heavy cream and cook for 6 to 8 minutes, until the liquid has reduced and the mixture has thickened.

3. Remove from the heat and then season with the coarsely ground black pepper and fresh sea salt. Serve warm.

SLOW COOKER CHRISTMAS HAM

Makes 10 to 12 servings
Active Time: 5 minutes
Start to Finish: 3½ to 8½ hours

---

6 to 8 lb cooked, spiral sliced ham

½ cup honey

¼ cup firmly packed brown sugar

¼ cup Dijon mustard

nonstick cooking spray

1. Spray the bottom of the slow cooker generously with nonstick cooking spray.

2. Place the ham flat-side down in the slow cooker.

3. In a bowl, combine the honey, brown sugar, mustard, and stir to thoroughly combine. Pour the sauce over the ham

4. Cover and cook on Low for 6 to 8 Hours or High for 3 to 4 Hours, finishing with a final 30 to 60 minutes on Low.

CHRISTMAS SUGAR COOKIES

Makes 2 to 3 dozen cookies, depending on the size of the cutters
Active Time: 30 minutes Start to Finish: 1¾ hours, including chilling the dough

¾ cup (12 tablespoons) butter, softened

¾ cup granulated sugar

1 egg

2 teaspoons pure vanilla extract

½ teaspoon salt

2½ cups all-purpose flour

1. Combine butter and sugar in a mixing bowl, and beat at low speed with an electric mixer to blend. Increase the speed to high, and beat for 3 to 4 minutes, or until light and fluffy. Beat in egg, vanilla, and salt, and beat for 1 minute.

2. Divide dough in half, and wrap each half in plastic wrap. Press dough into a pancake. Refrigerate dough for 1 hour or until firm, or up to 2 days.

3. Preheat the oven to 350 degrees F. Line two baking sheets with parchment paper or silicone baking mats.

4. Lightly dust a sheet of waxed paper and a rolling pin with flour. Roll dough to a thickness of ¼ inch. Dip cookie cutters in flour, and cut out cookies. Remove excess dough, and transfer cookies to the baking sheets. Reroll excess dough, chilling it for 15 minutes if necessary.

5. Bake cookies for 10 to 12 minutes, or until edges are light brown. Cool cookies for 2 minutes on the baking sheets, then transfer them to racks to cool completely. Decorate cooled cookies with Royal Icing, and candies if desired.

ROYAL ICING

Makes 3 1/2 cups   Active Time: 5 minutes   Start to Finish: 5 minutes

3 egg whites (3 ounces)

1 teaspoon vanilla extract

4 cups confectioners' sugar

Food coloring (optional)

1. Beat eggs with an electric mixer until frothy. Add cream of tartar and beat for 1 minute. Slowly add sugar, and beat for 2 minutes.

2. If tinting icing, transfer it to small cups and add food coloring, a few drops at a time, until desired consistency is reached. Stir well before adding more coloring.

CHOCOLATE WALNUT FUDGE

Yield: 80 pieces   Active Time: 25 minutes   Start to finish: 1 ¾ hours

1 cup coarsely chopped walnuts

3/4 pound (12 ounces) good quality bittersweet chocolate

2 ounces unsweetened chocolate

1/4 pound (1 stick) unsalted butter, sliced

2 cups granulated sugar

1 cup evaporated milk

1 teaspoon pure vanilla extract

Vegetable oil spray

1. Preheat the oven to 350ºF. Line a 9x9-inch baking pan with heavy-duty aluminum foil, allowing it to extend over the top of the sides. Spray the foil with vegetable oil spray.

2. Place walnuts on a baking sheet, and toast for 5 to 7 minutes, or until lightly browned. Remove nuts from the oven, and set aside.

3. Break bittersweet chocolate and unsweetened chocolate into pieces no larger than a lima bean. Either chop chocolate in a food processor fitted with a steel blade using on-and-off pulsing, or place it in a heavy re-sealable plastic bag, and smash it with the back of a heavy skillet. Place chocolate and butter in a mixing bowl, and set aside.

4. Combine sugar and evaporated milk in a deep saucepan, and cook over medium heat until sugar dissolves and mixture comes to boil. Continue to cook, stirring constantly, for 15 to 18 minutes, or until mixture registers 236ºF on candy thermometer, the soft ball stage.

5. Pour hot mixture over chocolate and butter, and whisk until smooth. Stir in walnuts and vanilla.

6. Spread fudge evenly in the prepared pan. Refrigerate, uncovered, for 1 to 2 hours, or until cold and set. Lift fudge from the pan with the foil, and cut into squares. The squares can be stored refrigerated for up to 1 week. Place them in an airtight container with sheets of plastic wrap in between the layers.

Variations:

• Add 1 tablespoon instant espresso powder to the milk for mocha fudge.

• Substitute pure orange extract for the vanilla, and substitute ½ cup chopped candied orange peel and ½ cup dried cranberries.

441

The Night Before Christmas

By Clement C. Moore

Twas the night before Christmas,
when all through the house
Not a creature was stirring, not even a mouse.
The stockings were hung by the chimney with care,
In hopes that St Nicholas soon would be there.

The children were nestled all snug in their beds,
While visions of sugar-plums danced in their heads.
And mamma in her 'kerchief, and I in my cap,
Had just settled our brains for a long winter's nap.

When out on the lawn there arose such a clatter,
I sprang from the bed to see what was the matter.
Away to the window I flew like a flash,
Tore open the shutters and threw up the sash.

The moon on the breast of the new-fallen snow
Gave the lustre of mid-day to objects below.
When, what to my wondering eyes should appear,
But a miniature sleigh, and eight tiny reindeer.

With a little old driver, so lively and quick,
I knew in a moment it must be St Nick.
More rapid than eagles his coursers they came,
And he whistled, and shouted,
and called them by name!

"Now, Dasher! now, Dancer! now, Prancer and Vixen!
On, Comet! On, Cupid! on, Donner and Blitzen!
To the top of the porch! to the top of the wall!
Now dash away! Dash away! Dash away all!"

As dry leaves that before the wild hurricane fly,
When they meet with an obstacle, mount to the sky.
So up to the house-top the coursers they flew,
With the sleigh full of Toys, and St Nicholas too.

And then, in a twinkling, I heard on the roof
The prancing and pawing of each little hoof.
As I drew in my head, and was turning around,
Down the chimney St Nicholas came with a bound.

He was dressed all in fur, from his head to his foot,
And his clothes were all tarnished
with ashes and soot.
A bundle of Toys he had flung on his back,
And he looked like a peddler, just opening his pack.

His eyes-how they twinkled!
his dimples how merry!
His cheeks were like roses, his nose like a cherry!
His droll little mouth was drawn up like a bow,
And the beard of his chin was as white as the snow.

The stump of a pipe he held tight in his teeth,
And the smoke it encircled his head like a wreath.
He had a broad face and a little round belly,
That shook when he laughed, like a bowlful of jelly!

He was chubby and plump, a right jolly old elf,
And I laughed when I saw him, in spite of myself!
A wink of his eye and a twist of his head,
Soon gave me to know I had nothing to dread.

He spoke not a word, but went straight to his work,
And filled all the stockings, then turned with a jerk.
And laying his finger aside of his nose,
And giving a nod, up the chimney he rose!

He sprang to his sleigh, to his team gave a whistle,
And away they all flew like the down of a thistle.
But I heard him exclaim, 'ere he drove out of sight,

"Happy Christmas
to all, and to all
a good-night!"

Menu 52

The end of the year is nigh, and it's a good time to reflect on what the past year has brought for your family. While the year's first menu was symbolic of prosperity and good fortune, this menu utilizes a wealth of eggs, symbolic of rebirth. They're fitting ingredients for the end of December, as we contemplate our resolutions for the coming year.

Cheesy Hash Browns

Quiche Lorraine

Garden Salad (page 65)

Maple Macaroons

CHEESY HASH BROWNS

Makes 4 To 6 Servings
Active Time: 20 Minutes
Start To Finish: 60 Minutes

---

4 tablespoons butter

4 large russet potatoes, shredded with a cheese grater and squeezed dry

1 teaspoon salt

½ teaspoon pepper, or to taste

6 eggs

½ cup milk

1 cup shredded cheese

1. Preheat the oven to 375 degrees F.

2. Add the butter to the cast iron skillet, and when bubbling, add the potatoes and season with the salt and pepper. Press the potatoes into the bottom of the pan. Cook for about 5 minutes.

3. In a mixing bowl, whisk the eggs and milk together. Pour the eggs over the potatoes, shaking the pan to help them penetrate to the bottom. Sprinkle liberally with the cheese.

4. Transfer the skillet to the oven and cook until just set, about 10 minutes. Serve immediately.

The best cheeses to use in this recipe are those that melt well. This includes cheddar, Swiss, American, mozzarella, Monterey Jack, or Provolone. Use a blend of these cheeses if you want, so long as they are all shredded.

QUICHE LORRAINE

Makes 6 to 8 servings   Active Time: ½ hour
Start to Finish: 1 hour

1 pre-made refrigerator pie dough

½ to ¾ pound bacon, cut into ¼ inch pieces

3 large eggs

2 cups heavy cream

¾ teaspoon coarse salt

¼ teaspoon freshly ground pepper

1. Preheat the oven to 400 degrees F.

2. Allow the refrigerated pie dough to come to room temperature. On a lightly floured surface, unroll and smooth it. Gently fold it and place in the cast iron skillet, pressing gently into place. Crimp the edges at the top of the skillet for a decorative touch.

3. Use a regular skillet or griddle to cook the bacon pieces, sautéing them until just crispy (don't overcook the bacon). The bacon will cook faster in pieces, so keep an eye on it. Transfer the pieces to a plate lined with a paper towel to absorb some of the grease.

4. In a large bowl, whisk the eggs and cream until thoroughly combined. Add the salt and pepper and stir.

5. Pour the egg mixture into the crust-lined skillet and sprinkle with the bacon pieces.

6. Put the skillet in the oven and bake for about 30 minutes or until the quiche is puffy and golden brown and the eggs are set. Use pot holders or oven mitts to take the skillet out of the oven. Allow to sit for 10 minutes before slicing and serving.

Variation: Use ham instead of bacon.

Use heavy cream for a suppleness and richness that you can't get from half-and-half. It may be more fattening, but it's also more delicious. It seems like cheese should be added to this, but the classic French quiche Lorraine does not have it. Voilà!

MAPLE MACAROONS

Makes 24 cookies, depending on size   Active time: 15 minutes   Total time: 40 minutes

1 14-oz package (about 5 cups) shredded, sweetened coconut

¼ cup maple sugar

¼ cup white sugar

1/8 teaspoon salt

3 egg whites

½ teaspoon maple extract

1. Preheat oven to 325 degrees and line two baking sheets with parchment paper.

2. In a medium bowl, combine the coconut, sugars, and salt.

3. In a separate bowl, beat the egg whites with an electric mixer on medium-high for about 3 minutes, until soft peaks form.

4. Add the egg mixture and maple extract to the dry ingredients and mix well.

5. Drop the dough by rounded tablespoonfuls onto the parchment-lined baking sheets. Bake for about 20 minutes, until golden brown. Don't overbake or your cookies will be dry rather than chewy.

6. Cool on a wire cooling rack.

Index

Index

Recipe Index

452

Recipe Index

F

G

T

V

W

Y

Metric Conversion Chart

US measurement	Approximate metric liquid measurement	Approximate metric dry measurement
1 teaspoon	5 mL	
1 tablespoon or $^1/_2$ ounce	15 mL	14 g
1 ounce or $^1/_8$ cup	30 mL	29 g
$^1/_4$ cup or 2 ounces	60 mL	57 g
$^1/_3$ cup	80 mL	
$^1/_2$ cup or 4 ounces	120 mL	$^1/_4$ pound/ 113 g
$^2/_3$ cup	160 mL	
$^3/_4$ cup or 6 ounces	180 mL	
1 cup or 8 ounces or $^1/_2$ pint	240 mL	$^1/_2$ pound/ 227 g
1 $^1/_2$ cups or 12 ounces	350 mL	
2 cups or 1 pint or 16 ounces	475 mL	1 pound/ 454 g
3 cups or 1 $^1/_2$ pints	700 mL	
4 cups or 2 pints or 1 quart	950 mL	

A RECIPE FOR:

Servings: Active Time: Start to Finish:

A RECIPE FOR:

Servings: Active Time: Start to Finish:

A RECIPE FOR:

Servings: Active Time: Start to Finish:

A RECIPE FOR:

Servings: Active Time: Start to Finish:

A RECIPE FOR:

Servings: Active Time: Start to Finish:

A RECIPE FOR:

Servings: Active Time: Start to Finish:

A RECIPE FOR:

Servings: Active Time: Start to Finish:

A RECIPE FOR:

Servings: Active Time: Start to Finish:

About Cider Mill Press Book Publishers

Good ideas ripen with time. From seed to harvest, Cider Mill Press brings fine reading, information, and entertainment together between the covers of its creatively crafted books. Our Cider Mill bears fruit twice a year, publishing a new crop of titles each spring and fall.

"Where Good Books Are Ready for Press"

Visit us on the web at
www.cidermillpress.com
or write to us at
PO Box 454
12 Spring St.
Kennebunkport, Maine 04046